I0130898

Cooperation

Is human nature cooperative?

Man is often said to be a social animal – but what does that mean? Michael Argyle believed that one of the most important components – our capacity to cooperate – had been overlooked and indeed that the whole notion of cooperation had not been properly understood.

Originally published in 1991 the author was critical of earlier approaches, he put forward a new and extended understanding of what cooperation consists of, showing the form it took in different relationships and its origins in evolution and socialisation. He offered new solutions to intergroup and other social problems and took a new look at language and communication as a cooperative enterprise.

Cooperation

The basis of sociability

Michael Argyle

Routledge
Taylor & Francis Group

LONDON AND NEW YORK

First published in 1991
by Routledge

This edition first published in 2013 by Routledge
27 Church Road, Hove, BN3 2FA

Simultaneously published in the USA and Canada
by Routledge
711 Third Avenue, New York, NY 10017

Routledge is an imprint of the Taylor & Francis Group, an informa business

© 1991 Michael Argyle

All rights reserved. No part of this book may be reprinted or reproduced or utilised in
any form or by any electronic, mechanical, or other means, now known or hereafter
invented, including photocopying and recording, or in any information storage or
retrieval system, without permission in writing from the publishers.

Publisher's Note
The publisher has gone to great lengths to ensure the quality of this reprint but points
out that some imperfections in the original copies may be apparent.

Disclaimer
The publisher has made every effort to trace copyright holders and welcomes
correspondence from those they have been unable to contact.

A Library of Congress record exists under ISBN: 0415035457

ISBN: 978-0-415-83812-2 (hbk)
ISBN: 978-0-203-78675-8 (ebk)
ISBN: 978-0-415-83819-1 (pbk)

Cooperation

Man is often said to be a social animal – but what does that mean? Michael Argyle believes that one of the most important components – our capacity to cooperate – has been overlooked and indeed that the whole notion of cooperation has not been properly understood.

Critical of earlier approaches, the author puts forward a new and extended understanding of what cooperation consists of. He develops his theme by analysing the evolutionary and cultural origins of cooperation, its early appearance and development in children, its manifestation in the main social relationships – family, friends and work, and in communication and conversation. Individual differences in cooperativeness are examined, and the failure of cooperation between groups is investigated and remedies suggested. Fresh solutions to inter-group and other social problems are offered and a new look at language and communication as a cooperative enterprise is suggested.

Michael Argyle is Reader in Social Psychology at the University of Oxford and a Fellow of Wolfson College. Among his recent books are *The Psychology of Happiness* (1987), *Bodily Communication* (2nd edition, 1988) and *The Social Psychology of Work* (2nd edition, 1989).

Cooperation
The basis of sociability

Michael Argyle

ROUTLEDGE

London and New York

First published 1991 by Routledge
11 New Fetter Lane, London EC4P 4EE

Simultaneously published in the USA and Canada by Routledge
a division of Routledge, Chapman and Hall, Inc,
29 West 35th Street, New York, NY 10001

© 1991 Michael Argyle

Typeset by Pat and Anne Murphy, Highcliffe-on-Sea, Dorset
Printed and bound in Great Britain by
Mackays of Chatham PLC, Chatham, Kent

All rights reserved. No part of this book may be reprinted or reproduced or
utilized in any form or by any electronic, mechanical, or other means, now
known or hereafter invented, including photocopying and recording, or in any
information storage or retrieval system, without permission in writing from the
publishers.

British Library Cataloguing in Publication Data

Argyle, Michael, *1925–*
  Cooperation: the basis of sociability.
  1. Competition & cooperation.
  I. Title
  302.14

Library of Congress Cataloging in Publication Data

Argyle, Michael.
  Cooperation, the basis of sociability / Michael Argyle.
  p.   cm.
  Includes bibliographical references (p.   ).
  1. Interpersonal relations. 2. Cooperativeness. 3. Social groups. I. Title.
HM132.A695   1991   90-8299
302'.14–dc20   CIP

ISBN 0-415-03545-7
     0-415-03546-5 (pbk)

For Ruby, Beatrice, Iona, Emil and Phoebe

Contents

Illustrations

Figures

Tables

Preface

'Man is a social animal', we often say, but what does this mean? One of the most important components has been widely overlooked, I believe, not only by the general public, but by psychologists as well. This is our capacity to cooperate, to engage in joint behaviour with others. The whole notion of cooperation has not been properly understood, it is more than a matter of working for some joint end product. More crucial than this, I suggest, is following a shared programme, which generates coordinated behaviour, which in some cases is an end in itself, as in games, music and dance. In such cases 'it takes two (or more) to do it', and all social behaviour contains a cooperative element in this sense.

I have tried to set out the evidence about the cooperative side of human nature, and have pursued its evolutionary, sociological and developmental roots, its manifestation in different relationships, and in language and communication, its variation between different personalities, and its application to inter-group problems.

I am indebted to many people for their ideas and comments. In Oxford this includes Nick Allen, A.H. Halsey, Yair Hamburger, Paul Harris, Thayne McCulloh, Joel Peck and Alison Clark-Stewart. During a lecture tour of North America a number of very useful suggestions were made by David Bakan (York, Toronto), Ralph Exline (Delaware), Jerry Ginsberg (Nevada), Barry Schneider (Ottawa), Ben Slugoski (Mt Allison, NB) and Jerry Wiggins (UBC). I have found the writings of a number of people particularly helpful, such as Margaret Clark, Judy Dunn, H.R. Schaffer and Harry Triandis.

Ann McKendry, now wizard of the word processor, typed this – about the twentieth book she has done for me – beautifully as ever.

Michael Argyle
Oxford

Part one

The study of cooperation

Chapter one

Introduction

'No man is an island' (John Donne)
'United we stand, divided we fall' (Aesop)
'Two heads are better than one'
'It takes two to do it'
'Many hands make light work'

Many thinkers have pointed to the importance of cooperation in human life. I want to go further, and argue that cooperation is central to human existence. And, unlike Aesop, John Donne and the rest, we now have extensive empirical evidence from the biological and social sciences to prove it.

Some species of animals display a great deal of cooperative behaviour, which is evidently necessary for their survival, and which is innate, the result of evolution. There is extensive cooperation and mutual help among humans too, and we shall see that there is evidence for some innate cooperative behaviour; for example, the bodily equipment for sexual cooperation and communicating, as well as the capacity of infants to slip easily into interaction routines with their mothers. However, behaviour patterns which are innate in animals are usually less so in humans, and cooperation is no exception. The role of social learning can be seen in the differences between cultures; it is necessary for moral and religious leaders to exhort us to be less selfish and love our neighbour as ourselves.

There is a sense in which all social behaviour is cooperative: it takes two (or more) to do it, whether this is playing on a see-saw, playing tennis, making most kinds of music, dancing, working together in a group, taking part in a conversation, or having a social relationship. In each of these cases there is some kind of social system, in which the activities of each member are coordinated to achieve a final product.

In this book we shall pursue the idea that cooperation is central to social behaviour. While there was a lot of early interest in cooperation, usually contrasted with competition, the term has almost vanished from the social science vocabulary. However, there is a lot of new research which suggests that it should be brought back. As will be shown later, cooperation is also the key to a number of practical problems, from social skills training to inter-group prejudice.

It is not being suggested here that cooperation is the whole story about social behaviour. What about situations of conflict or when people are being assertive or persuasive, acting as leaders? It is found that to be successful, leaders must be accepted by their followers, and they will only be accepted if followers think their leader shares their goals and will be effective in attaining them; this is a cooperative state of affairs. We shall see later that assertiveness and negotiation in conflict situations are most successful when there is concern for the goals of the other side, when a relationship is established and a jointly advantageous solution can be found.

I believe that the term cooperation has been used too narrowly in the past, to refer only to groups of people working at tasks for external rewards. The *Oxford English Dictionary* defines *cooperate* as:

1 to work together, act in conjunction (with another person or thing, to an end or in a work);
2 to practise economic cooperation.

Webster's *New Collegiate Dictionary* gives the following definition:

1 to act or work with another or others: act together;
2 to associate with another or others for mutual benefit.

This is certainly one kind of cooperation, and we shall have a lot to say about it. However, there are two other areas of social activity which are equally cooperative. In friendship, love, and other close relationships, people are motivated to strengthen and perpetuate the relationship, and are concerned with the welfare of the other.

Second, many kinds of activity cannot be carried out alone at all – playing on a see-saw, playing tennis, performing a string quartet, and so on, are all cases in point. Conversation and indeed all kinds of communication require close coordination between those involved. This gives us three main classes of cooperation – joint task activity, social relationships, and coordination over joint activities, communication and interaction.

Here is an attempt at a revised definition.

Cooperation: acting together, in a coordinated way at work, leisure, or in social relationships, in the pursuit of shared goals, the enjoyment of the joint activity, or simply furthering the relationship.

Note that shared *group* goals are mentioned. Two young men pursuing the same girl share *individual* goals, but this is not cooperation (Deutsch 1949).

If they both simply want to make her happy or teach her statistics, on the other hand, this could be cooperation.

These are the three main ways in which individuals may be cooperative.

1 *Cooperation towards material rewards.* Behaviour can be cooperative, competitive, individualistic, or altruistic; we shall describe ways of assessing such tendencies in individuals later (see ch. 10). It is possible to score free social behaviour for cooperation, and this has been done for children's play (see pp. 99ff.).
2 *Communal relationships.* Clark (1986) measured the extent to which people regarded a relationship as communal by a series of questions, such as 'Would you enjoy responding to the other's needs?' and 'Would you like doing things just to please the other?' Exchange relationships were identified by questions like 'If you had received something valuable from the other could you immediately return something valuable?' Research on love has used similar questions about the degree of altruistic concern. We shall deal with two kinds of close relationships, which have rather different origins. Love, marriage, and family life involve a kind of biological cooperation. Friendship is mainly for leisure, though it provides help and social support too.
3 *Coordination.* In a sense all social interaction and communication require a minimum level of coordination, even competitive games. It is necessary to keep to the same rules of the situation or game. Cooperation fails when there is an absence of social skills, especially extreme cases like schizophrenia and autism, where there is very poor synchrony and little gaze.

We shall be primarily concerned in this book with cooperation at the interpersonal and small-group level, rather than at the level of society as a whole. However, we shall look at cultures which differ in 'collectivism', and attempts to establish ideal cooperative communities. It remains to be seen whether cooperation can work in a similar way on the scale of whole communities.

Beyond the egoistic model of human nature

Most thinking in psychology has assumed that all behaviour is motivated by internal needs, and learnt by related reinforcements. Social psychologists have assumed this, for example in 'exchange theory', originally derived from economics; it is supposed that actions, such as staying in a relationship, are based on estimates of costs and benefits. Psychoanalysts encouraged their patients to satisfy their needs, and avoid what was believed to be dangerous repression. Later clinical theories, such as those of Maslow and Rogers, encouraged people to fulfil themselves by 'self-actualisation' – but without any reference to other people (Wallach and Wallach 1983).

We shall develop a non-egoistic view in this book; there is already a body of empirical research in support of an alternative to egoistic thinking. Here are some of the main examples:

1 Although biological ideas lay behind psychological assumptions about needs and their satisfaction, the animal world is full of examples of looking after others, sharing and taking risks in order to help others.
2 Ideas from economics lay behind rational and cost-benefit approaches in social psychology. But in sociology there is a long tradition of interest in 'communal' and *Gemeinschaft* relationships, where there is a close emotional tie, concern for the others' welfare, and no calculation of rewards and costs.
3 Bakan (1966) put forward an influential distinction between 'agency' and 'communion'. Agency is behaviour that is directed towards 'self-protection, self-assertion and self-expansion', Communion is 'being at one with other organisms, in contact, openness and union'. He argued that both are important, but the new point is the addition of communion.
 We shall see later that in love and close relationships there is great concern for the needs and welfare of the other, and a desire for intimacy with them. This is not well described as seeking individual rewards. Clark and Mills (1979) contrasted 'communal' relationships of this kind with 'exchange' relationships, where people expect to receive benefits comparable with what they contribute. There may be external rewards in relationships, but these are often not the main goals.
4 Helping another person may satisfy individual needs in various ways. Cialdini and Kenrick (1976) found that subjects who were told that their performance of a boring task would help the blind, needed little payment for their services. Batson (1987) carried out a series of experiments to find out whether helping behaviour is ever truly altruistic. He concludes that we do not yet know; nevertheless, the high percentages of subjects who agreed to stand in for 'Elaine' and take her electric shocks is impressive evidence that people often engage in behaviour where the situation is to help another, at apparent cost to self.
5 Most research on love and other close relationships has assumed that each party is trying to maximise his or her rewards. However, in these relationships we know that people are very concerned about the rewards received by the other. If a mother is rewarded by enabling her child to be rewarded, it becomes impossible to disentangle individual rewards. Similarly in games, music and dancing, while it might be possible to discover or invent needs that are being met, the more obvious goal is the joint production of the group performance.

Social behaviour requires more than one person

A great deal of research in social psychology has been done by studying subjects in total isolation. This is perhaps defensible if what is being studied is their perceptions, attributions or other judgements. The subjects see videotapes or read descriptions of samples of social behaviour and fill in rating scales to show for example, who they think was responsible for what happened. This is somewhat different from being amongst those involved in the action, but not perhaps totally different. However, when the object of study is cooperation, aggression, or inter-group behaviour, it is manifestly absurd to study subjects sitting in little rooms by themselves.

Missing from such laboratory situations are:

social interaction, by conversation or non-verbal communication
audience effects
self-presentation
agreed rules of behaviour
shared concepts.

Many kinds of social behaviour are literally impossible alone, such as behaviour linked to social relationships, and joint activities like tennis. Even individual items of social behaviour, as we shall see, are not accomplished alone, but require a sender and receiver, where a social act is planned to be received, and is often modified during delivery by back-channel signals from the other, whose verbal and non-verbal responses are closely integrated with those of the sender.

The limits of the cognitive approach to psychology

The dominant approach in social psychology during recent years has been cognitive. That is, it has been assumed that:

$$S \rightarrow cog \rightarrow R$$

Social interaction then consists mainly of one or more individuals thinking, taking turns to solve problems. A successful instance of this is attribution theory, where the attributions affect, for example, whether or not to help someone. Another is the prediction of health behaviour from health beliefs. Helping behaviour has often been explained as the results of a calculation of the rewards and costs of helping versus not helping. Cooperation has been explained in a similar way, in terms of group members perceiving that their own goals will be promoted when other members pursue theirs.

I believe that the cognitive approach can explain a lot about social interaction and social relationships if two extensions are made to it.

Figure 1.1 The limitations of cognitive psychology

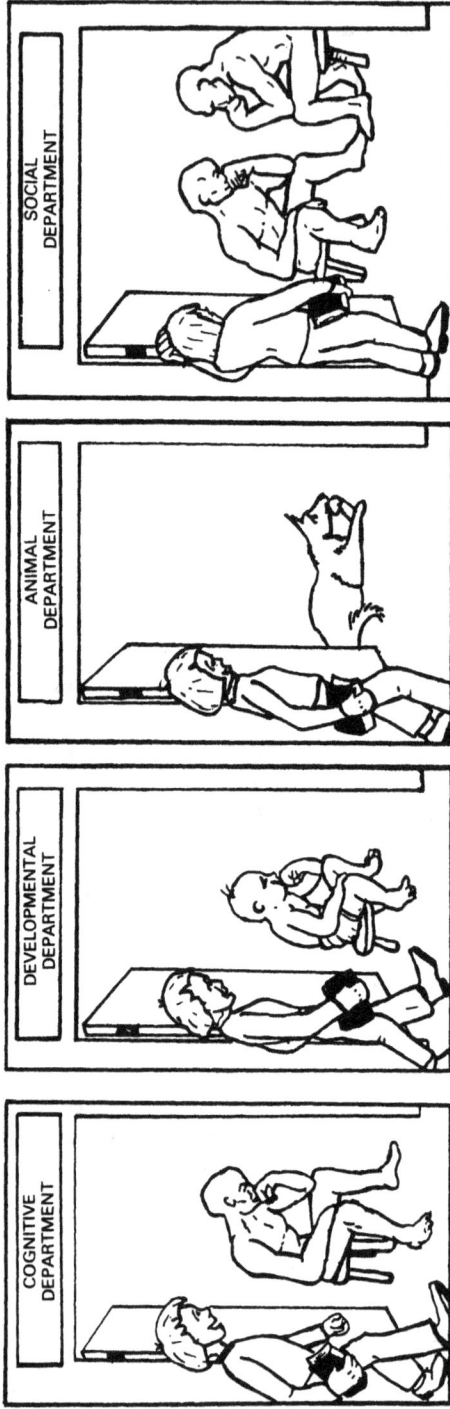

Source: The Psychologist July 1988

1 Interactors need to have shared cognitions; for example, two people cannot hold a conversation unless they have words with similar meanings, and they can't play a game unless they agree on the rules.
2 Interactors need to take account of the cognitions of others. We shall show later how cooperation requires such taking the role of the other, and how conversation and politeness also require this process.

There have been criticisms of the cognitive approach in social psychology already. For example, Bentler and Speckart (1979) found that behaviour is partly predictable from intentions, but it is also partly predictable from past behaviour and from attitudes, independently of intentions. Health-related behaviour (like taking exercise) was more predictable via this second route. Subjects said they were going to work harder, take more exercise, stop smoking and so on, but they often failed to do so; to predict their actual behaviour, past behaviour had to be taken into account.

Nisbett and Wilson (1977) documented the many areas in which subjects are unable to provide accurate reports which could explain their behaviour, or where these are simply mistaken, as in cases of subliminal perception and unawareness of the true causes of behaviour. This provides a serious objection to the (Harré and Secord, 1972) doctrine that the best way to explain social behaviour is to seek 'accounts' from participants.

The study of cooperation provides further instances of the limits of cognitive models. For example, children engage in several kinds of cooperative behaviour at a very early age: sucking at the breast and other forms of primitive interaction occur from birth onwards – long before any cognitive powers have developed. Attachment to the mother is a powerful emotional process, apparently unrelated to either rewards or cognition. The mechanism by which attachment takes place is not agreed: it could be imprinting, conditioning or 'psychobiological atunement', whereby the mother acts as a homeostatic device to regulate the infant's mood. Following Harlow's experiments, no one thinks that instrumental learning via food reward is involved, and no one has so far offered a cognitive theory. Early cooperative play, from the age of 12 months, also antedates the cognitive processes believed to be needed for it.

In a number of studies nursery school children have been asked why they had helped or shared; by four they often referred to the needs of others. However, this was not the only reason that they gave; they did these things simply as part of enjoyable social behaviour with friends (see p. 104).

There is no question of the importance of cognitive factors in social relationships. Our own work on rules showed that for every relationship there is a set of informal rules which it is widely believed should be followed, and which if broken often lead to a collapse of the relationship (Argyle and Henderson 1985). It was found by La Gaipa and Wood (1981) that disturbed adolescent girls who had no friends also had inadequate concepts of friendship, and had not appreciated the importance of commitment and concern for the other. However, there are several aspects of relationships which cannot be explained in cognitive terms.

Burnett (1986) asked subjects in detail, using a variety of methods, what they thought the differences were between, for example, 'friends' and 'sisters', and she found a very low level of awareness of the key features. Subjects found this task difficult, it made them uncomfortable or embarrassed, especially in the case of male subjects, and they showed a superficial understanding, mindlessness rather than thoughtfulness or expertise. Nevertheless, most of them succeed in handling a range of relationships, apparently without the need to understand them.

Of all relationships love has long been regarded as irrational, and this is probably correct. It has been found that a projective measure of intimacy motivation was a better predictor of intimate behaviour than a self-report questionnaire, and McClelland (1986) speculates that intimacy is based on non-cognitive right hemisphere activation.

There is extensive evidence that friends are an extensive source of positive emotions, indeed the most common source (see p. 153). However, the explanation of this is far from clear, and those involved can't explain it. One possibility is that the experience of closely synchronised interaction is intrinsically rewarding, the result of evolutionary pressures favouring cooperation. We shall see that synchrony of bodily movements leads to liking, and is probably enjoyable.

Social interaction, verbal and non-verbal, also involves extra-cognitive processes. Some non-verbal signals, like pupil dilation, are below the conscious threshold for receivers, and can't be controlled by senders. Many other non-verbal signals, like gaze shifts, head nods and small changes of facial expression, are of great importance but are scarcely noticed. Facial expression is partly under cognitive control, from an area of the motor cortex, partly driven by lower centres in the region of the hypothalamus – the source of spontaneous expression. Turn-taking depends on minor non-verbal cues which people are quite unaware of. 'Back-channel' signals from listener to speaker are most important here, though most people are scarcely aware of them. Interactors engage in a finely tuned 'gestural dance', in which their bodily movements are coordinated, as well as being synchronised with the words spoken.

There is no question that cognitive factors like following plans, goals, rules, and cognitive structure of all kinds are important for social interaction. It would not be possible to play or understand cricket without knowing the main rules, how to win, or without mastering such concepts as 'not-out', 'declare' and so on. Social behaviour is like such games in many ways. Social behaviour, like cricket, requires skilled performance, and the model of a motor skill can be applied to both. Motor skills have a hierarchical structure, and perhaps riding a bicycle is a simpler example than cricket.

The larger goal, such as cycling to work, leads to a conscious plan, which is affected by known rules of the road, and knowledge of geography – it is entirely cognitive. However, riding the bicycle without falling off is at a much lower, more automatic, less conscious level of skill. Trying to think about how it is done can result in falling off. On the other hand, skills training, including social skills training, often involves a period of conscious attention to lower levels of performance, such as how to look and smile properly, though this awareness is usually shortlived, and conscious attention returns to focus on the goals of encounters, not the minutiae of performance (Argyle 1983).

The history of research on cooperation

Before the Second World War

During this early period there was a lot of interest in the topic of cooperation, by psychologists, anthropologists, sociologists and economists. This culminated in a report for the American Social Science Research Council by May and Doob (1937) on *Competition and Cooperation*. Cooperation was a topic of great interest, particularly to American social scientists, and it was assumed to be the opposite of competition.

Psychology

Most research was done by developmental and educational psychologists. The kind of questions which they asked were:

1 Is man by nature instictively cooperative or competitive?
2 At what age levels, or during what period of growth in children, do competitive and cooperative behaviour develop?
3 Are American public school children more efficient in competitive or in cooperative situations?

Two main kinds of research were done: observing young children to see if their early play was cooperative or competitive, and comparing the effects of cooperation and competition on individual task performance. There was little theoretical basis to this work, it was restricted to individual tasks with external rewards, and it was not much concerned with the psychological processes involved. The only part of this tradition to be continued after the war was educational work in cooperation and competition in school (see p. 101ff.).

Anthropology

Margaret Mead (1937) made an important contribution by her edited collection of anthropological field studies of primitive societies, which she judged to be mainly cooperative, competitive or individualistic. In fact there were certain forms of cooperation in all of these societies, as we shall show later. This 'culture pattern' approach has since been discredited because it supposed that societies were homogeneous and could be described in terms of a single dimension or process. The special contribution of anthropology has been to show how different aspects of a society fit together, including the material culture, the educational system, kinship systems, and the religious ceremonies and beliefs. However, this early interest in the topic of cooperation has not been sustained as a major direction of research.

Sociology

The classical sociological theorists like Tönnies and Durkheim were very interested in the integration of society, and in comparing different kinds of society from this point of view, but they were not very interested in empirical research. However, other sociologists of this period collected data about utopian communities, of which many had been founded in the nineteenth century. All of these communities were based primarily on cooperative ideals, such as joint ownership of property, and involved breaking away from the competitive wider society. However, most of them failed, and there has been a lot of interest into the reasons for this. May and Doob concluded:

(a) The numerical size of the group deviates too far from the optimum.
(b) As membership changes, the original levels of aspiration change.
(c) Members begin to compete among each other in socially disapproved ways.
(d) Children do not become sufficiently cooperative.
(e) The group is too alien to American culture.

Post Second World War

By the end of the Second World War cooperation had largely disappeared from the vocabulary of social scientists, with certain exceptions. There were, however, a number of other developments highly relevant to this topic.

Social psychology – games

The dominant direction of research has been the use of the Prisoners' Dilemma Game (PDG) and other games. In all of them the subjects are given the task of maximising their gains while playing against another player – the motivation is for material reward, and the task is a cognitive one. Relationships and shared activities are excluded by the nature of the task. These experimental games have been criticised and later rejected by most social psychologists because of their lack of external validity: the players sit in isolation, they cannot speak, see each other or exchange non-verbal signals; they do not know one another, so there is no relationship; and they are limited to trying to score points. The theoretical basis of these games is a simple version of games theory, presented in pay-off matrices.

A number of other games were devised, some allowing speech and the formation of coalitions, others about bargaining and negotiation. This whole approach was abandoned by most social psychologists during the 1970s, as a casualty of the 'crisis in social psychology' – a heightened concern about the lack of validity of many experiments. The PDG was later given a new lease of life by Axelrod's contest (1984) between strategies, and the emergence of 'tit-for-tat' as the winner.

Deutsch's experiments (1949) were more realistic – arousing cooperation and competition by different incentives, though still based on external rewards. In the cooperative condition, if the group was successful (for example, in competition with another group), a reward would be shared equally among the members. In the competitive condition, the most successful individual in the group would be rewarded. This has become *the* way of creating cooperation and competition in many later studies.

These experiments on cooperation were based on a new theoretical model. A cooperative group was thought to have a 'group goal' where the members have the same goal *for the group*, that is a state of affairs which they all desire for the group. The group goal can be linked to individual goals and motivations, as in this case.

Animal behaviour

Meanwhile, the study of animal behaviour was moving very fast. It had long been known that animals display a great deal of cooperation. Birds give alarm calls, at risk to themselves, others respond by 'mobbing' the predator. Monkeys live together in large groups, collaborating over defence, nestbuilding and eating. Animals display a lot of helpful and apparently altruistic behaviour. They collaborate in sexual behaviour and looking after infants, to continue the species. They have the capacity to communicate by facial expressions, vocalisations, and in other ways.

The bodily equipment for all this behaviour – faces, voices and sexual organs – is obviously innate, so to a large extent are the related behaviour patterns, especially in lower animals. The evolutionary explanation of all this is that such cooperation is essential for the survival of individual and species. The origins of help and altruism, and to a lesser extent cooperation, have been something of a theoretical problem. An early theory was that helpful and cooperative *groups* were at an advantage for survival. However, it was argued that, in a helpful group, selfish individuals and their descendants would do best, so that unrestricted helpfulness is not an 'evolutionarily stable system'. Two quite different evolutionary models have now been put forward: the idea of 'inclusive fitness' – that individuals act to promote the survival of their *genes*, and hence help and cooperate with others who share their genes, that is their kin. The second model is of reciprocal altruism. Both will be explored in the next chapter.

Helping behaviour and altruism

Social psychologists meanwhile became more interested in helping than in cooperation. This was partly because helping behaviour posed a theoretical problem to those who believed that all behaviour was motivated by drive-reduction. Part of the solution was found to lie in empathy, the capacity to share another's emotional state, and especially states of distress. We shall see later that empathy is equally important for cooperation. Helping is greatly affected by social norms, which are taught to and internalised by children; again the same is true of cooperation. But what is the origin of such norms? This takes us back to sociology, and the emergence of rules in social groups, where rules are group solutions to social problems. However, helping is not the same as cooperation, though cooperation usually involves help.

Social relationships

The study of social relationships has developed rapidly during the last 10–15 years. At first it was dominated by ideas like exchange theory, emphasising individual gains. Social relationships were explained in terms of 'interdependence', where each party needs the rewards provided by the relationship with the other. However, doubt has been cast on this approach by the findings about altruism and attachment in love, and the importance of communal relationships.

Relationship research has not made much use of the concept of cooperation. However, it will be argued here that relationships provide the key to the main forms of cooperation. Work groups cooperate over large tasks, families cooperate over procreation, mutual care, joint eating, and shared domestic life. Friends cooperate over joint leisure, and in providing help and social support. In all relationships there are informal rules, and in the case of workmates there are rules to ensure cooperation.

The study of inter-group behaviour has shown how there is a strong tendency to favour in-group members rather than members of out-groups. The study of ethnic attitudes also shows that there are limits to how far cooperation normally extends.

Social interaction and communication

These have been studied extensively since about 1960, and it is increasingly evident that this is not a matter of individuals generating a kind of S-R sequence, or exchanging rewards. Language is no longer seen as words written on paper but primarily as speech acts uttered in social situations, intended to be understood by and to influence someone else. A sequence of interaction involves very close synchrony between those involved. This is another kind of cooperation, sometimes called 'coordination', but cooperation it surely is, towards the goal of communicating with each other.

The presentation of self, the establishment of a self-image, is part of a similar process, in that self-presentation requires cooperation from the recipients, who must be prepared to negotiate and accept the self-image presented.

A different intellectual tradition, symbolic interactionism, has also emphasised the joint construction of all social behaviour – for example, the negotiation of the nature of situations – though with less interest in empirical research, or in the details of the interaction processes involved.

Developmental psychology

Piaget (1932) had suggested earlier that cooperative play developed at the age of seven to eight in connection with playing marbles and other games with rules, and the necessary cognitive powers did not develop until this age. However, research on social fantasy play has found that this took place much earlier and was quite common by age three. What these investigators scored as 'cooperative' went beyond seeking material rewards; they counted behaviour such as mutual help, division of labour and achievement of a group goal, as evidence of cooperation (Marcus 1986).

A theory of cooperation

Operational definition

We gave a revised definition of cooperation as 'acting together, in a coordinated way at work, leisure, or in social relationships, in the pursuit of shared goals, the enjoyment of the joint activity, or simply furthering the relationship'.

One of the most widely accepted theories of cooperation is the games theory model embodied in the Prisoners' Dilemma Game. Some criticisms of this model were listed above, and will be developed more fully in the next chapter. I shall conclude that it does not make any useful contribution to understanding cooperation,

Another well-known theory is Deutsch's, that people cooperate towards shared group goals, which are linked to individual goals, and they decide to do this as the result of rational cognitive decisions (Deutsch 1949). This model has strong empirical support from his own experiments, and from others; for example, Hornstein (1982) measured motivational 'tension systems' by the amount of memory for an uncompleted task, and varied whether another member of a group was or was not expected to finish it.

In cooperative pairs 68 per cent remembered the uncompleted task, 28 per cent the completed. For competitive pairs 28 per cent remembered the incomplete task and 48 per cent the other. This fits one important kind of cooperation quite well – in working groups. Cooperation at work has further complexities however, which are not covered by this theory. People, and animals, cooperate in this way with others with whom they have some relationship. And since this kind of cooperation is so common, both among animals and among primitive tribes, it may be partly unlearnt; it is particularly common in hierarchical groups of males. And different individuals may have different goals, which may be partly in conflict, as in the case of supervisors and subordinates, management and unions, salesmen and customers, and many other combinations of roles.

I conclude that the shared group goals theory provides a partial account of one kind of cooperation. However, cooperation is needed for at least three different reasons. It is needed in the first place for many tasks in the material world – building houses, providing food, dealing with enemies, catching large animals, for example. These are all problems in the animal world as well as for humans.

Second, cooperation is needed to sustain the basic social relationships needed for life – between sexual partners, mother and child, leaders and followers in work and the community, between workmates and between neighbours. To ensure that these relationships occur there are partly innate (in animals entirely innate) motivational systems. As a result, cooperation in these relationships is rewarded by satisfaction and joy.

Third, none of this cooperation over work or relationships could occur at all without communication and social interaction. The physical equipment and the basic social signals are innate, but the cooperative skills for doing it need to be acquired. Much of the shared activity of friends engaged in leisure is similar, in requiring coordination over activities like dancing, music and sport.

Two hypotheses about cooperation will be put forward in this book.

1 It is proposed that cooperation leads to positive affect and other emotional rewards. We have found that marriage and other relationships are powerful sources of joy, satisfaction, mental health and health. Sex, one of the basic forms of cooperation is powerfully rewarding, so is affiliative behaviour, and it is suggested that the same applies to cooperation *per se*. The reason is that these forms of behaviour are of evolutionary importance, and so biological rewards have become linked with them.

2 It is proposed that cooperation leads to interpersonal attraction between those involved. Deutsch (1949) found that in his cooperative groups the members were more friendly, supportive, trusting and open to one another. One reason is that in cooperative groups the members help each other, which is rewarding. There may be a second process: the experience

of coordinated, synchronised interaction may itself be a source of rewards and attraction.

Cooperation and helping are not quite the same thing, though they are closely related. The two can be separated, for example in studies where subjects (in isolation) are asked to choose between cooperative, altruistic individualistic and competitive divisions of points or money between self and another. The cooperative choice is for maximum joint profit, the altruistic choice maximises the other's points. Cooperation usually involves help, but in both directions. And the purpose is not so much the welfare of the other as the joint group product.

What is the opposite, or absence of cooperation like? The traditional contrast was with competition. However, if we think about some games, like tennis, squash and table tennis, both cooperation and competition are clearly present. There is certainly a difference between a 'friendly' and a more serious (less cooperative) game, but there cannot be a game at all unless the players try to win. And even in a serious game there is a high degree of cooperation, in keeping to the rules; and there is a high level of coordination, and mutual accommodation, of anticipating and reacting to each other. Individualism is another important contrast. Individuals are constantly pursuing their own goals, but usually in a fairly harmonious way, within the rules, as part of a cooperative social system. We shall argue that there are social forces which keep most individual behaviour within such a harmonious system.

Failure of social skill is the cause of many failures of cooperation, especially in social interaction and relationships. Social skill consists in influencing others, in acceptable ways, which usually means taking account of their needs, so working within this cooperative system. Non-cooperative behaviour might be labelled as 'selfish', but from our point of view more usefully as lack of social skill.

Cooperation for external rewards

As we have seen, most thinking about cooperation has taken this as the main reason for cooperation, and the dictionary definition assumes that this is what cooperation is. It is certainly not the only basis of cooperation, since biological survival requires several other kinds. Nevertheless, this is one of the essential ways in which more than one person is needed. It happens in the animal world: ants cooperate in an elaborate social system, with several different castes; flocks of birds collaborate to drive off a predator. It happens in all primitive societies – to catch a hippopotamus, build houses, fight other tribes.

In the modern world there are many ways in which task cooperation for external rewards takes place. Industrial work could be seen as a large-scale kind of cooperation, though many workers do not share goals for the group, they are merely pursuing their own goals, working for wages and promotion. Nevertheless, they have aligned their goals and coordinated their activities sufficiently for a group product to be turned out, and this can therefore be regarded as cooperation, in the absence of shared group goals. A group goal can be created by offering a group bonus or incentive. It is found that the effectiveness of group incentive schemes falls off rapidly with size of group (see p. 120). Co-ownership, as in work cooperatives and communes are other cases of work cooperation (see pp. 81ff.). The most familiar case of joint ownership is, of course, the family. We shall look carefully at how far successful cooperatives, based on work or joint owner-ship, are possible on a larger scale than that of the family or small communes.

Very often work requires cooperation between individuals in different roles, who have rather different goals. Supervisors and subordinates are an obvious case; we shall see later that effective leadership requires cooperative skills. Management-union negotiation is a case of conflicting goals; we shall see that the best outcomes here too are produced by a collaborative relation-ship using 'integrative bargaining'.

Cooperation over work usually does not take place unless there is a social relationship between those involved, and cooperation *solely* for external rewards is rare; the closest example is probably some cases of negotiation or selling, and even here there has to be some degree of trust before any business can be done. This is especially true in Arab and Third World cultures where even the simplest sale has to be preceded by a period of tea-drinking and informal talk. In most cases of cooperation, one of two additional motivations is present, or both – based on relationship and shared activity. To these we now turn.

Cooperation in relationships

Relationships are needed for biological survival. There are some external rewards here, since people help each other, but there are also internal rewards. We carried out a study of these forms of satisfaction in different relationships, and came up with three main factors (Argyle and Furnham 1983: see p. 111):

1 material and emotional support
2 social and emotional support
3 enjoying shared interests and activities.

There are a number of motivations under the second factor, which are partly innate, the result of evolution, partly the result of socialisation.

Sexual behaviour usually needs two to do it. This is the most biologically-rooted kind of cooperation, since the equipment, the motivation and some of the behaviour patterns, are innate in humans as well as animals. The product is children, but there are more immediate rewards too: the coordinated activity is very enjoyable and so is the strengthened relationship. However, sexual behaviour is not all innate, and there are cultural rules about when, where and with whom to do it, and books of instructions on how to.

Mothers and infants are motivated to collaborate closely over feeding and caring for the infant; the behaviour patterns are partly unlearnt, both partners derive great satisfaction from the relationship, and it leads to powerful bonding between them. Marriage is found to be the most important of all relationships, in terms of the effects on happiness, health and mental health. This is partly because of sex, but even more the result of social support, and close cooperation over a wide range of domestic activities, plus shared concern for children and home. A high level of cooperation over everyday matters, and agreement over major decisions, is necessary. It can be achieved in two main ways – by following the informal rules which have commonly been found to work, and by developing the social skills of peaceful and constructive negotiation of differences.

Friendship is different from family relationships in several ways. It is motivated by social motives, like the needs for affiliation and intimacy, and extraversion, which can be regarded as an index of social motivation. We have the innate equipment to talk, to smile and laugh, to pat on the back, to eat and drink. The long-term product is probably social cohesion, and hence cooperation and help, and the inhibition of aggression, in the group. The immediate goal is enjoyment, and friends are one of the greatest sources of joy. The main friendship activities are conversation and leisure, where there is little or no end-product, but enjoyment of the activity or performance itself. There is cooperation in keeping to the rules of friendship, which include rules for handling the network, and the rules of polite behaviour.

Cooperation over shared activities

Task cooperation can be induced by means of interdependent tasks, as when members of a work team do different jobs. Cooperation over tasks, and cooperation to sustain relationships, both require communication as well as joint activity. This is the original motivational basis of the desire to interact and communicate, but such behaviour seems to have become fairly autonomous, an end in itself.

Leisure activities are the clearest example of shared activities as ends in themselves. Games and most forms of sport require two, at least, to play. Although there is often competition, as we have seen there is cooperation in keeping to the rules, and a high level of coordination over taking alternate turns. There is often cooperation in terms of a positive social relationship between the players. In the case of team games there is of course cooperation within the team.

Music and dancing also need a number of cooperators, and the product here is the performance, which is an end in itself, and does not need any audience or payment. There is precise coordination, more simultaneous than alternating, while different performers perform the same, or closely related, sequences. In each of these cases the cooperation requires quite accurate timing and coordination – a kind of social skill, and shared ideas and purposes. In each of these cases the result is a high level of joy and satisfaction, and enhanced attraction or bonding to the others involved. We are moving here to the hypothesis, for which a certain amount of scattered empirical support can be gathered. This is that coordinated and synchronised activity is intrinsically rewarding, a source of joy.

Communication, both verbal and non-verbal, is one of the most important joint activities, needed both for tasks and relationships. Cooperation here can be seen in the form of intricate coordination between two or more participants, at a level and timescale well below the moves in most games. There are bodily organs for sending and receiving in animals and humans; the capacities to send and receive via facial expressions, vocalisations, posture, and other non-verbal signals have evolved together.

Verbal communication shows further dimensions of sender-receiver cooperation. To begin with they must share some common vocabulary, and in addition shared assumptions and information; these all become extended during the course of conversation. When someone speaks, he anticipates that someone else will be able to decode it, and designs the message accordingly. While someone is speaking, the listener is also active, indicating that he is attending, and more important provides back-channel feedback, his comments on the utterance, and he sometimes helps the speaker, for example, by finishing a sentence for him.

When people interact they need to agree on the 'definition of the situation', and in particular on their role in it. These roles are closely linked to their self-images and some of their behaviour can be seen as 'self-presentation', behaviour intended to project a self-image. But this has to be acceptable to the others present, so that self-presentation becomes a process of negotiation of identity.

The three basic roots of cooperation

We have now suggested that there are three sources of motivation:

1 for external rewards
2 in relationships
3 over shared activities.

Often they occur together, but they can also operate one or two at a time.

For example, *external rewards alone*, is rare, but approximated by temporary collaboration between strangers; for example, at a road accident, or during negotiation or a sales transaction between strangers. *Relationships alone* is also rare, but the early stage of romantic love is close to it. *Coordination alone* can be seen in a casual conversation, or dance, or music-making, between strangers.

The origins of cooperation in individuals

We shall see that cooperation in ants is entirely innate, and in higher mammals largely so, and we mentioned above the evolutionary models involved. However, because some behaviour is innate for animals it does not follow that this is true of humans. An obvious example of an innate cooperative capacity in humans is sexual behaviour where there is a physiological basis for the drive, and the behaviour leads to strong reinforcements. In the case of communication we possess the necessary bodily equipment for sending and receiving social signals by vocalisations and facial expression.

Other evidence in favour of genetic origins of cooperation comes from research on infants. At a very early age they show signs of sympathy for others in distress, and are able to establish communication and interaction sequences with their mothers. They appear to be born prepared to cooperate and communicate. Sociobiological theories of inclusive fitness predict that we should be most cooperative and helpful to those who either share our genes, or help us to produce offspring. Research on relationships finds that a high level of serious help is given to close kin.

However, human beings are born more open, less complete, than animals, and with a far greater capacity to learn. The extent to which cooperative tendencies are acquired, and the form they take depends partly on the culture. Later research suggests that there are other cultures where independence is the dominant style (Bethlehem 1982). We shall look particularly at cooperative primitive societies, and also at less primitive ones where cooperation is emphasised; for example, in the Israeli kibbutz, and in Russian collectivism.

It may be a universal experience of childhood that children have to learn how to keep to rules, take turns, reciprocate, and divide things up fairly, in other words to cooperate. Children spend a great deal of time playing games where such principles are essential. They also spend a lot of time in fantasy play, in which two or more children cooperate closely to play out such fantasy roles as doctor and patient, teacher and naughty pupil. They establish conversational skills, and learn how to work towards group goals. Cooperation, like altruism, individualism or aggressiveness can become a social norm, a value, which is taught by parents and educators, and subsequently accepted and internalised. The influence of parents is important here, in providing models to follow, by giving instructions and providing learning opportunities. A warm relationship, especially with the mother, leads to social extraversion, helpfulness and other aspects of cooperation. The effect of siblings is more complex, and quite surprising.

Cooperation and concern for others are taught by most religious and moral leaders. Innate helpfulness does not extend far beyond the immediate group, and perhaps religious and other commandments are needed to extend it further. These ideas may come from outstanding moral leaders. They may also come from a kind of group problem-solving, generating rules to solve social problems, rather like the rule of the road. In either case such rules are subject to a kind of social evolution, and only the ones which seem to work survive in each society.

The psychology of the cooperative individual

We have argued that cooperation is partly innate, partly the result of socialisation experiences. Both components would be expected to generate individual differences in cooperativeness. As with other dimensions of personality, this would be expected to vary with situation factors, but also explain consistent tendencies across situations. It should be measurable by rating observed behaviour, and by self-report questionnaire. In this case a further measure is available – performance in game experiments, though we may doubt the validity of these.

What aspects of personality would we expect to generate cooperation, on theoretical grounds?

1 Social motivation, as measured by extraversion, for example, should generate a variety of kinds of cooperation.
2 Empathy, the ability to recognise another's emotions and understand their point of view.
3 A number of social skills will be needed especially the skills of coordination and interaction.
4 Are women more cooperative than men, as traditional stereotypes suggest?
5 There are various kinds of individuals who are not cooperative, are aggressive, delinquent, or psychopathic. They may lack the social skills to persuade others within a cooperative framework, and they may lack empathy, the capacity to see others' points of view and appreciate their feelings.

External conditions for cooperation

There are various external conditions, which either exist in nature, or can be created by man, which encourage and support cooperation. The basic one is the need to carry out large tasks such as building houses, but in advanced cultures there are many more. Cooperation leads to, and is also encouraged by, division of labour between individuals who specialise in different parts of the job. Tasks can be interdependent in other ways, when the actions of two or more are coordinated – using a two-handled saw, bricklaying, piloting and navigating an aircraft are like this. Further encouragement to cooperate can be added by group incentives.

If cooperation is socially valued in a culture, cooperative rules can be enforced, both by reward of social approval, and by punishments for failing to cooperate. We have found evidence of such rules to sustain cooperation, especially in working groups. Studies of highly cooperative cultures and subcultures have shown how such rules can be backed by sanctions.

Cooperative relationships can be encouraged and strengthened by a number of external conditions. Sheer proximity, from working or living together is the most basic. In the family there is joint ownership of property and income, as well as proximity. Larger groups are held together by social networks, creating a flow of information and help, and joint activities.

Wider implications of the study of cooperation

The study of cooperation is important because of its broader implications. While most of these go beyond the scope of experiments in social psychology, they will be borne in mind, and we will see what can be contributed.

1 *Is human nature cooperative?* We have already seen that there are innate components to human cooperativeness. Cooperation is generated in another way, by the emergence of rules and other external props to encourage it. However, there are considerable cultural and individual variations in how much cooperation there is.
2 *Inter-group behaviour.* Hostile attitudes between groups, sometimes leading to aggression, is one of the world's most serious problems. Psychological research so far has succeeded in explaining it, but not in curing it. The cooperative forces which we have described operate most strongly within families and other immediate groups, and to a lesser extent in larger social groups. So what, if anything, can be done about inter-group conflicts? The study of cooperation *does* provide a number of practical solutions. Sheer contact is effective under the right conditions, especially equal status and cooperation. Training in cooperative groups, with members from more than one group, and training in inter-cultural communication, are two important methods.
3 *Social skills training (SST).* We suggested above that cooperation requires special social skills, and that these skills may be central to a lot of human behaviour. SST can be provided to help people establish and sustain

relationships – in marriage, friendship and at work. At the level of joint activities and social interaction, the skills required involve synchronised performance at quite a small timescale, so that social skills training may be necessary at a finer level of analysis than hitherto.

4 *The possible benefits of cooperation.* We have suggested that cooperation has both short-term benefits (like joy), and long-term ones (like production, social integration). Are there more basic benefits, e.g. to health, mental health, and happiness?

5 *Cooperatives.* Does research on cooperation offer any support for co-ownership, as in workers' cooperatives and utopian communes? The key question here is of scale, since there is no doubt that cooperation in small groups, like families, is no problem, but there is considerable doubt over whether it can work on a large scale.

6 *Ethics.* Christian ethics focuses on 'love your neighbour as yourself', which is a very lofty ideal. Social psychology's concern with helping behaviour reflects the Christian attitude. It has recently been discovered that this has a 'dark side', in that the recipient of help may feel humiliated or constrained, and the donor may do it partly in order to control or display his superiority. Cooperation has no such negative consequences.

Research on the Prisoners' Dilemma Game has come up with 'tit-for-tat' as the most effective strategy here. Tit-for-tat has now been offered as a moral or strategic guide to conduct; we have expressed serious doubts about the usefulness of the PDG as a model, and therefore also doubt the value of the winning strategy.

Is it possible that cooperation could be another moral principle, more likely to be followed than Christian ethics, and known to result in positive relations between those involved?

Chapter two

Experiments on cooperation

There have been many experiments on cooperation, many of them using 'games' which were designed to model the underlying processes involved in cooperation. Some of these experiments studied the conditions under which cooperation is most likely to occur; for example, the rewards and costs, or the relations between people. Some have studied the strategies or skills which make another person cooperate. Some have studied the success of cooperation, and how a cooperative group behaves.

One question which some investigators have asked is 'How often do people choose to cooperate?' In the Prisoners' Dilemma Game, for example, the level of cooperation starts at about 50 per cent, then declines rapidly, slowing rising again to about 60 per cent by 300 trials (Rapoport and Chammah 1965). However, as will be shown below, most of these experimental games have very low external validity, in the sense that they are very different from most real-life occasions for cooperation, though sometimes real-life parallels can be found. For this reason they cannot provide an answer to the question 'How often?' A much better source of information on this issue is the study of actual groups, at work or leisure, and these will be the topic of later chapters.

The Prisoners' Dilemma Game

This is the most famous experimental model for the study of cooperation. Over 1,000 studies have been published by social psychologists; it has been adopted as a model in evolutionary theory (Chapter 3), and widely used as a method of research in peace studies, published in the *Journal for Conflict Resolution*. It is a prime example of the approach to psychology which was criticised in the last chapter: it is entirely cognitive, it assumes that people are solely seeking external rewards for themselves, and it studies people essentially in isolation.

Two suspects are taken into custody and separated. The District Attorney is certain that they are guilty of a specific crime, but he does not have adequate evidence to convict them at a trial. He points out to each prisoner that he has two alternatives: to confess to the crime the police are sure they have done, or not to confess. If they both do not confess, then the District Attorney states he will book them on some very minor trumped-up charge such as petty larceny and illegal possession of a weapon, and they would both receive minor punishments; if they both confess they will be prosecuted, but he will recommend less than the most severe sentence; but if one confesses and the other does not, then the confessor will receive lenient treatment for turning state's evidence, whereas the latter will get 'the book' slapped at him.

(Luce and Raiffa 1957: 95)

The game can be represented by pay-off matrices, as in Figure 2.1. Here C stands for cooperate (i.e. not confess), D for defect (i.e. confess). This model, with variations, has been translated into a laboratory game, in which two players, usually in different rooms, and nearly always strangers, and who cannot see one another or communicate, choose which of two

Figure 2.1 Two representations of the prisoners' dilemma

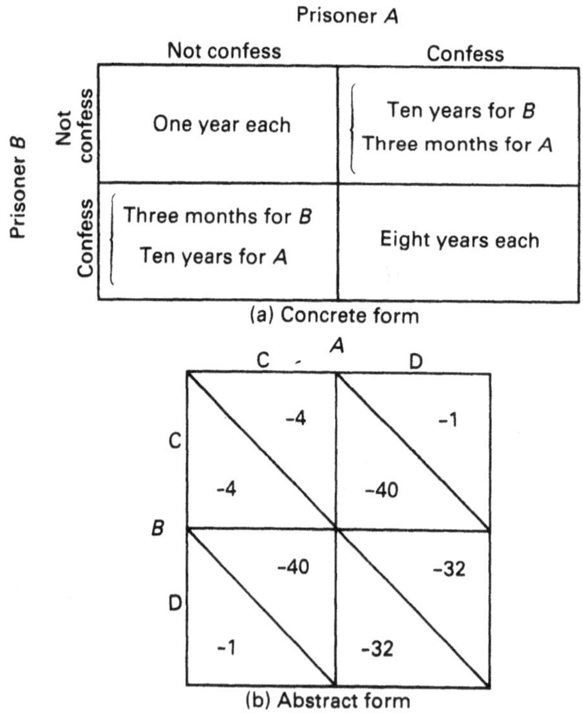

(a) Concrete form

(b) Abstract form
(scaled in three-month units)

Source: Deutsch and Gerard 1967

buttons to press on each trial, corresponding to C and D, without knowing what the other will do. The goal is to win as many points as possible, sometimes real money, often over a series of trials.

The PDG, as it is usually called, contains a curious paradox. The rational, 'minimax', strategy for each player is D: for each choice by the other player, he will do better with D than C. However, if both choose D, they both do badly – eight years in prison; while if both choose C, they do much better – only one year in prison. However, a C choice is risky, since the other might choose D, with disastrous consequences, and he must be trusted not to do so.

Proponents of the PDG believe that everyday life is like this – it is necessary to cooperate, but other people can't be trusted. Closer parallels come from international affairs; for example, trusting another country to reduce oil production, in order to keep oil prices down, though this is really an n-person PDG, which will be discussed shortly. Other examples have been suggested which also lie in the field of economic competition. Two person examples are rarer, because there is usually communication, and two people can usually work out a joint solution. Negotiation of this kind will also be discussed later.

I shall argue that the PDG is *not* a good model of cooperation in real-life. First, however, let us see what has been found out about cooperation in those 1,000 experiments. To begin with, which do the players actually choose? They start with a little over 50 per cent of C choices; this then declines as the trials proceed, but after about 30 games C choices increase again, up to 60–65 per cent by 300 games (Rapoport and Chammah 1965). This U-shaped pattern has been widely found. Players often reciprocate C choices; they also reciprocate D choices, leading to what has been called the 'DD lock-in effect', and they get stuck in a long, reciprocated sequence of non-reciprocated moves. It normally starts because one player distrusts the other. It persists because a C move when the other is likely to choose D would lead to even greater punishment. As mentioned above, there may later be a slow recovery period, perhaps reflecting the growth of a slow, 'unarticulated collusion' (Colman 1982a).

When are players most cooperative?

1 *When there is a positive relationship between them.* In a number of experiments it has been found that there is more cooperation if a positive relationship exists or is created experimentally. There are more C choices if (a) subjects are already friends, (b) they are similar to each other, or (c) if they are simply told that they are similar or are members of the same group. It has been found that husbands and wives make 100 per cent C choices, compared with 65 per cent for friends and 22 per cent for strangers who had been briefly introduced in a somewhat similar laboratory situation, which

offered a choice between cooperative and individualistic responses (Marwell and Schmitt 1975).

When there is a positive relationship, the players' motivation changes; they are no longer trying to win regardless of or at the expense of the other, but want to maximise the gains of both.

2 *When they can talk to one another.* Usually no communication is possible in the PDG, apart from the sequence of choices made. Games theory makes it clear that there is a great advantage in communication in a game where cooperation is possible – whereas there is usually no such advantage in a zero-sum game, where one wins what the other loses. Deutsch (1958) found that with no communication 11 per cent of C choices were made; with simple messages expressing the wish to cooperate this rose to 39 per cent for the sender and 22 per cent for the receiver; with more elaborate messages promising both retaliation and later absolution, C choices rose to 89 per cent and 72 per cent for senders and receivers respectively. Other studies have found that C was more common if both players could see and hear each other (Wichman 1972).

There are more C choices if promises can be made, and these are more effective than threats. In most real-life conditions, people are able to converse, negotiate and persuade, and would have little difficulty in arriving at the cooperative solution to the PDG.

3 *The effect of the other player's strategy.* If A is always cooperative rather than defecting, B will make more C moves. There is more C, if the other becomes more cooperative in later games, after initial defection, i.e., is a 'reformed sinner'. However, 'tit-for-tat' is even better – see below.

4 *When C and D choices are presented more clearly.* The PDG is a rather confusing game to play. Messick and McClintock (1968) devised another way of presenting the same matrices, as 'decomposed games'. An example is given in Figure 2.2. This makes it easy for each player to see the direct consequences of his choice in terms of pay-offs for himself and the other. The total pay-off depends also on what the other chooses. There are various alternative decomposed matrices; some show very clearly, for example, how each player's rewards depend on the other, and this leads to increased cooperation.

Figure 2.2 PDG and two derivative decompositions

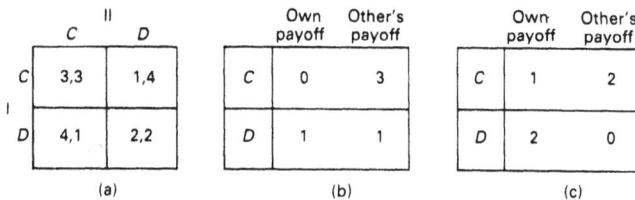

	II C	D
C	3,3	1,4
I		
D	4,1	2,2

(a)

	Own payoff	Other's payoff
C	0	3
D	1	1

(b)

	Own payoff	Other's payoff
C	1	2
D	2	0

(c)

Source: Colman 1982a

5 *Individual differences in motivation.* Although the game and instructions are designed to encourage individuals to seek rewards entirely for
themselves, it turns out that players do not all have the same motivation;
some are trying to gain the most points for themselves, some trying to do
better than the other, some trying to maximise the points won by both
together. It is possible to obtain measures of these individual motivations
using decomposed matrices, where subjects are asked to choose between a
higher individual score, a maximum advantage over the other, or a
maximum total for both together (see pp. 195ff.). Kuhlman and Marshello
(1975) assessed subjects in this way, and then put them in the PDG, with the
results shown in Figure 2.3.

Figure 2.3 Cooperation and social orientations

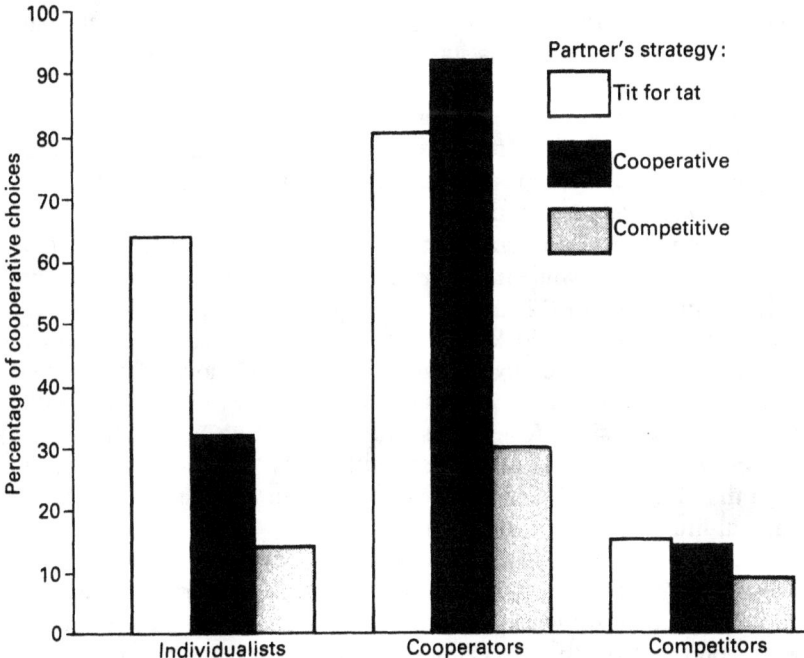

Source: Based on Kuhlman and Marshello 1975

It can be seen that the competitors were consistently non-cooperative with
all partners – they always elicited D choices from the other. Cooperators,
on the other hand, were only competitive with competitive people, and were
more aware of the variability between different players. Kuhlman also
found that persistent cooperators were observed on another occasion to
smile more, giving some support to our theory that cooperation produces
positive emotional rewards. There is a rather surprising gender difference –

women cooperate *less* than men (see p. 210). And there are some interesting cultural differences (see p. 38).

6 *Subjects' perception of partner.* If subjects are told that they are playing against a machine, their level of cooperation is much lower than if they think it is a person (Arbric 1982). If subjects are told that their partner is a selfish, boastful person, they cooperate less than if they think he is kind and modest.

Which is the most effective strategy?

Perhaps the most interesting finding with the PDG is the discovery of the best strategy. Axelrod (1984) organised a computer tournament, to be played over 200 trials by computer simulation between rival strategies. The winner was Rapoport's now famous tit-for-tat strategy, which defeated other more complex ones. This starts with a single C move and thereafter does what the other player did on his previous move. This result has been widely replicated, and has been offered as a guide to international affairs, and even to life in general. Most experiments show that this strategy is more effective in eliciting C responses from another than any other strategy, and it is better than consistent cooperation, which may be seen as weak and be exploited. However, consistent C play can do better with partners who are basically cooperative, while tit-for-tat does better with those who are competitive or individualist (Figure 2.2). There can be a problem with tit-for-tat, however, that the DD lock-in takes place and the other never makes a C move. This can be avoided by starting with several C moves. Other experiments have found that most success is obtained if there is slow retaliation (for D moves) and slow 'forgiveness' (for subsequent Cs) (Pruitt 1981).

Before we take these findings too seriously, I want to question the usefulness of the PDG itself. There are several respects in which it is very different from real-life cooperative situations.

1 *Simultaneous play, ignorance of other's move, risk if other fails to cooperate.* These are all key features of the PDG, but very rarely apply in real-life as we shall see when we come to study them. It is particularly odd that the players have to move simultaneously rather than taking turns. In defence of this game it has been argued that:

It seems to capture some of the essential characteristics of social situations in which an individual must choose whether to work together with others, or to 'cheat' by accepting the fruits of other people's labor without contributing to the collective good . . . it is assumed that the best possible outcome from an individual's point of view is to behave uncooperatively while the other individual cooperates.

(Peck 1989)

The model does not fit the great majority of cases of two-person coopera-tion. If person A decides *not* to dance, play tennis, etc., he gets no pay-off at all. If he decides *not* to take part in joint hunting or housebuilding, his pay-off is again zero. So the pay-off matrix more often looks like that in Figure 2.4.

Figure 2.4 Pay-off matrices for real-life cooperative and uncooperative choices

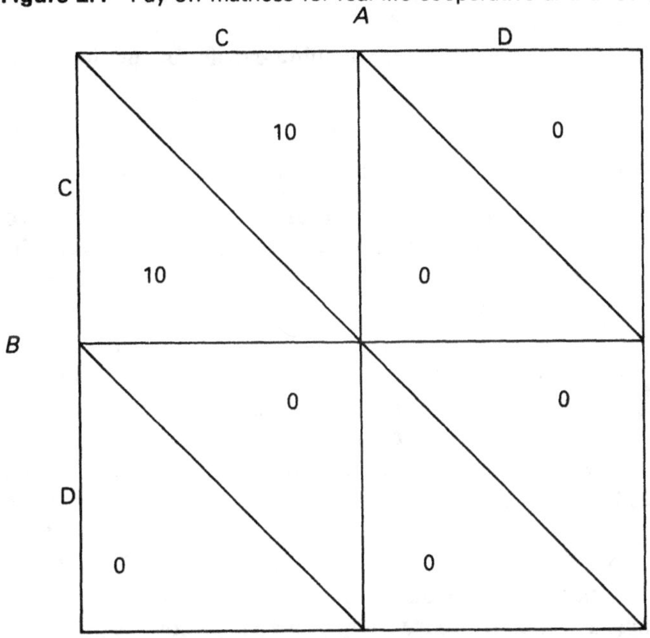

2 *The game itself is too abstract.* Eiser and Bhavnani (1974) devised less abstract translations of the PDG into an economic, an international and an interpersonal problem. Subjects were told, for example: 'This experiment simulates some aspects of interpersonal behaviour − friendly or unfriendly interactions − between pairs of individuals'. It was found that in the economic condition there was *less* cooperation than usual, since it seemed to provide an excuse for exploitation and self-interest, but in the other conditions there was *more* cooperation.

3 *There is usually no communication.* As we have seen, the more com-munication is allowed, the more C moves there are.

4 *The players are usually strangers, and invisible to one another.* As we have seen, the stronger the relationship, the more cooperation.

5 *Absence of social norms.* This is a game without rules. We shall see in Chapter 5 that children learn during socialisation to conform to cooperative norms in appropriate situations. The PDG has little similarity to any familiar social situation, to which such norms apply, so that the effects of socialisation on cooperation will be muted. There is, however, evidence

that some subjects value fairness in the distribution of pay-offs, and, for example, prefer a lower joint profit if it is more equitable (McClintock and Van Avermaet 1982).

Despite its lack of face validity, the PDG has produced quite an interesting pay-off in terms of experimental results. With this peculiar situation at least, cooperation depends on communication between players, a positive relation between them; there are individual differences in cooperativeness, and cooperation is achieved even with an unwilling partner by the tit-for-tat strategy.

Social traps and dilemmas

Social traps are situations in which individuals are tempted into courses of action which offer them short-term advantages, although if others do the same there will be long-term costs for all. An example is the 'tragedy of the commons'. It is a story about a group of farmers: each has one cow of 1,000 pounds on the common, which will only support six cows. If one farmer put a second cow on the pasture he would end up with two 900 pounds cows, but if they all did this they would each have two 400 pounds cows, so that all are worse off than before. This does model some real-life situations, where one person could do better for himself at very small loss to the public good, but if everyone did it the result would be disastrous. Examples are: not paying taxes, not joining the union, increasing family size in overpopulated countries. It is rational, though 'selfish', for any individual to increase his rewards in this way, provided that others don't all do the same. Another kind of social trap is a 'collective fence', when there is a short-term reward for *not* doing something, like shovelling snow after a blizzard, helping with the Christmas party. A third kind of dilemma is the problem of public goods, such as (in the USA) benefiting from public TV without paying. Most cases of breaking the law are similar, if the risk is small enough: not paying taxes or bus-fares, for example.

A number of experimental versions of these social traps have been used. The n-person PDG is one. Another is a laboratory situation where players share a pool of resources (counters, nuts, etc.), and try to accumulate as many as possible by helping themselves on each trial, while the pool is replenished at a certain rate and taking too much means less for everyone later (Messick and Brewer 1983).

An interesting, and less abstract, version of this game was devised by Mintz (1951). Subjects were asked to pull aluminium cones by strings from a bottle, whose neck would only allow one cone out at a time. Sometimes the bottle slowly filled with water, and subjects were paid if they extracted their cone before it got wet. Under this condition the subjects all tried to get their cones out at once, and the cones frequently became jammed in the bottle neck – thus modelling people getting stuck in the exit from a blazing theatre. But if the task was described as a 'measure of cooperation', subjects took turns; if discussion was allowed beforehand the number of jams was reduced.

Figure 2.5 The Mintz experiment

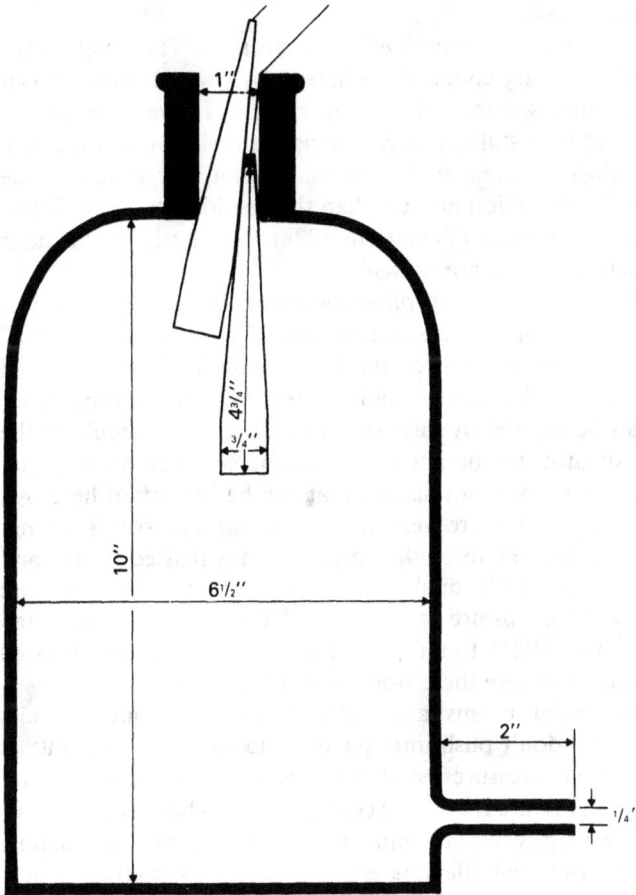

Source: Mintz 1951

A more realistic version of this experiment has recently been carried out by Muir and Marrison (1989) in simulations of escape from a crashed aircraft. In one condition subjects were paid £5 if they were among the first 50 per cent of passengers out. This led to violent competition to get out, and people frequently being jammed in the exits if these were too narrow.

In real-life social dilemmas, many individuals are found to contribute to the public good – in a way that economic or self-interest theories would not expect. For example: workers join unions, students join demonstrations, drivers use lead-free petrol, people donate money to charities, work to set up play facilities for children, or to run community leisure centres, join the army, when they could be 'freeloaders' and leave it all to others. Some, of course, do become freeloaders. The explanation of this kind of cooperation can be explained by a number of processes which have been studied in experiments (Marwell 1982).

1 *Rewards for cooperation, sanctions for defecting.* The single most effective way of encouraging cooperation here is by rewards and punishments, and experimental groups will establish these if given the opportunity. If more money is at stake, players cooperate less, but they are also more likely to develop a system of sanctions, so that, for example, the immediate rewards for defection are less than the resulting sanctions, thus removing the original dilemma (Yamagishi 1988). However, in the cases listed earlier no such sanctions are present.

2 *Social relationships, concern for other members.* In some groups, like families, there is no problem – members are concerned about the welfare of other members. Experiments, however, have used groups of strangers, and have found that subjects will cooperate only if they can trust the other to do the same. Trust can be created by interaction which gives a sample of the others' behaviour, or information about their probable restraint. In-group identity is another feature of relationships that can be important here. All the processes discussed so far are heightened if group identity is strong. Conformity pressures are greater, other members are trusted more, and expected to be cooperative. Individuals are more concerned with the welfare of others, so that public goods are valued more. Kramer and Brewer (cited by Messick and Brewer 1983) found that if the instructions emphasised group identity or common fate there were more C choices.

3 *Social norms.* Social norms and rules develop to control social dilemmas – don't steal, don't push into queues, and so on. Conformity is brought about by social pressures, and the sanction of disapproval and rejection. Behaviour in private is also affected if the norm has been internalised, which depends on a positive attachment to the group; the sanction now is loss of self-respect. In social dilemma experiments a cooperative norm is often established. Feedback about the behaviour of others can strengthen or weaken conformity. If a player starts by competing, but then learns that the others are not behaving as he had expected, he shifts towards this apparent norm (Wilke and Braspenning 1989).

4 *Communication* leads to greater cooperation, especially if the group is not too large, as was found by Mintz, and in a number of other studies. Communication is effective here for a number of reasons: norms can be established, members learn that others are committed to cooperating, individuals can be persuaded by being reminded of their responsibilities, and discussion of the shared problem can increase group identity and hence cooperation (Messick and Brewer 1983).

5 *Group size*. Cooperation is considerably less in larger groups, over the range 2-12. This may be because the impact of one individual on group outcomes is less in larger groups – a little like diffusion of responsibility in helping behaviour, or de-individuation in other studies, where individuals feel more anonymous and less accountable and responsible. There is less cooperation if de-individuation is increased by anonymous conditions. Reduced C in larger groups may be because it is more difficult to control what is happening; for example, it is no good using tit-for-tat. And there may simply be more uncooperative 'bad apples' in larger groups (Colman 1982a).

6 *Individual differences*. As with the PDG, some players are more cooperative than others. Cooperators expect that others will cooperate more than defectors do (68 per cent v. 24 per cent in one study). If a player expects the others to cooperate, he will do the same.

Social dilemma experiments take us nearer to cooperation in the real world than the PDG did. However, cooperative behaviour has turned out to depend partly on positive social relations within a group, which have rarely been incorporated in the experiments, but to which we turn in later chapters.

The Trucking Game

In the original version of this game subjects were given road maps (Figure 2.6) and a control panel (Deutsch and Krauss 1960). They were asked to imagine that they were in charge of a trucking company carrying perishable goods. On each trial the players received 60c each, but a deduction was made for each second that the journey took. There was a short one-way route, and a longer alternate route; it would cost at least 70c to use this route. Subjects were in separate booths and could not see one another. They played 20 trials. If no gates could be operated, cooperation developed rapidly, and by about five trials they were taking turns to use the shorter route. But if each player could control a gate, as shown in Figure 2.4, frequent blockages occurred and there was little development of cooperation. The investigators concluded that having a gate creates the assumption that it will be used, thus arousing competitive motivation.

Why did cooperation break down when gate closure was possible? Was it because this was a threatening and competitive situation? Certainly the availability of gate closure often led to retaliation, even at cost to self. However, Shomer *et al.* (1966) devised a version of the game which separated the use of threats as a signal and the capacity to fine the other player. It was found that threats used as signals led to greater joint profit, i.e. a form of cooperation, while fines led to smaller profits. And Gallo (1966) found that if subjects stood to earn real money from the experiment, they used their gates less, and engaged in five times as much cooperative alternation behaviour.

Figure 2.6 The Deutsch and Krauss trucking game. Top: the road map; bottom: the display panel to indicate moves

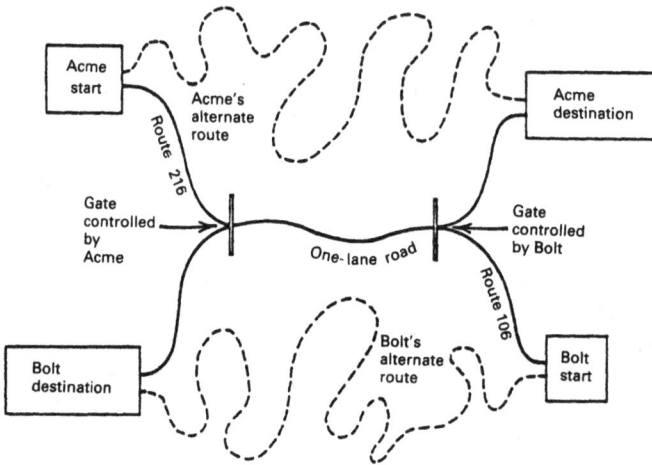

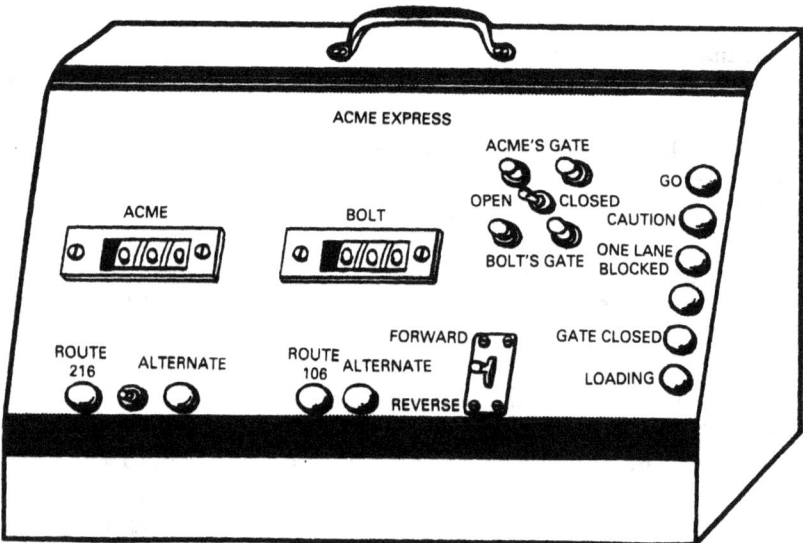

Source: Deutsch and Krauss 1960

Coalition games

This is another experimental analogue of cooperation and with a clear similarity to certain real-life situations. A typical procedure is to use a board where players throw dice to decide how many squares they can move their pieces towards Home. There are at least three players and each is given a weight, e.g. 2, 3, and 4, by which their dice throws must be multiplied. However, players are allowed to talk and negotiate, and above all may form coalitions where, for example, a pair share one piece and can use their combined weights; they must also agree how their winnings are to be divided, if they win.

Coalitions are sub-groups which are formed to use joint resources to achieve a common goal, where there is initially some conflict of interest between those forming the coalition. There are several theories about which players will form coalitions; in the 2, 3, 4 example above, for instance, the players with weights 2 and 3 usually combine against 4, and win; the initially stronger player loses. The theory with most support is Gamson's 'minimal resource theory' (1964), that a coalition will form from the cheapest winning combination of players, that is 'where the total resources are as small as possible while still being sufficient'. This happens because players think that they should divide their winnings in proportion to their weights. The paradoxical result is that the player with most resources loses. However, players do not divide their winnings in this way; it was found that Australian students simply divided them equally. Another theory proposed that coalitions would contain the smallest number of *members* needed to win; it has been found that the majority of coalitions in these games do not in fact have any surplus members.

The main point of interest from our point of view is the extent of 'non-rational' play, or 'total confusion', of players not trying to maximise their winnings.

1 *Relationship between players*. They are often concerned to keep good relationships with one another, especially in the case of female players, so unnecessary coalitions may be formed. If they like one another, it is more probable that they will form coalitions. Players may also fail to change partners, if they have come to trust a previous one.

2 *Status and competence effects*. A player with a stronger weight is sought as a coalition partner if winning is emphasised, but less so if the subsequent bargaining over dividing the winnings is emphasised.

3 *Concern with parity*. Many subjects show a concern that all should receive equal rewards in the end, with the result that they are happy to combine against highly weighted players to share out coalition earnings equally, and generally not maximise individual gains, especially if they are to meet afterwards (Tedeschi *et al.* 1973).

The closest parallels in the real world are in politics, especially in forming ruling coalitions from two or more small parties, and in international affairs. Some of the findings from laboratory experiments have been confirmed; for example, the disintegration of surplus majorities (Colman 1982a).

Children's cooperative games

Madsen (1971) devised a number of games suitable for children to play in groups of two or four. The Madsen Board has four strings, one from each corner, and attached to a pen at the centre; rewards depend on how often the pen marks each player's target. In the Marble Pull Game two children can each pull a marble which they can keep, but if they both pull, two magnets separate and neither gets a marble. In the Cooperative Box two children must cooperate if they are to open a hinged box fastened by four latches. The Circle Matrix is a board with circles marked, in each turn a child can move the piece one step, but without cooperation neither can score.

The tests have been given to samples of children in a number of cultures, with the following results:

1 The original finding was that Mexican children aged 4–11 cooperated more than American children, who were competitive to the point of being self-defeating.
2 In several cultures rural children were more cooperative than those from cities. This may partly explain the first result since the American children were from Los Angeles and the Mexican ones from a village. However, Mexican city children were still a little more cooperative than the Americans (Mann 1980).
3 Israeli kibbutz children were more cooperative than Israeli city children.
4 Cooperation was high in a number of primitive cultures – Aboriginals, Canadian Indians, Maoris, Kikuyu, Korean villages, and Polynesians, but was lower among groups which had become educated or urbanised.
5 Competition was high among American, Japanese and Greek children.

In each of these games children have to learn how to cooperate, if they are to obtain any rewards. Cooperation here involves turn-taking in the first two games, as well as skilled coordination of physical movements. The main findings from these games are from comparisons of different cultures, and these will be reported in Chapter 5.

Economic games

These are games between 'buyers' and 'sellers', who are each trying to do as well as they can by agreeing a price and quantity of goods to be sold. Two tables are drawn up, showing the profit to each for a given price and quantity; usually the players do not know the contents of the other's table. These tables are constructed so that a certain range of decisions will give a 'maximum joint profit' (i.e. a cooperative solution), though the players do not know this.

To give a simplified example, suppose that A is selling a secondhand car to B; A would not sell unless he could get £1,000 for it, though he hopes to get £1,500, and B would not pay more than £1,300, though he would like to get it for £900. What happens is that A asks £1,500 and B offers £900. They then make systematic concessions, and discover that an agreement is possible in the range £1,000–£1,300. Outside this region neither party will come to an agreement. Further concessions are made until the two parties meet, somewhere within the common region. An individual player can do better for himself by 'tough' bargaining, i.e. making a high initial demand, small and diminishing concessions. Each player learns something about the other's bottom line, and what his own profit will be at each point, though the other may be bluffing. If either is too tough, however, there will be no agreement.

To show the concept of maximum joint profit (MJP) we need the matrices used in these experiments. Table 2.1 shows one used by Siegel and Fouraker (1960) which is based on realistic economic assumptions. The amount the subjects were actually paid depended on the profits which they made in the experiment.

What happens is that one player suggests both a price and a quantity, then the other makes a different bid, varying both the number of items and the price. With the matrices provided there is an MJP of 1080, which can be achieved in several ways, e.g. nine items at 180. This was achieved more often than chance, especially when the players had information about each other's matrix.

Kelley and Stahleski (1970) maintained that the MJP would be found if each side started with quite high aspirations, and made a series of small concessions, until agreement was reached. It is probably more accurate to say that this strategy will lead to a *fairly high* joint profit (Pruitt 1981). However, the MJP is not obtained if the two players behave in a cooperative manner, or if one makes regular concessions, not contingent on the other doing the same. It is necessary for both sides to pursue their own advantage, in this situation at least, for the cooperative solution to be discovered.

This game suffers from the same difficulties as the PDG – no communication, no relationship and so on. It is, on the other hand, a lot nearer familiar real-life situations, and is probably able to tap into the strategies which people actually use.

Table 2.1 Bargaining movement hypothesised by Fouraker

	Seller's Profit Table					Buyer's Profit Table			
	Quantity					Quantity			
Price	8	9	10	11	Price	8	9	10	11
240	1190	1350	1430	1430	240				
230	1120	1260	1320	1300	230				
220	1050	1170	1210	1170	220				
210	980	1080	1100	1040	210	50	0		
200	910	990	990	910	200	120	90	33	
190	840	900	880	780	190	190	180	143	91
180	770	810	770	650	180	260	270	253	221
170	700	720	660	520	170	330	360	363	351
160	630	630	550	390	160	400	450	473	481
150	560	540	440	260	150	470	540	583	611
140	490	450	330	130	140	540	630	693	741
130	420	360	220	0	130	610	720	803	871
120	350	270	110		120	680	810	913	1001
110	280	180	0		110	750	900	1023	1131
100	210	90			100	820	990	1133	1261

Source: Adapted from Siegel and Fouraker 1960

Negotiation

We now turn to more complex kinds of negotiation than buying and selling: for example, where one advantage can be set off against another, and where it is possible to solve problems and arrive at new solutions. Again, this is partly a matter of competing interests, but is at the same time cooperative, since a solution can be found which maximises the overall gains – a kind of MJP.

Most research on negotiation has been done in the laboratory, with role-played situations, modelling management-union bargaining, for example; a scenario is presented to subjects who try to come to an agreement which is advantageous to their side. There are also field studies, based on close observation of real-life negotiation. And there has been some study of two other spheres of negotiation – international affairs and marriage.

Negotiators are often representatives of other people or organisations, like management and unions. They are also often quite closely involved with the negotiators on the other side, and may know them well. British research has found that negotiations often go through three phases. First negotiators (Ns) make speeches, taking their roles as representatives, making out a strong case; second, the two sides get together in an informal way, explore possible concessions and solutions; now the relationship between them is uppermost; and third, they return to their representative roles, and resume serious bargaining, until a settlement is reached (Morley and Stephenson 1977). If agreement is difficult to achieve the chairman or some other third party may come in to mediate, and suggest a compromise solution. Pruitt (1981) has argued that negotiators should aim for 'integrative agreements', which reconcile the interests of both sides, and give maximum benefit to each, and that this can be achieved by adopting a problem-solving approach. The other is more likely to make concessions and move towards an agreement if there are going to be advantages for him too.

How agreement is reached

1 *Bargaining*, as described under Economic games, may be the first phase. Each side starts by stating its position, and then there are a number of reciprocal concessions, until an agreement is reached – if both sides are sufficiently keen to come to an agreement.

2 *Information exchange*. During the second, informal phase of negotiation, each side may learn something about the other side's position: what their bottom line is, which of their goals is most important, what their constraints are, for example. This is a necessary antecedent for integrative problem-solving. Although negotiators may be reluctant to reveal too much, their proposals may be informative, they may state preferences, and they can indicate directions or dimensions along which they would like an offer to be improved. Their non-verbal reactions to proposals may also be informative – showing whether they are willing to make some concession.

3 *Problem-solving*. We suggested above that a problem-solving approach should be adopted, and that it often takes place during the second, more informal phase of negotiation. It is a much more cooperative process than bargaining proper, and both sides consider the other's point of view. Often a new solution can be found which is acceptable to both sides. One type of problem-solving has been described as 'log-rolling', where there is an exchange of quite different concessions. One side gives way on X, the other on Y. This is not possible in simple buying and selling, but is in more complex cases.

Neale and Bazerman (1985) found that subjects who were instructed to think in terms of the positive gains which they might make, rather than their losses, made larger concessions, resolved more issues and obtained more favourable settlements.

4 *Compensation for the other party*. One way of negotiating an agreement is to elicit concessions from the other side in exchange for some kind of compensation. This may take the form of finding how to cut the other's costs, face-saving for the other side, or compensation for any losses

41

incurred by him. This may involve some degree of trust, if the compensation is to take place later.

5 *Social relationships between negotiators*. As in other kinds of game discussed earlier, a positive relationship makes it much easier to arrive at a jointly advantageous solution. We described how there is often a change of roles during the second phase of negotiation when the opposite sides engage in cooperative problem-solving. Even during the periods of harder bargaining it is important that they should not interpret disagreement as dislike or antagonism (Morley and Hosking 1984).

Research on bargaining over the telephone has found that here the person with the stronger case nearly always wins, whereas in face-to-face conditions this is not always so. The reason is that when people can see each other, interpersonal forces such as the desire to be liked become activated and may lead to larger concessions being made unnecessarily (Rutter 1987).

6 *Help by third parties*. Often two sides are unable to reach agreement and they seek help by a third party. This may be an arbitrator whose decision, it is agreed in advance, will be accepted, or it may be a negotiator who helps them find an acceptable solution. Negotiators can help simply by being there. The two sides are now under some pressure to be on their best behaviour, and not to be aggressive or unreasonable – in family disputes, for example. The third party can induce a problem-solving attitude, create a good atmosphere by means of humour, improve social relations between the two sides, improve communication between them and educate them in the process of negotiation. The third party can also help in the actual solution of the problem; for instance, by suggesting a solution, perhaps a new one, or suggesting to each side what concessions the other side might accept, and making sure that the self-esteem of each side is protected.

Effective negotiating skills

Some negotiators are found to be more effective than others – in being able to arrive at advantageous and integrative agreements.

1 *Toughness, stubbornness*. Do tough and inflexible or conciliatory negotiators do better? We saw that, in buying and selling, a relatively tough stance is advantageous both to an individual negotiator and in coming to the MJP. In more complex negotiations a combination of flexibility and rigidity has been found most effective. That is, negotiators are fairly rigid about their goals and give them up gradually or not at all, but are flexible in adopting a problem-solving attitude towards the means and are open to the exploration of different solutions.

2 *GRIT* (Graduated and Reciprocal Initiatives in Tension-reduction). Osgood (1962) proposed a strategy designed to resolve hostilities between two countries. This is intermediate between military action and unilateral disarmament. It goes as follows:

1 Announce the intention of reducing tension by making a number of concessions.
2 Announce each move in advance.
3 Invite the other side to reciprocate.
4 The concessions are continued for some time regardless of reciprocation.
5 Initiatives are risky but do not reduce the capacity to retaliate if necessary.
6 If there is no reciprocation, the level of concessions is increased.

GRIT has mainly been tested with the PDG. It is quite similar to tit-for-tat, but usually beats it, in generating C responses and increasing trust. The main failures are when there is strong conflict between the two sides, or there is a power difference or if there is no trust between them. Lindskold and Han (1988) found that GRIT not only produced cooperative responses from partners in the PDG, but in a subsequent negotiation task led to more integrative bargaining and more frequent discovery of the optimal solution.

It seems likely that GRIT has actually been used in international affairs, for example between the USA and the USSR. Concessions made by Kennedy during the Cuban missile crisis in 1962 were reciprocated by the Russians (Lindskold 1986).

3 *Skills of negotiators.* They are more successful if they have established a reputation for honesty. It is found that negotiators were rated most positively and produced larger concessions and greater collaboration when their actions seemed to be based on sincere beliefs about the value of their departments (Baron 1986). Negotiators are also successful if they can reduce anger or other negative feelings on the other side (Kabanoff 1985). These are part of a more general interpersonal style of creating a cooperative relationship.

4 *Personality of negotiators.* Many studies have been carried out to find which kind of personality makes the best negotiator, and a number of consistent results have now emerged. Rubin and Brown (1975) proposed a dimension of interpersonal orientation (IO), where a high IO person is very responsive to interpersonal aspects of relationships with others. They found in a series of laboratory experiments that bargaining was more effective in producing greater cooperation and mutual gain when both sides were cooperative – either in personality, or induced by experimental instruction. It was also found that bargaining was more successful if performers had higher IO, and where there was little power difference between the two sides. However, neither these nor other classifications of people have located a kind of personality that is consistently successful in negotiations (Lewicki and Litterer 1985).

Conclusions from game experiments

In our view most of these experiments are poor models for cooperation. In all cases the situation is rather abstract and artificial, and unrelated to the real concerns of subjects, although in some cases they stand to gain different amounts of money. In several games there is no communication between the players, and when this was allowed it was a major predictor of cooperation. In several cases there was no relationship – the other player was an invisible stranger, or even non-existent; when relationships were introduced the level of cooperation was greatly increased. It was assumed that players would simply try to maximise their own gains; some did, but others behaved in an altruistic way, to produce gains for the other person as well. Initially these games had no rules or norms. However, if a cooperative norm could be established, a high level of cooperation followed, as in the social dilemmas. And none of these games involved any joint activity, as real games, work and leisure do, and where the rewards are found from the joint activity itself. Such activities will be discussed in Chapter 7.

These games have produced a lot of interesting information, however, about the skills which can be successful in bringing about cooperation in these situations. The PDG is the most constrained and least realistic of them. Cooperation can emerge only in the course of a series of trials; tit-for-tat is the most effective strategy here – more so than constant cooperation, since this may be exploited. In the social traps situation, if communication is allowed, it is possible for players to establish a cooperative norm, persuasions to conform or sanctions for deviance. The economic games introduce the possibility of maximum joint profit, based on knowledge of the other player's matrix. Negotiation situations open up the possibility of more intricate joint problem-solving, or 'integrative bargaining', where each may give way on issues which are of less importance to that side. A special skill which is important here is GRIT.

Part two

The origins of cooperation

Chapter three

The evolution of cooperation

Cooperation in animals

Many species of animals cooperate, while others cooperate very little – just enough to produce the next generation. Some species cooperate very closely, more than the human species. We will start by looking at the main kinds of cooperation found in animals. These will be arranged under the three main forms of cooperation which we discuss in this book – family, work and shared activities, including communication.

Family

1 *Sexual behaviour.* Copulation requires male-female cooperation, with mutual willingness and coordinated behaviour. It does not need a great amount of love: the mantis eats her mate starting with his head while copulation is proceeding. Sex is the most basic, and biologically essential, kind of cooperation.

2 *Care of young by parents.* This is perhaps better described as 'altruism', since it is largely one-way. However, as we shall see in more detail for human infants, the young are programmed to interact with parental care-takers, and can be seen as taking part in cooperative routines. In addition, the parents cooperate with one another, for example by taking turns to guard the nest. Care of young is hard work, and entails frequent feeding, as well as nestbuilding and protection.

3 *Helpers at the nest.* This is help with the young by animals other than the parents. They help with feeding, nestbuilding and protection, and delay producing young themselves. As the term 'nest' implies, this is often found among birds.

Work

4 *Division of labour.* In the case of ants there is division of labour between the queen, males and sterile female workers. Less extreme divisions

are found between different kinds of workers – parents and helpers, leaders and followers, are examples. More spectacular is taking turns for guard duty by meerkats (see p. 56).

5 *Group hunting.* A group of lions, for example, are more successful if they hunt together; they share the spoils afterwards. The cooperation here involves some coordination; for example, driving prey into an ambush where others are waiting. Cooperation over food-gathering is mainly found in carnivores.

6 *Group attack on a predator.* Birds and mammals commonly mount a joint attack on a predator, known as 'mobbing' in birds. In meerkats these attacks are very closely coordinated.

7 *Help in fight within group.* One animal may come to the help of another, for example, in a fight over a female, as has been observed in baboons. Dolphins and whales will come to the help of another animal injured in a fight by swimming between this animal and the attacker, and by supporting and carrying it to safety.

8 *Warning calls.* One animal sees a predator approaching, and instead of hiding gives a warning call or a visual display to other members of its group, at some risk to itself. The others may hide or make a joint attack on the predator.

9 *Maintaining spatial structure.* A school of fish or a flock of birds move about with fixed distances between them, and they move and change direction in a highly coordinated way. A group of baboons or other monkeys on the march have a definite order, with the dominant males towards the front, children with their mothers, females with their mates.

Joint activities

10 *Grooming.* Non-human primates and other animals, spend a great deal of their time together cleaning each other's hair and skin. This is biologically important, but is also a sociable activity.

11 *Play.* Among non-human primates younger animals spent a great deal of time playing, chasing each other or pretending to fight. It takes two or more to do this, and they have to signal their intentions by the 'playface' or its equivalent.

12 *Communication.* Animals are equipped with the means of vocal, facial and other forms of communication with each other (Huntingford 1982).

Three theories of the evolution of cooperation

The Darwinian theory of evolution was about the survival of the fittest – the fittest individuals, that is. Why should cooperative tendencies evolve? Three main explanations have been put forward.

Kin selection

Darwin's theory of evolution said that any inherited property which helped its bearer to have more offspring would increase in frequency in the population. An animal is said to have greater 'inclusive fitness' if it causes its own genes to survive, which it can do either by producing a lot of offspring, or by helping other relatives – looking after grandchildren and cousins, for example. Inclusive fitness could be increased by a gene or genes to help or cooperate with relatives – this has come to be called 'kin selection' (Hamilton 1964).

The theory supposes that animals are in some sense able to estimate the degree of relatedness of other animals; this is deduced partly from physical similarity, partly from observation of who lives in the same nest; in some way they calculate the ratio of costs to increased benefits of the other. The degree of relatedness (r) of the two animals is the percentage of genes which they share – usually a half for children and sibs, a quarter for grandchildren, nephews and nieces, and half-sibs, and an eighth for cousins. This 'calculation' of costs and benefits is highly approximate, and involves no more mathematics on the part of those concerned than when a child catches a ball (Dawkins 1976). Animals do not pursue a purpose of maximising their biological fitness; an organ or a pattern of behaviour survives because it conveys a biological advantage, and hence is selected in the evolutionary process. It is human beings who make conscious plans for the future.

Animals are often able to recognise relatives or categories of relatives. In some bees, for example, one of them guards the entrance to the nest, and admits others in direct proportion to their degree of relatedness. Recognition here is based on similarity of appearance (Greenberg 1979). Another way in which kin are recognised is by knowing siblings, for example, in the nest. And there can be evolutionary development of the capacity to recognise kin. In humans as well as other animals the parent-child relation is closer than that between siblings, although the genetic resemblance is the same – 50 per cent in each case. However, the parent-child link is more certain. Similarly, the mother-child link is more certain than the father-child one, especially in promiscuous cultures; this explains why the mother-child link is usually closer. Parents do more for children than vice versa; this too can be explained – since parents can do more to promote their genes by looking after the next generation (Dawkins 1976).

There is quite a lot of evidence in support of the kin selection theory. First, bees recognise kin, on the basis of smell, and admit others to the colony if sufficiently related. Second, in ants (see pp. 54ff.), sisters share about three-quarters of their genes, brothers only a quarter, while brothers and sisters are almost unrelated. There is highly cooperative group life, based on the females, who are all sisters, in most species. Third, ground squirrels often give warning calls, although this is very dangerous. These calls are most often given by adult females, when defending an area also occupied by sisters, daughters and half-sisters, not by cousins, nieces or grand-daughters. Fourth, in Japanese macaques spatial proximity and frequency of grooming are closely correlated with genetic closeness, and this predicts grooming even when proximity has been taken into account.

An interesting example of kin-related cooperation has been found in the Florida scrub jay, a bird only found in Florida. Pairs are mated for life, which is up to eight years. They produce a brood every year, and stay within their territory for the year. A permanent territory of 10–30 acres is occupied and defended. There is cooperative breeding, in which the parents are helped by others in about 50 per cent of cases, mainly by males since the females leave to breed elsewhere. Most help is given by sibs or other close kin, and to single parents of the same sex. Woolfenden (1973) found that these helpers increase the survival rate of broods by about 65 per cent. This is not due to better food but to better defence against predators, and also to some increase in size of territory.

Evidently helpers at the nest improve the survival of the brood – to whom they are related. But why don't they breed themselves? They may have difficulty finding a mate or territory, and may do better to wait to inherit the parental territory. Meanwhile, they are acquiring breeding expertise, and can look forward to being helped themselves in the future (Emlen 1984).

In the Florida jays there is a clear hierarchy in each family, the breeding male coming top, even over his own mother unless she has a mate. Males dominate females, older ones over younger. If the breeding male leaves or dies, the next male in the hierarchy takes his place.

However, kin selection is not the only genetic basis for cooperation. There are a number of species in which cooperation and help take place with non-kin. In dwarf mongeese, for example, there are helpers at the nest who are not closely related. But the most spectacular case is symbiotic cooperation between completely different species.

Reciprocal altruism

Trivers (1971) suggested another possible origin of altruism and cooperation – that the altruistic act is later reciprocated by the recipient, and that such reciprocity itself could be selected as an evolutionary strategy. He supposed that this reciprocity could build up over the course of a long period of association between two animals, or in a group of animals, and there would be discrimination against cheats – those who failed to reciprocate.

The benefits of reciprocal altruism are shown in the case of mice: if kept in isolation they cannot prevent sores on parts of their heads which they cannot reach to groom themselves; in groups they can lick one another's heads (Dawkins 1976). Vampire bats regurgitate blood to one another, when the other has failed to feed and is very hungry, and this is done on a reciprocal basis. Another example is chimpanzee males who help non-kin to secure a female.

Symbiotic relations between organisms of different species, and who are certainly not kin, can be explained in terms of reciprocal altruism. These relations are most common between different kinds of insects, and we shall discuss ants and aphids later. This is probably because insect social systems are based on impersonal cooperation, which can be extended indiscriminately to another group (Wilson 1975). Examples of symbiosis from higher up the evolutionary scale are crocodiles and birds who pick their teeth in exchange for protection, and fish with smaller 'cleaner' fish who remove their parasites, or provide camouflage. There are mixed flocks of birds where a well integrated flock is joined by another species, for protection against predators and better foraging. These examples are encouraging news for those who think that sociobiology has entirely pessimistic implications for peace between different human groups.

Reciprocal altruism would be expected to develop under certain conditions: long life, small and stable groups, low dispersal, little hierarchy, and, above all, ability to recognise other individuals. Trivers (1985) argues that these conditions can be found among primitive men, so that this may be an important basis for human cooperation.

A serious problem with reciprocal altruism is the danger of others cheating, that is not reciprocating. The models discussed later suggest that cheating is not an evolutionary stable system, since 100 per cent of cheaters form a very unhelpful group, and because cheats lose out against tit-for-tat grudgers. There are, however, short-term benefits of cheating, and longer-term ones if it is not detected. There are probably selection pressures to identify cheats and remember who has cheated in the past. Trivers cites the example of male songbirds who have established neighbouring territories, and tolerate each others' singing. However, if a bird moves to a different piece of territory, this is treated as cheating, and he is attacked.

Trivers (1985) argues that human cheating is restrained by the formation of friendship relationships, since helping behaviour and liking cause each other. Friendship and its emotional rewards ensure the continuation of cooperation and help. We shall argue later, however, that external rewards play quite a small role in the formation of close relationships (Chapter 7). Trivers also believes that the prevention of cheating, and keeping up reciprocity, lie behind the human concerns with fairness, justice and the punishment of offenders.

How cooperation becomes established – Axelrod's theory

In an initially asocial, selfish community, there is a problem about how cooperation or altruism ever get started in the evolutionary process. Cooperation may be beneficial for communities, but usually individuals can do even better for themselves by letting others cooperate while they cheat. Axelrod and Hamilton (1984) see this as an example of the Prisoners' Dilemma Game; in their game-playing experiments tit-for-tat was the winning strategy against all others; that is, cooperate if the other player does, but cheat if he does, over a long series of games. How could the positive cycle start, or break in to a community of non-cooperators? It could happen if the other is recognisably kin, so that there is a part-interest in his pay-offs. It could also start by clustering, so that a small group of non-kin could establish a positive tit-for-tat sequence between themselves. The amount of cooperation would be enhanced if there is to be a long series of future meetings, with no known end-point, if cheating is punished, if individuals can be socialised to care for one another, if they are taught reciprocity, and if they are good at recognising individuals and detecting cheating.

Further research in the PDG tradition has used computer modelling to see which strategy is the most successful. Continual cooperation does quite well, but is beaten by other strategies; for example, strategies that punish the opponent for not cooperating. Tit-for-tat generally holds up against other strategies, but if it is opposed by constant cooperation, the ESS is a mixture of the two (Hirschleifer and Coll 1988). Dawkins (1976) tried out computer models of different strategies, and found that over a long series of games what he called 'grudgers' won over 'suckers' and 'cheats'; grudgers were using the tit-for-tat strategy, and he argues that this is the dominant evolutionary strategy.

However, it can be argued that this kind of work is entirely irrelevant, since the PDG may not fit the biological situation that it is supposed to model. The decision to cooperate may be made because the probable pay-off is greater than that from acting alone – as in the case of lions hunting; the main costs are due to the loss of freedom.

Looking over the twelve examples of cooperation with which we began this chapter, how far would it be possible for example to 'cheat'? It would be possible to beg for food when hungry but not reciprocate, to be groomed but fail to groom in return, to be helped in an in-group fight but not help in return, or to benefit from warning calls but never give any. However, none of these involves simultaneous moves, in complete ignorance of what the other is going to do, and cheats would not prosper for very long. In several cases animals seek and evidently are rewarded by the relationship (e.g. with mates, offspring), or the activities (e.g. sex, grooming). These relationships and activities have important long-term consequences as well. Presumably the enjoyment of relationships and of the joint activities may be due to evolutionary pressures to encourage cooperation.

Group selection

This theory suggests that *groups* which are cooperative (or altruistic, etc.) will be more likely to survive and proliferate because of the biological advantages of cooperation – helping to defend against predators, looking after young, and so on. This has been offered as an explanation for some otherwise puzzling kinds of animal behaviour. Among langurs, for example, an adult male will displace another male attached to a group of females, after which this new leader tries to kill infants in the group up to six months of age. This could be explained as being in the interest of the whole group by reducing overpopulation in relation to food supply. However, this pattern of behaviour could also be explained in terms of the inclusive fitness theory, explained above; the new leader saves energy in looking after unrelated offspring, and makes the female ready for bearing his own (Hrdy 1977).

There is a difficulty with this as an explanation of altruism, however, that a selfish individual in an altruistic group would prosper and his genes would multiply at the expense of those of the others. Altruism is not an evolutionarily stable strategy. For group selection to work at all, against individual selection, the conditions would have to be just right. These are: the existence of a large number of small groups or colonies, very little migration between them, and high rates of extinction or disintegration of these colonies due to an unfavourable environment (Maynard-Smith 1974).

Something like these conditions have been found for mice in haystacks, and have been created experimentally in beetles. However, it is still not known how often the right conditions for group selection occur in nature, and the present balance of expert opinion is that group selection is probably less important than the two other evolutionary origins of cooperation and altruism.

A number of biologists have been attracted to group selection theories to explain human cooperative behaviour. The reason is that humans often cooperate in groups of non-kin, such as ethnic groups and political parties. The conditions for group selection may have been right for food-foraging hominids during the late Pleistocene period (300,000–100,000 B.C.) when they went about in small, partly isolated groups (Hamilton 1975). During this period great evolutionary changes were taking place, such as an increase of brain size from 400–500c.c. to 1400–1700c.c. During this period there were small groups of kin, hunters and gatherers, on the grasslands of East Africa for example. Groups of males hunted increasingly large animals with gradually improving weapons. This required both intelligence and cooperation. Dominant males ruled families and hunting groups; they needed to be 'controlled, cunning, cooperative, attractive to the ladies, good with children, relaxed, tough, eloquent, skilful, knowledgeable and proficient in self-defense and hunting' (Fox 1972). At a later stage, when tribes and countries engaged in intermittent warfare, other qualities were demanded and selected – team play, altruism, patriotism and so on (Alexander 1979).

Tiger (1969) suggested that it was the males who developed cooperation, through centuries of hunting in groups, where the more cooperative groups would be successful and survive. This cooperation entailed the formation of male dominance hierarchies, and male bonding. This kind of organisation is found in baboons and other primates, in primitive societies today, and, Tiger suggests, in many modern social institutions. Politics, sports teams and social clubs often have a similar structure.

It is true that among humans there is a tendency for males to form larger, task-oriented and more hierarchical groups than females do, and that there is no known explanation for this in terms of socialisation.

A quite different version of group selection was put forward by Boyd and Richerson (1985). They believe that the human tendency to form groups with non-kin is difficult to explain by genetic models, and suggest that group selection is responsible, but through *cultural* not genetic selection. What is meant by cultural selection is that an element of culture is introduced, it becomes popular, is taught to children and perhaps enforced by sanctions. The spread of fashions, new ideas, and items of behaviour of all kinds, have been analysed in this way. Boyd and Richerson extend their theory by observing that the phenomenon of conformity leads to greater homogeneity in groups, so that the conditions are right for selection of cooperating groups through extinction or disintegration and redistribution of the others. Again the theory is attractive but as yet unproved. Meanwhile there are several versions of the group selection theory which are possible explanations of cooperation in human groups between non-kin.

Examples of cooperative animals

Ants, bees and wasps

There are many species, including 10,000 of ants, and all display an extra-ordinary degree of cooperation. They are also very successful – the weight of the world's ants exceeds that of all land vertebrates, and they have been described as 'the actual owners of the Amazon basin' (Trivers 1985). One nest may contain a million ants and weigh several tons. The degree of cooperation is so high that in many ways an ants' nest is like a single organism – all members may be the offspring of one queen or of a very small number of them, food is shared, and the temperature is regulated jointly (Dawkins 1976).

Above all, there is a high degree of 'reproductive altruism', by the non-reproductive, wingless, female workers. There is an unusual reproductive system: the queen acts as an egg factory, and can produce either fertilised or unfertilised eggs. The unfertilised ones become males, who have only one set of chromosomes; the fertilised eggs become females who have two. This leads to a peculiar set of genetic resemblances. In particular, sisters share three-quarters of their genes when there is a single queen, since they are like identical twins on their father's side, and like ordinary siblings on their mother's. On the other hand, sisters share only one-eighth of their genes with their brothers. This gives an explanation of the close cooperative relations between the worker-sisters, their concern for their mother (since she can produce more sisters), and their successful manipulation of their mother to produce more females than males, in the ratio of 3:1 (Hamilton 1972).

The delayed reproduction, or absence of it, and the colossal amount of work done by the workers is in their genetic interest, since although they do not reproduce themselves, their new sisters share three-quarters of their genes, whereas for those few females who become queens, their offspring share only half of their genes. The study of ant colonies has provided the most telling support for the kin selection theory.

There is further division of labour and cooperation among the workers. Several specialised castes have evolved, such as soldiers – large ants with big jaws, living larders – who hang motionless and swell up to a large size when full, and agricultural ants – with further subdivisions for cutting leaves and caring for fungus gardens. What is interesting for our purposes is the development through evolution of these different castes, all of them non-reproductive, in the interest of the colony as a whole.

A further kind of cooperation is through 'slavery'. In a number of ant species, the workers do very little work, but instead make raids on the nests of other ants of a different species, led by their soldier ants, overcoming the others, and carrying off the worker pupae to their own nest. Once they have been born, these slaves are put to work cleaning the nest, foraging for food, and caring for young, 'blissfully ignorant of the fact that they are unrelated to the queen and to the young they are tending' (Dawkins 1976). When the young are mostly reared by slaves the sex ratio is 12:1 rather than 3:1. Presumably female worker slaves try to produce a preponderance of females in order to share the work, following their own genetic programme, but they are outwitted by the queen whose interest is to produce equal numbers.

In addition to keeping slaves, some ants have an equivalent of farm animals, such as aphids like greenfly, which suck juice out of plants and excrete a sugary substance, which can be 'milked'. The aphids can suck sap out of plants, which the ants cannot. Going further down the animal scale, ants keep plants, by cultivating fungus gardens, sometimes on a large scale, excavating as much as 40 tons of soil (Wilson 1971).

Meerkats

We turn from the very broad category of organisms just described, to a particular species, which has been found to display a very clear pattern of cooperative behaviour.

The meerkat is a kind of mongoose, found in the Kalahari Desert, and lives in highly cooperative groups of six to nine. The most interesting feature is their division of labour, between digging holes for snakes, scorpions and grubs, and being on guard duty, on the look-out for eagles, jackals, foxes and other predators. It is difficult to look for predators, while your head is down a hole, and taking turns solves the problem. The meerkat on guard duty climbs to the top of a tree or termite mound, adopts an erect posture, and keeps a very keen watch – for up to 90 minutes in the intense desert heat, and exposed to attacks from eagles. When the guard is changed, a second animal takes up post within 10 seconds. Certain animals do more frequent guard duty, and for longer spells than others.

There is also cooperation over defence against predators. With large animals like jackals and Cape foxes, the meerkats bunch together, bark, and then charge in a close group. Each kind of predator is dealt with differently, but always in a highly coordinated manner. One meerkat alone would be quite unable to take on these predators, who are much bigger than they are.

Digging for food is also cooperative. They form a line to move sand, and they dig together and share whatever is found at the bottom of the hole. Only one female is allowed to breed at a time, and cheats are punished, so that there is some female migration. Other females do long spells of baby-minding, for up to two days at a time, while the mother is foraging. These babysitters suckle the young, protect them from predators by lying on them, and regurgitate the best food for them.

There is division of labour for guard duty, leading attacks on predators, childbearing and babysitting, and several animals are needed for some of these tasks. In a very small group like four there would not be enough helpers to go round. In a very large group there is not enough food to be found in the territory, hence the size of group actually found (Macdonald 1986).

Non-human primates

Most species of monkeys and apes are highly social and cooperative.

> The majority of primates live their whole lives in close association with others. The social group occupies a range, shares knowledge of local foods, paths and dangers, and offers opportunity for play, grooming, and close association. In the group the young and females are protected and dominance gives an order to society.
>
> (Washburn and Hamburg 1965: 4)

In addition to the joint product of biological goals, monkeys and apes spend a great deal of time in social activities like grooming and play, or just sitting in bodily contact. They also develop long-term relationships, with children, mates and between leaders and subordinates. Baboons will risk their lives while defending other monkeys against fierce predators like leopards. Cooperation is not just within the immediate family group, but extends to large groups of up to a hundred in the case of baboons.

The family

Monogamy, between mating couples, is found in some kinds of apes, such as gibbons, and in several kinds of monkeys, such as marmosets, though these are in a minority. It is very interesting that monogamy occurs in 92 per cent of bird species, probably because all eggs need to be watched, and a mate is needed to find food. It is not understood why some primates are monogamous and others not, since not all of the former provide paternal help. There are other biological benefits, such as sharing the nesting place and giving an early start to breeding. And monogamy is more common when food or nesting places are scarce, and is more common among forest-dwelling animals where the competition is more intense (Clutton-Brock and Harvey 1976). Polygamy is more common: families consist of one male, several females and their children, and these relationships may be long-lasting, as with gorillas, but not with langurs. This kind of family tends to evolve when there is an abundance of food, especially during the breeding season, when females can keep young in feeding grounds hidden from predators, there is longer life so that males can defer breeding, and there are nested territories so that several families can live in the male's territory.

Multi-male groups, with a number of both males and females and their young, and some degree of promiscuity, are found in baboons and chimpanzees. A final arrangement is the solitary one, where mates do not cohabit at all, as with orangutans (Wilson 1975; Passingham 1982).

Pair-bonds are established in birds by courtship displays and rituals, which can be elaborate and prolonged. Chimpanzees and gorillas also use elaborate courtship displays, with rhythmic hooting and chestbeating. The sexual behaviour itself is probably an even more potent source of bonding.

Many species of mammals, including most primates, are polygamous; the basic group again consisting of a single male, several females and their offspring.

The mother–infant bond

In all creatures some learning is necessary, if only to find out where the nest is and to recognise their mother. Mothers look after, feed, and protect their young during this learning period. For most mammals this is a matter of a few weeks; wolves, jackals and hyenas will go hunting at six weeks. However, for the primates it is far longer; chimpanzees and gorillas are not fully adult until they are 10–14 years of age, nearly as long as for humans.

Infants of many species become attached to their mothers, that is they have a special affection for her, shown by clinging or otherwise seeking proximity, gazing and vocalising towards her, distress at separation, and sustained contact at reunion. Attachment of infants to their mothers is found in 9–10 per cent of mammalian species, and has the functions of protection against predators and provision of food, hence promoting survival of infants. It is found under certain conditions; for example, where the young are mobile at an early age and liable to stray, and when several females share a male's territory, so that infants might become confused with one another.

Mothers become attached to their young, partly through the process of giving birth and eating the placenta, which produce hormone changes that stimulate maternal behaviour. The infant's clinging, sucking, crying, looking and other signals are further stimuli for caretaking. Infants become attached to their mothers because they in turn have the right kind of skin; baby monkeys appear to find physical contact with their mother comforting, they seek it when anxious, and in the absence of their mother will cling to cloth of the right furry feel, as the Harlows showed (1965). Mothers lick, groom, feed and provide warmth, and soon establish interactive routines, which appear to be the basis of grooming.

Cooperation in larger groups, and between non-kin

Pairs of male baboons will form coalitions beginning with one male helping another to gain access to a female, which might otherwise be impossible. Help is solicited by head-turning signals, and is reciprocated. Sometimes such coalitions are between kin, but often they are not and appear to be cases of reciprocal altruism. Vervet monkeys will reciprocate grooming, but only to non-kin. Male baboons may also help a female who is being attacked, and this leads later to sexual access to her (Packer 1977).

Baboons, rhesus monkeys, and other monkeys, live in quite large groups, of 50–100; smaller than this for chimpanzees and gorillas. These groups share a territory, go on the march together, and cooperate over defence against predators, giving warning calls, and in sharing food. Where a large group moves about together they adopt a characteristic spatial pattern. The dominant males, with females and their infants, are in the middle, with less dominant males around the edges, and some ahead of the group by 200–400 yards to give the alarm.

Stable and generally cooperative groups of baboons and others are based on a hierarchy of males, where females take the social status of their mates, and high-ranking males have greater access to the females. The dominance relations between males are established by fights or threat displays, and the alpha animal becomes the leader of what may be a large group. He occupies a central place in the territory, and others look towards him in an 'attention structure', so that if he suddenly decides to move, all the others follow at once. In chimpanzees the alpha animal establishes his position through a series of alliances, with both males and females. In exchange for the support of females he defends them and acts as a peacemaker. A rival male may try to separate the alpha animal from his supporters by attacking them (De Waal 1982).

The formation of a dominance hierarchy seems to be a device for turning aggression and competition in groups of males into a stable, peaceful and cooperative social system, in which the aggression is usually invisible. In primates there is an additional feature of the system, that some 'control animals' or strong leaders, prevent fights between the others. In insect societies the hierarchy goes further, so that there is division of labour — those at different levels doing different jobs. Aggression may occur in primate groups when a newcomer appears on the scene, threatening the social order until he has been forced to the lowest status. Inferior position in the hierarchy is signalled by submissive postures, lower ranks doing more grooming and being mounted.

The extent to which cooperative behaviour will evolve, and the forms it takes, depend on the nature of the environment. The non-human primates evolved in savannahs or in heavily forested areas. There was quite a lot of food, mainly from vegetable sources, but also danger from large animals. Since nearly all primate species are cooperative, the advantages must be greater than the costs.

Shared activities

So far we have been thinking mainly about cooperation which has a serious biological purpose – like finding food, looking after young, defence against predators. There are other kinds of social behaviour which appear to be wholly social and cooperative, and which do not seem to have any immediate biological purpose.

Grooming consists of cleaning another animal's fur and skin, to remove parasites and clean wounds. In higher primates this is done mainly by hand, though the mouth is used as well to lick wounds, for example. Grooming is often reciprocated, and most of it is directed to parts of the body which an animal can't reach itself. However, grooming has become mainly a ritualised form of positive social behaviour, in some cases entirely so; for example, when grooming areas which *can* be reached. A great deal of time is spent on this activity by primates, though also by insects and birds, especially in species where there is a lot of bodily contact. Although grooming is reciprocated, it is done more to higher status animals and is partly a signal for appeasement, used in tense situations to avert aggression. It is also done between animals in close relationships, like mothers and their young. It is solicited in various ways, such as lying down, and presenting the back and neck (Wilson 1975).

Play is a kind of non-serious activity, which is enjoyed for its own sake, using or copying activities from more serious activities. It is like exploration, in seeing what can be done in some situation or with some object, often in a new way. Play is only found in higher mammals and is believed to have a socialisation function in developing skills of young animals. It often consists of mock-aggression and chasing, which is of course cooperative in this context. Invitation to play needs a 'play face'. Monkeys can also play alone by leaping, climbing and swinging, though these can also be done together.

Greeting. Many species of animals, when they meet, use some kind of greeting behaviour, apparently to reassure each other about their friendly intentions. In the primates this may consist of lip-smacking, touching hands, a play face, embracing, putting lips together, or putting a hand to the lips of the other (Passingham 1982).

Singing duets. This is done by mating pairs, or families in more than 200 species of birds. It is found especially in tropical birds, who have prolonged pair-bonds and year-round territory. It has the functions of helping the male to defend the territory, enhancing bonding, coordinating defence and preventing misdirected aggression. It is an interesting case of cooperation based on close coordination. The nearest primate cases are the chorus of howler monkeys and the calls of gibbons. Choruses of much larger groups are found in frogs and crickets (Farabough 1982).

Communication

> By far the greatest part of the whole system of communication seems to be devoted to the organization of social behaviour of the group, to dominance and subordination, the maintenance of peace and cohesion of the group, reproduction, and care of the young.
>
> (Marler 1965: 584)

In these ways animal communication is used to enable cooperation towards biological goals to take place.

A lot of animal communication is directly related to the pursuit of these biological goals. Animals may beg for food, bees give information about where food is by means of the bees' dance, a leader may initiate a move in search of food, worker ants have to coordinate their work to obtain and store food. None of this cooperative activity would be possible without the necessary social signals to influence and coordinate. Genes would not be passed on unless females could signal their sexual readiness and attract males, and unless males could put on a suitable display to make them acceptable to the females. In some birds complex and coordinated courtship rituals are then needed to produce the necessary bonding. The care of young requires complementary sets of maternal and infantile signals; these interlocking signals prepare both sides to cooperate in giving and receiving maternal care. Izard (unpublished) carried out an experiment in which the facial nerves of several young monkeys were severed, with the result that these animals were neglected by their mothers and never succeeded in establishing social relations.

Some alarm calls evolve so that animals can tell members of their own group, especially kin, of the arrival of predators by signals which do not give away their own position.

Animal communication uses a wide range of signals – facial expression, vocalisations, touch, gaze, gestures and other bodily movement, posture, spatial position and movement, smell and taste, and appearance. Let us look at facial expression in monkeys and apes to see how the ritualised meaning of these signals has evolved. A rather non-cooperative signal is the simplest case: threat signals. An animal who was about to attack would open its mouth, with teeth visible, in order to bite; this later became ritualised as an 'intention signal', so that simply showing the teeth acts as sufficient threat. Smiling is a little more obscure: it may have originated from the play face with mouth relaxed and teeth covered, used as an invitation to play; or it may have come from the 'bared-teeth scream face', used as a signal for appeasement and submission.

An interesting study of the use of vocalisations in chimpanzees and gorillas was carried out by Marler (1976). Chimps use about 13 categories of sound, gorillas 16, and there are clear equivalences. Groups of chimps vocalise 10–100 times per hour, mainly when separated individuals and groups renew contact, and for keeping in touch at a distance; for example, reporting meat-eating. Gorillas vocalise much less often. They keep together in small groups, the sounds are mainly made by adult males, mostly belching, during feeding, grooming and play (Argyle 1988).

Some animal communication is *not* cooperative – e.g. signals in threat and aggression, although these are used in the interests of the kinship group. Most animal communication involves cooperation over sending and receiving messages – there is no point in sending unless someone receives. However, sometimes there is deception, though this is relatively rare. The most striking case is perhaps camouflage to hide from predators, as in the case of insects which look like leaves. In aggressive encounters some animals can enhance their threat diplays by appearing to be bigger than they are, or to have larger claws than is really the case (Trivers 1985).

There are several different kinds of communication.

1 *Expressing emotions and interpersonal attitudes*. This includes sexual signals, maternal-infantile, and affiliative signals. In each case the

purpose of the communication is to influence the other, but within a system of cooperative behaviour.

2 *Identity signals*. These indicate which species the sender belongs to, which group, and which individual he is. Bird songs show all this very clearly so that a bird can return to the right nest, sometimes among thousands. Ants can tell whether visitors belong to the nest, and should be allowed in, by means of chemical signals. Other signals indicate the status of the sender in the group – by a monkey's posture, for example.

3 *Sending information about the outside world*. Most signals are about the internal state of an animal, but also have the function of influencing others. Other signals are about matters outside the sender. Alarm calls are about predators, food calls indicate that food has been found, and the bees' dance tells the others where it is (Argyle 1988; DeVore 1965).

Is human nature cooperative?

There are three aspects of human nature from the evolutionary point of view. First, there are those features which are mainly unlearnt, the result of evolution, like the features of animals described earlier. This includes not only bodily features like faces and voices, but may also include patterns of behaviour, such as facial expressions, which have given a selective advantage. Second, some features of human behaviour may be very widespread, but due to cultural evolution, as described earlier. Wearing clothes and watching TV may be widespread but are obviously not the result of genetic evolution. Third, other features are universal, but require common human experiences, such as close contact with a caretaker or with other children, for them to appear. The incest taboo is an example, since in the Israeli kibbutz it becomes extended to all members of a child's age-group. This taboo presumably gave a selective advantage because it prevents inbreeding. Other marriage rules give similar advantages.

We might decide that something was genetic in addition to being universal if (a) there is a clear physiological basis, as in the case of facial expressions, (b) twin studies show that it is mainly or partly inherited, (c) it is found in infants, like the capacity to interact, and (d) it is found in non-human primates, though this is a less reliable argument, since something which is innate for primates may be less so for man. There can be a problem, however, that the same gene might manifest itself differently in different environments. We might decide that a feature was the product of cultural evolution if its history could be traced, to particular innovators, and occasions for it had developed too rapidly for genetic evolution.

Family

The clearest example of universal and innate aspects of human nature which are relevant to cooperation lie in the sphere of the family.

Sexual cooperation

Males and females have sexual needs, which result in mating and the procreation of children; intercourse is intensely rewarding. There is some degree of bonding between partners, and the nuclear family is found in all societies. In all human societies so far there has also been some division of labour between males and females. Females look after children and family. Males hunt, do heavy work and fight in groups with other males. This is partly due to the females' greater involvement in childrearing (see below), and to evolutionary pressures for males to compete for females and consequently to become larger and more aggressive, but also because parents rear boys and girls differently to maintain these patterns (Hinde 1984). Buss (1989) in a 37-culture survey found that women wanted a mate who was rich, hardworking and ambitious; men wanted a mate who was young and attractive. Women look for support and security, men for fertility. There is evidence that people tend to marry others who are genetically similar to themselves – giving a further boost to the genes involved (Rushton 1989).

Mother-child relations

In all human societies there is a long period of childrearing. Infants are ready to feed, interact and relate to mother from very soon after birth. There is powerful bonding between mothers and infants. Children are more important to mothers than to fathers, partly because mothers are more certain which are her children, but also because mothers do the early feeding and probably become more strongly bonded. Although child abuse does take place, this is mostly to adopted, foster, or stepchildren, rather than to natural children (see Figure 3.1).

Father-child relations

The nuclear family is universal, men stick (more or less) both to their wives and to their children. However, in cultures where there is a high level of promiscuity, husbands do little for their wives' children (who may well have a different father), and more for their sisters' children, who are certainly related to them. Flinn (1981) found a strong correlation between confidence in paternity and care for wife's children, across 289 societies.

Kinship

In all cultures there is recognition of kinship, and this affects who may be married (which kind of cousin, for example), and creates obligations to look after various categories of kin. While kinship is less important in modern societies, more major help is given to kin than to friends, as would be expected from inclusive fitness theory (Argyle and Henderson 1985). Kinship has also been the basis of groupings larger than the nuclear family, especially since settled agriculture started. The rule about clan exogamy, that is marrying outside the clan, has the effect of creating bonds and

Figure 3.1 Incidence of validated cases of neglect (*N* = 64,544) and abuse (*N* = 26,304) of children in USA for 1976 according to household composition and age of victim

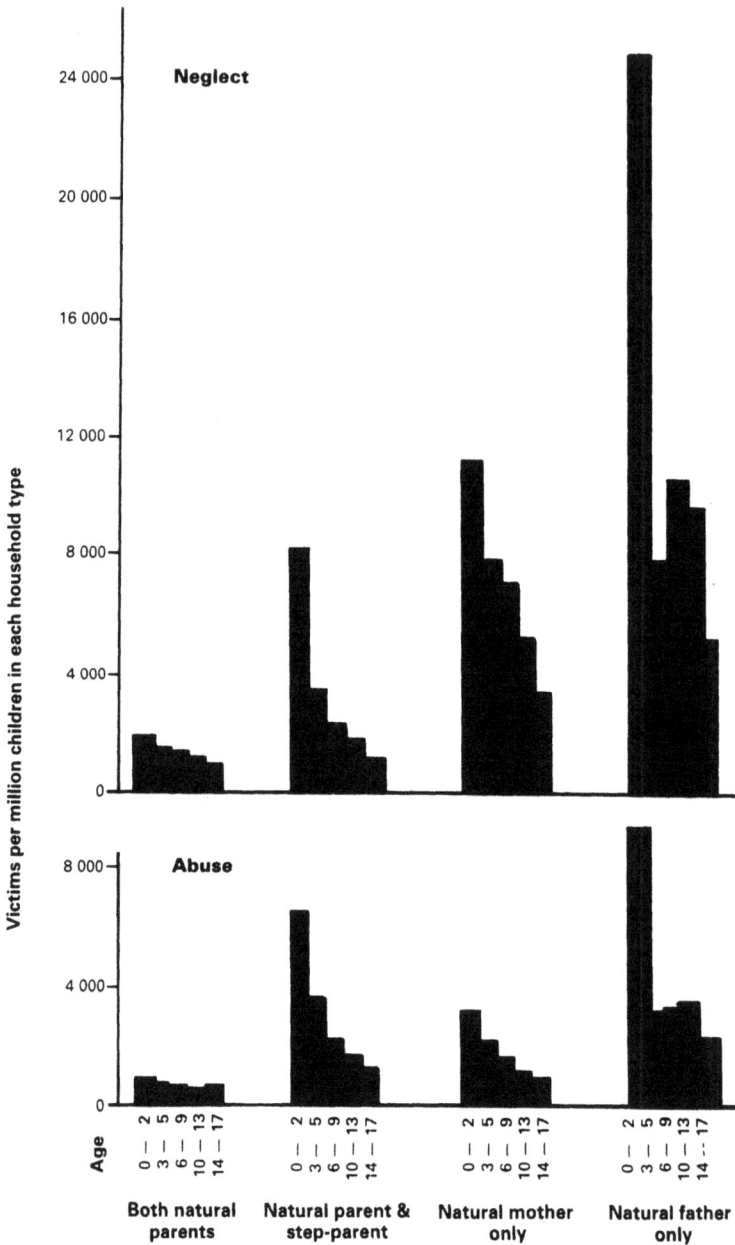

Source: Daly and Wilson 1988

generating cooperation between a number of clans, with obvious military advantage in a context of intermittent tribal warfare. Inheritance of property is mainly to members of the family – 55 per cent in the USA (Rushton 1989).

Work and cooperation in larger groups

We have just seen how kinship bonds developed, by a combination of genetic and cultural processes. We discussed earlier some theories of group selection, one being that many years of cooperation over hunting had led to the selection of cooperativeness on the scale of the small band. These bands provided mutual protection against predators, enabled cooperation in hunting, and mutual help with tasks like housebuilding. These bands also came into competition with each other; a tendency for groups to engage in aggressive conflict with other groups has been a pervasive feature of human history. Alexander (1979) suggests that this created a selection pressure to combine in progressively larger groups. And there has been a gradual tendency during human history for this to happen – from the band to the tribe, chiefdom and state. In view of the relatively short timescale, however, it is likely that *cultural* evolution was involved, where identification with increasingly large groups (such as England, Britain, Europe), is taught to the young, and maintained by literature, history, language and so on.

Finally, there is an apparently universal cultural development of rules and sanctions to enforce different kinds of cooperation, as described in the next chapter.

Shared activities and communication

Sociability

Sociability is found in all cultures; for example, in the form of conversation, dancing, music and games. A common feature of all of these activities is shared and coordinated bodily movement. We shall see in Chapter 5 that children, from a very early age, are able to take part in cooperative play, the main form of sociability in the early years. They also show an early concern at the distress of others and often try to relieve it. Humans and animals are distressed at the sight of others suffering. Weiss *et al.* (1971) found that when human subjects were able to turn off a shock which was being received by another, this acted as a reinforcer of the behaviour involved, and the response became rapidly faster, compared with other subjects who were not reinforced.

Non-verbal communication

NVC depends on the use of bodily signals, such as facial expressions, which are innate, though modified by learning. From an early age infants are able to use these signals, and do so to communicate in a way which is synchronised with other interactors (see Chapter 5).

Verbal communication

It is generally agreed that language is too complex a system to be learned unless there is some preparedness to do so. Nevertheless, learning from parents plays an important role; at the same time children learn turn-taking and the whole system of communicating by means of voice, face and gaze.

Individual differences in sociability

Extraversion is correlated with physiological structures in the brain; need for affiliation is correlated with strength of the immune system (see p. 207). Twin studies have been carried out on altruism, empathy, nurturance and extraversion – traits which are closely associated with cooperativeness, and found the percentages of heritability as shown in Table 3.1. This table shows the relative importance of inheritance for various traits, as derived from the greater correlations found between identical twins as compared with fraternal twins.

Table 3.1   Inheritance of cooperative traits (percentage heritability)

Trait	%
altruism	51
empathy	51
nurturance	43
extraversion	50

Source: Rushton et al. 1986; Floderus-Myrhed et al. 1980

Chapter four

Cultural differences in cooperation

It is very interesting to see how far cooperativeness varies between different cultures. This can show whether cooperation, or different forms of it, are universal and therefore possible innate features of human nature. It can also show the conditions under which cooperation is more prevalent.

Anthropological case studies

Margaret Mead (1937) looked at the anthropological materials available at that time, and selected thirteen primitive societies, of which she rated five as primarily cooperative, three as competitive, and four as individualistic. In her edited volume she invited a number of anthropologists to describe these tribes. At a much later date Bethlehem (1982) had another go at a rather different list, but with one overlap. Mead's cultures came mainly from the American Indians and the Pacific islands, Bethlehem's from Africa.

The 'culture pattern' approach of Mead and Benedict has been criticised, especially by British social anthropologists, on the grounds that it does not do justice to the complexities of cultures. Nevertheless, primitive societies are much more homogeneous than modern ones, and there are some big differences between them. We shall pursue them to see what can be learnt about cooperation.

Mead thought that the Zuni Indians of New Mexico were the most cooperative society then known. They live by agriculture and keeping sheep in a rather hard environment; there is cooperation over working the fields, looking after sheep, and building houses; religious ceremonies consist of rituals; education emphasises cooperation and sobriety. There is little accumulation of wealth, and it is redistributed by gifts and in ceremonies. On the other hand among the Zuni, there are many quarrels, and some hatred of the priests, as if the inhibition of individuality and initiative has gone too far.

Mead's next most cooperative tribe were the Bathonga, a large Bantu group in South Africa. They live in larger villages of 1,000 or more, controlled by a hierarchy of chiefs, headmen, and fathers, though there is a high level of cooperation and sharing. There is a lot of sociability, especially among men, who engage in games and drinking, and strangers are welcome. There is polygamy, and wives have to be bought, but there is no conflict over this. There is very harsh indoctrination and initiation of boys, to break undisciplined personalities. However there is rivalry in the form of sorcery and warfare, and in struggles for kingship, and there are misfits who have not learned to fit in and cooperate; these become magicians or artists.

Bethlehem's cooperative groups also came from Southern Africa: the Bushmen from the Kalahari Desert in Botswana and Namibia, and the Mbuti in Zaire. Both are hunters and gatherers, living in small, fluid groups; the hunting is cooperative and the proceeds are shared; there is a lot of mutual help in building huts, and there is no accumulation of property; helpfulness and cooperativeness are greatly valued, and there is a high level of warmth and friendliness.

Some other cooperative societies are quite different. For example, the Swazis, also from Southern Africa, are more settled, live in villages, grow crops and keep cattle, and have centralised leadership. Cooperation takes place not only within the large households, but in work parties which are organised for large enterprises, under a leader, unpaid to help a neighbour or kinsman. Here and amongst the Chewa, ambition and wealth are disapproved of and lead to unpopularity. In these peoples, 'cooperation, sharing, a respect for the rights and feelings of others, generosity, sociability, mutuality among people, are valued' (Bethlehem 1982: 253). Baumann (1987) studied another cooperative society, the Miri in the Sudan. This is a small tribe living in villages in the Nuba mountains. They have a strong sense of identity, and are strongly committed to mutual help within each village. Work parties in the fields include some kin but are mostly just neighbours. There is 'selfless hospitality', sharing food, drink and bed. This intense village cohesion is sustained by festivals of music and dance in which the whole community take part and share a powerful emotional experience, almost to a state of trance, generating strong feelings of group unity.

May and Doob (1937) drew a number of conclusions from Margaret Mead's collection of studies. Cooperation is based on a group which is defined by the culture, usually family, kin or village. Other aspects of the culture affect cooperation; for example, in the Bathonga, to catch a hippopotamus a man first has intercourse with a daughter, then takes drugs, and then gathers up some others to help him; the Batciga have to build a house in one day for ritual reasons, which makes cooperation essential. The main occasions for cooperation are catching large animals, building houses and seeking company, but the particular purpose – for instance which animal is to be caught – is culturally prescribed. Cooperation has to be learnt, and it is passed on by education, and enforced by rules and sanctions. There are always a few deviates for whom socialisation has failed, and cultures deal with these in different ways.

Margaret Mead also found some very competitive societies, of which she considered the Kwakiutl of Vancouver Island the most competitive, with their 'potlatch', in which rich people throw elaborate, ritual feasts, with very expensive presents for well-to-do visitors, everyday things for poorer ones, more food than they can eat, music and dancing, and speeches from the guests praising the generosity of their hosts. Goldman said 'Property is accumulated only to be redistributed or destroyed in a game in which prestige and self-glorification are raised to an egomaniacal pitch' (1937: 180). Life is dominated by competition, not only for material property but also for non-material things like titles, names and rights. Children are given early training in the manipulation of property, and have 'potlatches' with blankets. However, there is some cooperation over fishing, and for house-building, which takes 14 men, who get paid for it.

Mead and Bethlehem both thought that the Ifugao of the Philippines were very competitive too; they also struggle for status, by accumulating wealth and giving expensive feasts and sacrifices. However, in all these competitive societies there is still some cooperation: members cooperate over large tasks, they help each other during famines, and there is sharing and help within the family.

Mead's most individualistic society was that of the Ojibwa Indians in Ontario. Each male hunts on his own hunting ground while the women work alone at home; couples are self-sufficient and in winter they are completely isolated. Marriages are short and stormy, and property is owned separately by family members. However, there is cooperation between spouses, neighbours are invited into private land for sociability, and there are villages with tenuous coherence for the same purpose. There is also some competition, in children's games and for women. Another individualistic society are the Eskimos of Greenland. They live in small family units during the summer hunting season, but in settlements of related families in the winter. Again marriages are short and unstable, and other social relationships are weak. There are quarrels over women, and a high murder rate, but no sanctions to control people, and there is little care of the old. However, there is cooperation over a number of jobs which require more than one person – whale hunting, reindeer drives, seal hunting (which needs two), and again housebuilding.

Bethlehem gives first prize for individualism to the Ik of East Africa, who had been described by Turnbull (1973), and are now famous in anthropological circles for their apparent total lack of sociability and cooperation. At the time of Turnbull's visit there were about 2,000 of them, but their numbers were falling fast because of severe food shortages, and inability to cope. Even the family had all but disappeared – there was no sharing of food, even with spouses, children were pushed out at the age of three and left to fend for themselves in gangs, the old and sick left to die. There was some cooperation over hunting, but acrimonious quarrels over the division of spoils. Bands of children went about together, given some protection only by their numbers. There was no friendship with other members of the Ik, though some with people from other tribes. Gifts were given, but only to create obligations. However, the Ik are probably a special case, of a society on the point of collapse, mainly due to famine, leading to the disintegration of most of the usual forms of cooperation.

Margaret Mead and others have concluded that there is no simple relationship between cooperation and any particular sociological or ecological conditions. However, as Bethlehem points out, cooperation is common among the hunting and gathering societies of sub-Saharan Africa. When food is short competition increases, and when it is very short indeed the whole social system can break down as in the case of the Ik. But in all societies there are primary groups, of family or kin, within which there is cooperation, sharing of food and shared property, and even the Ik have nuclear families. We have seen how cooperation persists even in otherwise non-cooperative societies for tasks which are too big for one man, like catching large animals, and housebuilding. There is also friendship and sociability, including games, and there is collaboration over religious and other ceremonies (May and Doob 1937).

If we were to include Western Civilisation in this comparison, it would probably be described as individualistic and competitive, compared with most primitive cultures. In the next section I shall describe the shift which has taken place from collective village life to industrialised city life. First we should consider another line of anthropological thought. Mauss (trans. 1985) showed that the concept of 'self' or of individual persons is not found in many primitive tribes, like the Pueblo Indians or the Australian Aboriginals. There are names for clans but not for individuals, each person 'acts out the preferred totality of the life of the clan'. They play roles and they wear masks on ceremonial occasions. The concept of the conscious, responsible, self-directing individual is the result of slow historical development. Similar observations have been made of the nature of the self in American Indians, Africa, Japan, India, Melanesia, Morocco, and Southern Italy: the self is not 'decontextualised, autonomous and unique', but embedded in social relationships, blended with the environment and other people (Dittmar 1989). Clearly, cooperation is going to be a quite different matter when those involved see themselves as individuals rather than simply part of a group.

The decline of collectivism and cooperation in modern societies

Tönnies (1887, 1959) made a major contribution to sociological thought by his distinction between *Gemeinschaft* (community) and *Gesellschaft* (society). Gemeinschaft refers to groups and societies based on shared experiences, like families and neighbours in villages; there is cooperation and coordinated action towards a common goal, there are close social relations in which others are valued for themselves, and each needs the others, people act out of consensus and tradition, and members of the community share a common fate. In Gesellschaft individuals are isolated, live in a state of tension against all others, and collaborate in terms of their rational interests as in the market place, linked by contacts. Tönnies recognised that these were ideal types, and that actual groups and societies would lie on a continuum between them. However, he identified Gemeinschaft with the social life of family and village, in a domestic and agricultural economy. Gesellschaft began with city life based on trade and industry, capitalism, and state and national life.

Loomis and Beagle (1950) constructed an 11-point measure of this dimension, using a series of scales on which particular societies could be located. Tönnies is implicitly criticising modern industrial society for lacking the cohesiveness and social support of earlier folk society, though Gemeinschaft seems to imply a lack of individual freedom and creativity. We shall see later that economic growth is highly correlated with individualism, not collectivism.

Durkheim (1893, 1960) had similar ideas to Tönnies. He described earlier forms of society as 'mechanical', consisting of assemblies of people grouped solely by their homogeneity, and controlled by repressive penal laws; there was strong social support and no anomie, but individuals were subjected to the 'tyranny of the group', and there was no freedom of expression. Modern society on the other hand is based on 'organic' solidarity, in which people are linked by their independent roles in the division of labour; law is mainly civil law, based on restitution rather than punishment. He hoped to solve the conflict between individualism and social cohesion in this way, and did not recommend a return to earlier forms of society, to solve the problems of isolation and anomie (Giddens 1982).

Many later sociologists have pointed to differences between present, and pre-industrial society. For example, Riesman *et al.* said 'The tradition-directed person hardly thinks of himself as an individual' (1950: 33). There was a high degree of conformity, almost no social change, obedience to tradition, dependence on family and kin organisation, and no sense of making choices or plans, or taking control over their own lives. All these contrasts are exaggerated and oversimplified; there is a lot of Gemeinschaft in modern society, in families and in groups of all kinds and a great deal of social support, as we shall see in later chapters.

Collectivism versus individualism

This dimension was introduced to describe some of the differences between the cultures of East and West; for example, China and the USA. In a collectivist culture 'individuals may be induced to subordinate their own goals to the goals of some collective, which is usually a stable in-group (e.g. family, band, tribe)' (Triandis *et al.* 1988). A survey of 81 social scientists from all over the world asked how they thought collectivists and individualists would behave towards various others. The greatest differences were that it was thought that collectivists would consider more the implication of their actions for other members of their group, were more willing to share material resources, and non-material resources like time and affection, accept social influence more, and be more aware of the interdependence of outcomes. However, this concern for others was much greater for members of the in-group (see Figure 4.1) (Hui and Triandis 1986).

Figure 4.1 Individualists' and collectivists' concern as a function of familiarity

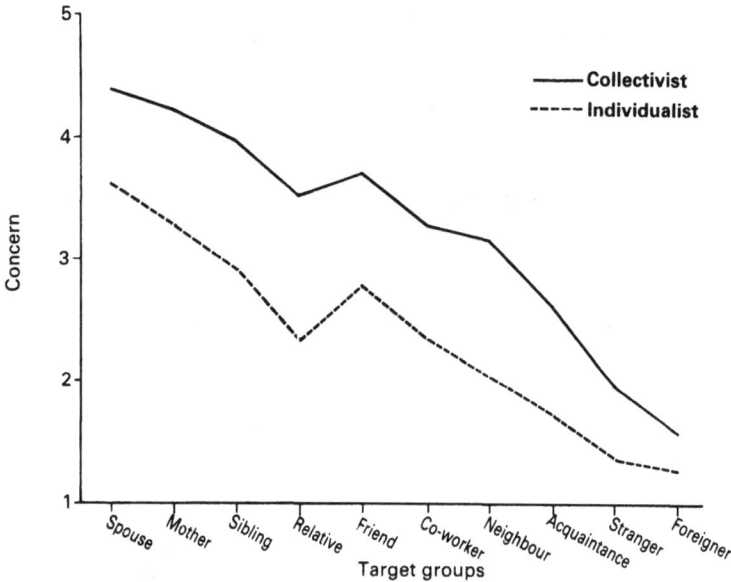

Source: Hui and Triandis 1986

A cross-cultural study of altruism found that Korea, which is a collectivist culture, had a *low* score for altruism in situations mainly involving strangers; Egypt had a *high* score, probably because of Moslem rules about charity (Johnson *et al.* 1989).

Triandis *et al.* (1988) studied further a particular aspect of collectivism – attitudes towards the in-group. In collectivist societies, they proposed, individuals are attached to one group, to which they subordinate their own goals; there is a high level of conformity and cooperation, which is rewarded with love, status and service, but not by money or goods; relationships are both with equals and with others of higher or lower status; there is a lot of social support, but everyone outside the group is treated as an out-group member. In individualistic societies, on the other hand, people are more loosely attached to a number of different groups, there is less conformity, cooperation or social support, relationships are mainly with equals, e.g. with friends or spouse, and fewer people are regarded as being in the out-group. These authors found that Americans were higher on individualism than Japanese or Puerto Ricans, but that there was more than one dimension here, and the factors were not the same in different cultures. However, the central themes of collectivism were found to be: self-definition as part of the in-group, subordination of personal goals to the group, concern for the integrity of this group, and intense emotional attachment to it.

Wheeler *et al.* (1989) provided a clear example of some of these differences in a comparison of social encounters reported by samples of students in Hong Kong and an American university. The Chinese had fewer social interactions a day on average (2.45 v. 5.99), but these were more often with groups, lasted longer, were more task-oriented and involved more disclosure. Forgas and Bond (1985) studied the dimensions used by students in Hong Kong and an Australian university to classify social events and situations. The Chinese students were concerned with and valued power differences, social usefulness, and communal feelings; the Australians were more concerned with individualism, whether events were enjoyable, competitiveness, self-confidence and freedom.

Other research has shown the importance of not causing another to lose face. Experiments have found that Chinese students avoid open disagreement in groups, by conforming or by keeping quiet. However, this does not create conflicts between public and private views, since it is easy for the Chinese to accept and internalise group norms. They are preoccupied with keeping social order and harmony, and conflict over resources rarely occurs. This is done by the emergence of hierarchies, and by strict obedience to superiors (Bond and Hwang 1986).

The concern for group harmony in collectivist cultures was shown in a study by the author and co-workers on the rules for relationships in two Eastern and two Western cultures. In Japan in particular, though also in Hong Kong, there was greater concern with rules for maintaining harmony in groups, than in Britain or Italy. There was more endorsement of rules for obedience to authority, not joking or teasing, keeping up positive regard, avoiding public criticism and restraining emotional expression (Argyle *et al.* 1986).

Other studies have been made of 'individualism', which has often been contrasted with collectivism. In the USA individualism is greatly valued – though Riesman and colleagues were concerned that it was being replaced by another directed preoccupation with peer-group acceptance. In China, however, individualism is commonly regarded as selfish, undisciplined and evil, since it places personal interests above those of the group. Mao stressed these ideas strongly, and they are a Chinese tradition, though they now have their critics. However, cross-cultural studies have found that individualism and collectivism are *not* opposites, but better regarded as separate factors – so that a culture could score high on both.

Hofstede (1980) carried out a study of individualism at work – how far individuals want to keep their independence and autonomy. He developed a questionnaire measure of individualism-collectivism in this sense, the individualism dimension being most clearly defined by questions such as: 'How important is it to you to . . . ?', answers being given on a five-point scale.

1 Have a job which leaves you sufficient time for your personal or family life.
2 Fully use your skills and abilities on the job (–).
3 Have training opportunities (to improve your skills or learn new skills) (–).
4 Have considerable freedom to adapt your own approach to the job.

These questions were used in a massive social survey of 40 countries and no less than 116,000 respondents. The national individualism scores are shown in Table 4.1. China was not included in this study, but Hong Kong, Taiwan

Table 4.1 Country individualism index (IDV) values based on the factor scores of the first factor found in a 14-work goals, 40-country matrix

Country	IDV actual	Country	IDV actual	predicted
USA	91	Argentina	46	
Australia	90	Iran	41	
Great Britain	89	Brazil	38	
Canada	80	Turkey	37	
Netherlands	80	Greece	35	
New Zealand	79	Philippines	32	
Italy	76	Mexico	30	
Belgium	75	Portugal	27	
Denmark	74	Hong Kong	25	
Sweden	71	Chile	23	
France	71	Singapore	20	
Ireland	70	Thailand	20	
Norway	69	Taiwan	17	
Switzerland	68	Peru	16	
Germany (F.R.)	67	Pakistan	14	
South Africa	65	Colombia	13	
Finland	63	Venezuela	12	
Austria	55			
Israel	54	Mean of 39 countries	51	50
Spain	51	(HERMES)		
India	48			
Japan	46			

Source: Hofstede 1984

Note: Work goal scores were computed for a stratified sample of seven occupations at two points in time.

and Singapore were, and all had high scores on collectivism, while the USA had the highest score for individualism. In all such studies the most individualistic cultures are North America, Northern Europe, Britain and the old Commonwealth; the most collectivist are China, South America, Asia, Greece and Southern Italy.

Individualist countries are more prosperous. Hofstede (1980) found a correlation of 0.82 between individualism and GNP. He found a number of correlates of collectivism, comparing 40 countries:

less economic development;
less social mobility, less development of a middle class, nearer the
    equator;
traditional agriculture, less industry and urbanisation, extended families;
more children per family;
traditional educational system for a minority of the population.

The most interesting exception to all this is Japan, though the Chinese societies and Korea are similar. In Japan a high level of industrialisation has been achieved, while using traditional social structures – hierarchical leadership, close-knit groups, and strong identification with the larger group, in this case the firm.

On the other hand, collectivism is associated with better health, probably because there is stronger social support and less competition. Figure 4.2 shows the rates of heart attacks in some collectivist and individualist cultures.

The education and socialisation of children play a key role in passing on collectivism and other attitudes. Later in this chapter we shall describe the training of children in the Israeli kibbutz (see pp. 85ff.), and in the next chapter there is an account of the Russian collective schools which are attended by about 10 per cent of children up to the age of seven, and the collective boarding schools, and rather similar 'schools of the prolonged day', attended by about 5 per cent of children from seven to 18. Great emphasis is placed on training in 'communist morality', following educational ideas mainly due to Makarenko (Bronfenbrenner 1970).

Shouval *et al.* (1975) studied the effect of collective upbringing by a questionnaire with 10 items asking for degree of agreement with examples of anti-social acts which might be urged by friends, such as cheating in a classroom test, or stealing fruit. In Russia the children from collective schools gave more moral answers than other children, but in Israel there was no difference. There were considerable national differences in scores, as shown in Table 4.2. Children in Russia and other communist countries scored very high, and those in Israel quite low. These scores are the 10 items each scored from 2.5 to -2.5, where 0 means conforming neither to the peer group nor to parents. The children were given the test under different experimental conditions – being told either that their answers would be

Figure 4.2   Heart attack rates per 1,000 inhabitants in selected samples

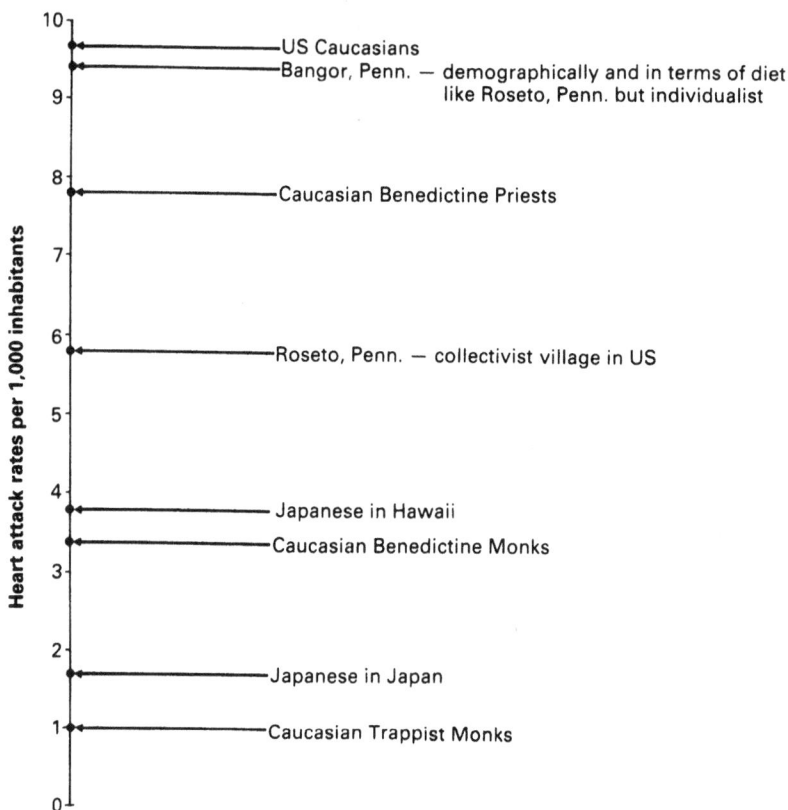

Source: Triandis et al. 1988

shown to their parents or to the peer group. Adult minus peer scores show how much more conformity to adult values there is in the parent condition. The main finding of interest is that the Israelis were more moral when *alone*. Shouval and colleagues interpret this in terms of the tradition of independence and individuality and aversion to conformity in Israel. The kibbutz schools allow daily contact with parents where the Russian schools do not, and they produce an even higher level of conformity than the regular Russian schools.

Cooperation and cohesion in modern life

There has been much concern among British sociologists about a decline in the close cohesiveness, mutual help and social support which was found in traditional working-class life, in the East End of London, for example.

Table 4.2 Dilemmas experiment: means for experimental conditions in various cultures

Country	Experimental condition				
	1: Average score	2: Base	3: Adult	4: Peer	5: Adult minus peer
USSR					
Boarding	14.83	13.82	15.62	15.04	0.58
Day	12.20	11.81	12.49	12.32	0.17
Hungary	14.06	13.28	15.17	13.74	1.43
Czechoslovakia	9.46	10.36	10.38	7.64	2.74*
Poland	6.14	6.94	7.60	3.90	3.70**
Japan	3.76	3.77	4.62	2.90	1.72*
Canada	2.92	3.58	4.27	0.91	3.36**
West Germany	2.83	1.79	4.43	2.26	2.17*
US	2.22	2.43	2.96	1.27	1.69*
Israel					
Kibbutz	1.56	2.26	1.80	0.62	1.18
City	1.50	2.77	1.22	0.52	0.70
Holland	1.18	1.27	2.10	0.16	1.94
Scotland	0.40	1.31	1.77	− 1.89	3.66**
Switzerland	− 2.09	− 1.59	− 0.76	− 3.91	3.15**

Source: Shouval *et al.* 1975

Note: * $p < .05$.
      ** $p < .01$.

In comparison modern middle class and suburban life shows much less Gemeinschaft – friends live further away, neighbours do not pop in, there is more privacy and social distance (Bulmer 1986). How far there really has been a substantial shift away from cooperation and mutual help is not known.

There is quite a lot of variation between neighbourhoods. Sampson (1988) surveyed 10,905 people in 238 UK parliamentary constituencies. The density of friendship ties was greatest when residents were older, working class and, above all, when there was little movement in and out. Other studies have found that help and cohesion between neighbours is strongest under the following conditions:

1 in long-established neighbourhoods
2 when the houses are close together, but in houses rather than apartment blocks
3 in villages compared with towns
4 in working-class areas
5 for women, especially those with young children.

(Bulmer 1986; Argyle and Henderson 1985)

Our own research has found that neighbours form the weakest of all social relationships. Nevertheless, they still form social networks and provide a lot of mutual help. In a MORI poll in Britain it was found that 22 per cent could name over 20 neighbours, 47 per cent could name 11 or more, and only 16 per cent could name three or fewer (MORI 1983). The same survey found that quite a high level of mutual help was reported (see Figure 4.3).

Figure 4.3 Minor help by neighbours over the last year (percentage of sample)

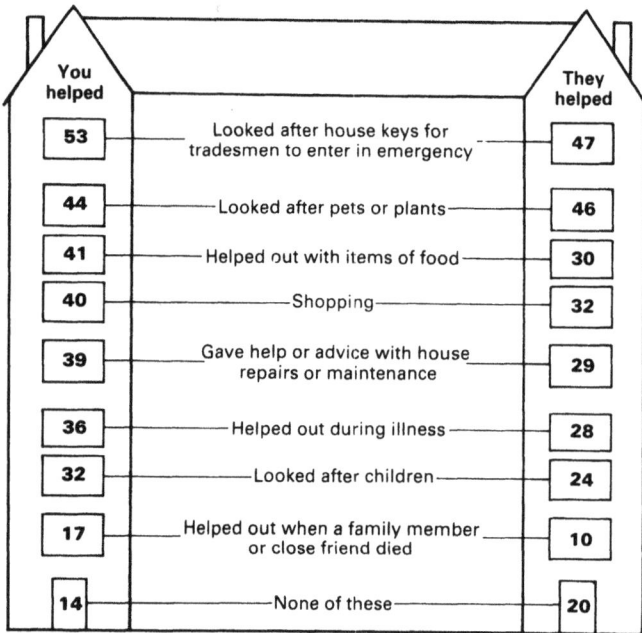

You helped		They helped
53	Looked after house keys for tradesmen to enter in emergency	47
44	Looked after pets or plants	46
41	Helped out with items of food	30
40	Shopping	32
39	Gave help or advice with house repairs or maintenance	29
36	Helped out during illness	28
32	Looked after children	24
17	Helped out when a family member or close friend died	10
14	None of these	20

Source: MORI 1983

The links between neighbours and others in a community can be analysed in terms of networks. Networks can be traced by asking all the people in a neighbourhood to name those whom they feel closest to, or interact with most often. More details can be obtained about the nature of the link, whether it involves help and support or is purely sociable, whether it involves information and advice, influence, e.g. in getting jobs, material or financial help, doing things together, and so on. Networks are important since they are the routes through which all this information, help and support flow.

In dense networks there is more social influence, and a pair of individuals, like husband and wife, who share the same links, are held together by the network. While such networks can be very supportive, looser networks also have their advantages – there is less conformity pressure, for example. Similarly there are advantages in networks based on a variety of different kinds of linkage, since they provide access to a wider variety of others who might be useful in some way.

Social networks provide social support. Research on social factors in health and mental health has shown the great importance of network support as well as close confidants.

A particular form of cooperation in modern communities is the formation of mutual help groups. This is something of a new social movement from the USA. It consists of the organising of local groups of people who share a similar problem. To some extent it has been going on for a long time – groups of young mothers who help each other with childminding, and who can give one another useful advice, for example. One of the first kinds of organised groups was Alcoholics Anonymous. Now there are groups of widows, the recently divorced, parents of handicapped children, families of prisoners, neurotics, gamblers, obese people, and others. These groups sometimes have an inspirational, almost religious air about them. About 6.25 million Americans belong to these groups, which threaten to rival psychotherapy as the preferred treatment for a number of problems, partly because they are much cheaper. They can also be seen as a replacement for the family, as a source of social support, and hence of health and mental health. A curious feature of the groups is that many members never leave (Jacobs and Goodman 1989).

Another kind of neighbourhood cooperation is in clubs, classes, churches and so on. These are mainly based on local neighbourhoods, and are more formally organised than the groups we have considered so far. The extent of this activity is shown in Table 4.3.

The Young and Wilmott (1973) survey of Londoners found that 53 per cent of married men working full time were active members of at least one club, and that 16 per cent were officers of clubs. In addition, 52 per cent of them went to a pub once a month or more, and 15 per cent to church regularly. The MORI survey (1983) shows that for many people those they know best are found in pubs and clubs of various kinds. Bracey's study (1964) of young families in the suburbs of Bristol found that men were more often members of athletics and educational groups than women. There was a famous study of 'Yankee City' by Lloyd Warner which found very extensive club membership. He found that many of these associations and branches were quite small – 28 per cent had under 10 members, 54 per cent had 20 or fewer (Warner and Lunt 1941).

Workers' cooperatives

These are working enterprises, inspired by the ideals of cooperation and equality, where the members own at least some of the capital value, and have an equal share in decision-making. There may also be non-members, limited to 50 per cent in European schemes, but they usually become

Table 4.3 Membership of voluntary associations

Survey by Young and Willmott		
Active members of one or more clubs		53%
Officers or committee members		16%
Church (at least once a month)		15%
Survey by Bracey	*men*	*women*
Members of social clubs	17	14
Members of athletic clubs	9	1
Members of parent-teacher associations	–	3
Attend evening classes, or other educational and cultural groups	6	1
'Social Trends' survey		
Dancing (in last 4 weeks)	14	16
Watch football	7	1
Bingo	2	6
Darts	15	4
Social and voluntary work	8	9
Amateur music/drama	4	3
	People known best	
MORI survey	*men*	*women*
People at local pub or club	23	10
Members of church	7	12
Members of sporting club	11	5
Members of club associated with hobby or interest	10	7
Members of a voluntary association	2	3

Source: Argyle and Henderson 1985

members within six months or a year. Workers' cooperatives developed in the last century under the inspiration of Robert Owen, William Morris and early socialist ideas. There has been a lot of further development since World War II, especially since 1970, as a result of rising unemployment. These firms have been given government and local government support, by way of both loans and advice. Several large cooperatives were set up in Britain by Tony Benn, then Secretary of State for Industry in a Labour Government, during the 1970s – the Meridien Motor Cycle cooperative, the Scottish Daily News and Kirby Manufacturing and Engineering (KME). All went out of business after a fairly short time; the largest, KME, employed 1,100 workers and lasted five years.

This is now definitely a minority movement, employing only about 12,000 in Britain, in 1986, in 1,300 firms. The average size is therefore small, about nine, but the typical size is smaller since there are one or two large ones. Only about 50 have more than 20 members. One of these is the Scott-Bader Commonwealth, a Quaker chemical company founded in 1951, and employing 430 workers. The movement has gone further in Italy and France, where there are a number of quite large cooperatives. The largest and probably most successful are the group of cooperatives in the town of Mondragon in Spain, employing 18,000 workers.

Many members are ideologically committed to cooperative participation, together with the idea of producing better working conditions, and socially useful products. Other members, however, have simply seen this as a way of getting a job, and have invested their redundancy pay this way.

These schemes are cooperative in several ways. First, their joint ownership. One of the main sources of capital is loans from members, which are in principle returnable. This generates commitment to the firm, but can also lead to status differences. Second, their democratic control. If the membership is small, all can take part in decision-making meetings (up to 19 in one scheme). Larger concerns need elected representatives of some kind. There are problems: many members are inexperienced in such participation, are not able to take constructive criticism, and lack the skills of conducting meetings.

How successful are they? There has been a failure rate of nearly 20 per cent, but many new small firms also fail. They have had great difficulty in competing with larger, better capitalised and therefore better equipped firms. There is said to be 'self-exploitation' – working long hours for low wages. On the other hand, working conditions and job satisfaction are thought to be higher than elsewhere (Mellor *et al.* 1988) though no precise data are available. They are attractive to those who work in them because of the cooperation and participation, the good working environment, and because they provide work.

There have been a number of common problems. (a) Lack of finance and capitalization has restricted the work to low tech areas like cleaning, renovation and craft work, otherwise the firms are uncompetitive. (b) With more than a very small number of workers, there is a need for some supervision and management. However, many of the members dislike hierarchies, and accuse any manager of being too big for his boots, too bossy, and so on. (c) We referred to the need for participation and chairman skills above. (d) The position of women has disappointed the female members, when they find that the men still run things. In the Mondragon companies there is a high level of financing, partly through each worker having to invest in his company, and a traditional management structure. In the Scott-Bader Commonwealth there is also a familiar type of management, democratic control, and a kind of joint ownership in that shares are held in trust for the workforce (ICOM 1987; Mellor *et al.* 1988).

What can we learn about cooperation here? That certain social skills are needed, and that it is necessary to have a management structure, although this eliminates equality.

Communes

These are groups of people who have withdrawn from the wider society in order to create a new kind of society, that is cooperative, egalitarian and free, where property is shared and where the members live together, rather like a large family. There have been many such communes, especially in Britain and the USA, during the last two centuries. The number of them depends on how they are defined; Abrams and McCulloch (1976) visited 67 of them in Britain, and report that the size varied from five to 25 adults and their children. Some of the religious communes are larger than this, and we will deal with them later.

A number of communes based on strict ideological principles were established in the USA, and a smaller number over here, in the nineteenth century. In Britain 30 communes existed in 1942, but all had disappeared by 1974 (Rigby 1974). During the 1960s a large number of new communes began, inspired by the counter-culture of the time. While all communes have common themes, which will be described here, there is also a lot of variety. Some are primarily 'doing their own thing', some providing mutual support, some seeking radical social change, some providing practical help with housing and living costs, some providing therapy, and there are also religious communes (Rigby 1974).

There is a similar ideological basis in all cases, of middle-class radicalism – vegetarianism, feminism, CND, anarchy and so on. There are also religious ideas, from East and West, an interest in Jung, Timothy Leary, Aldous Huxley. Above all there is a rejection of 'straight' society: the family is thought to be oppressive; normal and especially industrial work is meaningless; capitalism is evil, authority unacceptable, life in the wider, mass society impersonal and inhuman. In tune with counter-culture ideas, drugs have been common, and sexual promiscuity widespread.

Only a certain kind of person is attracted to commune life. Most members are in their twenties, though a few are in their thirties, usually after divorce or separation. Nearly all are of middle-class origins, may have started or finished a degree, but then dropped out of orthodox society.

Communes are a particular kind of experiment in cooperation, and they are indeed cooperative in several ways. (a) Communes are a kind of alternative family, but with greater freedom and equality. They are also groups of close friends, and spend a lot of time developing and discussing their relationships with one another; a lot of time is spent in just 'sitting around', in pure sociability. (b) Ideally there is shared property, as in families. In practice the buildings and land are owned by one or more individuals or families. (c) There is division of labour over the work and earning: some have jobs outside, some raise food, some do domestic work, others do handicraft work or run a health shop, and so on. The economy is usually assisted by social security. (d) There are communal meals, and shared use of cooking, eating and leisure areas. (e) There is a great deal of fun and play; domestic and other work is combined with sociability and play – rather like work before the industrial revolution (Abrams and McCulloch 1976).

What attracts some people to such experiments in cooperation? Three main motivations have been suggested. First, for some members the main attraction is the companionship and close relationships, which they have been unable to find outside. Some have experienced isolation and loneliness, probably through lack of social skills, others have had a major disruption in their social world, such as divorce. Second, a widespread motivation is a quest for identity, being able to enjoy a period of 'moratorium' or suspension of identity, while experimentation is possible, being accepted by a supportive group of like-minded young people, since identity requires recognition and confirmation by others. Third, radical activists are people who have abandoned their middle-class origins, education and sometimes jobs, and had a kind of conversion experience in which the simple life seems preferable to now meaningless regular work (Rigby 1974).

How successful are communes? In terms of continued existence they are not at all successful. The average length has been estimated as five years, and in fact many only last for two (see Figure 4.3). What are the reasons for breaking up? This is important for us since it shows some of the problems which may accompany cooperation. Briefly the main ones are:

1 *Economic.* There is difficulty raising the initial money to buy land and buildings; they are often owned by one family, which creates inequality. There is shortage of income, since craft work can't compete with regular manufacturing. The ban on private property is a source of tension.
2 *Management.* The desire for equality makes it difficult to establish any leadership or decision structure. The desire for freedom makes it difficult to make or enforce rules. There is often friction between members over sexual rivalry, laziness, or over different ways of doing things, but there are no rules or authority to deal with it.
3 *The position of women.* Despite the emphasis on equality, and the rejection of the family, the position of women in the commune has remained unchanged in many communes.

What can we learn about cooperation from these communes? Many young people find life in normal society unsatisfying and they seek small, cooperative groups of friends, where they can develop close relationships, in a supportive and egalitarian structure. This enables them to mature, to achieve an identity, and before long to return to the normal world. However, as social organisations these communes are shortlived, and are very unsuccessful from that point of view.

Utopian communities

These are larger bodies, typically about 200 strong, established with a definite religious or other basis. There have been many such groups in the USA, perhaps 100 at any one time, involving over 100,000 people. The

Shakers had 6,000 members in 18 groups; other well-known ones were the Hutterites and the Oneida community. In Britain there have been a smaller number including Findhorn, Beshara and Kingsway. More recently there have been a number of cult communities, attached to the Moonies, the Jesus Movement, the Bhagwan, and TM. As well as being larger than the communes described earlier, the religious communities last longer – an average of 50 years, some over 100, and 50 per cent lasting more than 20 years (see Figure 4.4).

Figure 4.4 Percentage of religious and non-religious communes surviving first hundred years

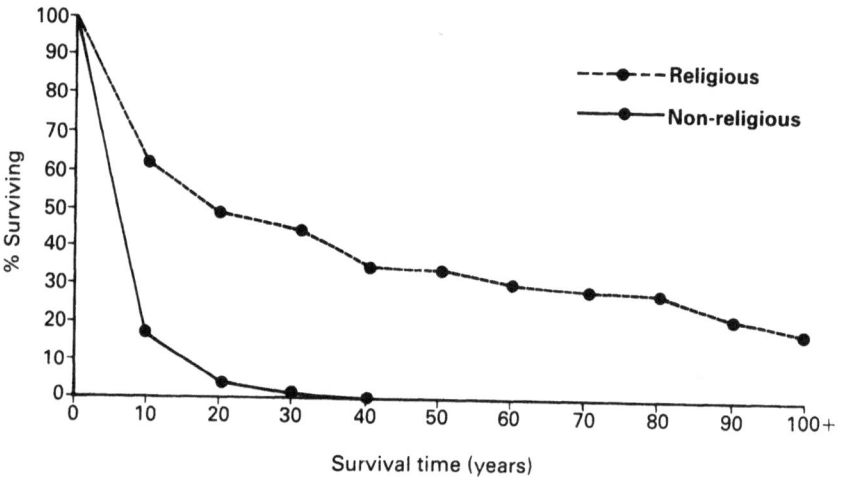

Source: Stephan and Stephan 1973

These are not just staging posts for young people, but are joined for life by many of their members. Some of these communities were established in the last century, especially in the USA, but the movement is now in decline, though new ones continue to be founded.

There is a strong ideology in these communities, usually Christian (though not attached to any church), mystical, occultist, Buddhist, or communist, often with some rather strange ideas. The Oneida community abolished marriage, while others have demanded asceticism.

Cooperation is more formal in these larger better-established groups. New members are usually expected to hand over all their possessions, and in exchange are supported for life. There is division of labour, where each member uses whatever skills he may have in the service of the community. There are frequent group meetings, for decision-taking, mutual criticism, and other regular rituals. The family is usually retained, but weakened, in that domestic activities are shared, and emotional (often sexual) bonds outside marriage are encouraged.

There has been some research into the conditions under which such communities are successful. We have already seen that religion is a major positive factor. Kanter (1968) compared nine successful and 21 unsuccessful ones, and concluded that a number of 'commitment mechanisms' were important, such as various kinds of abstinence, renunciation and mortification. Hall (1988) re-analysed that data using multiple regression, which shows the factors having independent effects. These were: a common ethnic background, homogeneity, confession, and a spiritual hierarchy. Abrams and McCulloch (1976) are critical of Kanter's emphasis on commitment mechanisms, which they see as similar to brainwashing, and inducing too much conformity and personality change. This has been widely reported to happen in some of the new cults like the Moonies.

Several other factors have been suggested as important for the success of communes. (a) Strong leadership. Religious groups often have a charismatic leader, who is seen as a kind of father. (b) Strong norms. There is a paradox here in that the members have often joined to escape the rules elsewhere. However, these are self-imposed, there is participation in establishing and changing them. (c) Regular meetings are needed to keep up cohesion, and to deal with frictions and disagreements, sometimes by mutual criticism, or encounter groups. (d) When there is a religious basis this gives shared values, creates more acceptance of authority, regular rituals, and the kind of commitment mechanisms emphasised by Kanter.

What can we learn here about the conditions for successful cooperation in these larger groups? They need to share beliefs and ideals, they need leadership, and they need to have clear rules, which members participate in deciding. Powerful social influences may help the group to survive, but the cost may be too great (Kanter 1973; Holloway 1966).

The Israeli kibbutz

These were originally farming collectives, though now partly industrialised, employing about 120,000 people, 3.6 per cent of the Israeli population in 1987. The size varies from 250–500 adults, together with as many children. They first started in 1910, and now produce 40 per cent of Israel's food, and through associated industries 7 per cent of her exports. There is a strong ideological basis, of devotion to Israel and to cooperative and socialist ideals, or in some cases religious ones. Here they are unlike the other cooperative experiments described in this chapter, since the kibbutz represents the highest ideals of the society outside, rather than rebelling against them.

There are several kinds of cooperation here. (a) The land and the means of production all belong to the state; only furniture and minor personal items belong to individuals. (b) The work is hard and unpaid; members are expected to turn their hands to what is necessary, though most have regular jobs, and experts may keep to their expertise. (c) There are collective meals, also library, pool, and club room. (d) The ideology is reinforced by lectures, debates, annual festivals and other community events, though it is said to be declining. (e) Each kibbutz is managed by elected committees, a weekly meeting of all members, and various elected officials and managers. No special status is attached to these offices and there is no great enthusiasm to occupy them; it was originally believed that manual work is the highest form of work. On the other hand, the agricultural and industrial managers have some real authority, and tend to form a higher status group. (f) Most important of all, however, is the socialisation of the children. Kibbutz children from an early age spend most of their time in the children's house, looked after by a special caretaker, the *metapelet*, with about five other children of the same age. They visit their parents every evening, and may sleep at home, but they regard the children's house as their real home. The result is that kibbutz children have a less intensive attachment to their own parents and siblings, a more diffuse identification with a number of adults and in particular a strong attachment to the other children in their house group by age 3–4 and, as with real siblings, do not marry them later. However, there is emphasis on group solidarity, and intimate relationships between two or three children are discouraged. The education of these children places great importance on collective values, cooperation with peers and other kibbutz members, and on the value of manual labour.

Objective tests, of the kind described above, confirm the cooperativeness of kibbutz children. They are also found to take more part in group games than Israeli city children. Studies with personality tests have found that kibbutz members have a 'diffusion of intimacy', and are more able to form cohesive groups than intimate relationships (Greenbaum and Kugelmass 1980).

How successful has the kibbutz movement been? It is economically quite important, as shown above. It still attracts 3.6 per cent of the population. But it has difficulty retaining young people, 50 per cent or more of whom leave. There is little to attract the highly educated, who don't want to do agricultural work.

There are a number of problems. The kibbutz movement is said to be in a state of 'crisis', with many members losing faith in the ideals of cooperation, togetherness and equality. There has in fact been some retreat from the old ideals:

1 There has been a shift towards individual wages, for about 40 per cent of consumption; some members have private sources of income; there is concern about retirement pensions.
2 There has been increased interest in private possessions, and wanting another room in the house.

3 There are demands for more leave, including extended leave.
4 The family has become more important, kibbutz families have become larger, with three or four generations; parents want children transferred to their house.
5 Women are not content with their lower status which is due to doing domestic rather than production work.
6 There has been increased stratification and decline of equality: the top people are the managers, those who have been there longest, and those who have inherited wealth from outside.
7 Members have wondered whether cooperative and egalitarian values are impairing their standard of living; some are interested in better jobs and higher education (Ben-Rafael 1988; Yizher 1989).

This has been interpreted as a retreat to private life and self-fulfilment.

Chapter five

Communication and cooperation in children

There has been a lot of interest in the social behaviour of infants, since this may throw light on the innate capacity to communicate, cooperate, and form relationships. The conclusion of many research workers is that children show signs of a capacity and a wish to engage in social behaviour from a very early age.

Infants are very responsive to faces, or to discs with human features painted on them – two eyes and a mouth, and this preference has been found in the first weeks of life, though infants' vision is poorly developed at this age. However, they can see quite well at a range of 50 cm, roughly the distance of the mother's face during feeding. They are particularly interested in eyes, and eye-like patterns; they focus on an observer's eyes and make eye-contact at 25–28 days. At two months a mask with two dots will produce a smile, but a real face with eyes hidden will not. Infants are also responsive to human voices, prefer the higher-pitched female ones, and have been found to recognise the mother's voice by three days. There is some evidence that by one month infants discriminate between sounds in terms of their phonetic features.

The earliest social signal sent by infants is crying. It is generally regarded as a biological survival mechanism, for eliciting material care. There are also positive vocalisations – cooing, and later laughter. The first facial expressions is the startle reaction found in the newborn. Smiling first occurs during sleep, and at faces by two-and-a-half months. Newborn infants display a slight smile to sweet tastes, and a closed mouth with corners down to a bitter taste (Ganchrow *et al.* 1983). At this age these are simply physio-logical reactions to physical stimuli, startle to loud noises, crying to hunger, pain or physical restraint, smiling to groups of dots of the right shape, and some kinds of touch, taste and sounds.

As well as perceiving and emitting social signals, infants engage in some cooperative social interaction. In the feeding situation, mother and infant make moves which are closely coordinated. The infant searches for the breast by rapid side-to-side movements followed by sucking; mother and baby rapidly adapt to each other. During feeding there is a kind of turn-taking, where the mother is quiet and inactive during bursts of sucking, and more active when the baby is quiet (Kaye 1977).

'It can now be accepted that the infant is in a number of ways preadapted to interact with other people' (Schaffer 1984: 34). One of those ways is in treating people and objects differently. Some investigations have reported that very young infants are more relaxed when with people, and have a more mobile face and gesture-like mouth movements, of a speech-like nature. However, infants behave more in these ways to their mothers, compared with peers or strangers (Schaffer 1984).

There is now extensive evidence from developmental psychologists that there are individual differences in temperament between infants – in sociability, irritability and so on, just as there is evidence from twin studies for the heritability of extraversion and other traits (see p. 66). Infants contribute to their relationship with their parents, mothers respond to their baby's personality, and they have to establish a working relationship between them (Clarke-Stewart 1988).

Social behaviour at two to five months

By two months infants can see better, and are particularly interested in people. Mutual gaze takes place; this is sought and enjoyed by mothers, and is also sought by infants. They alternate looking with looking away; experiments show that looking away is used to reduce the level of arousal. Mothers look far more than in normal adult interaction, the infants in glances of about 1.3 seconds.

> What is significant is that the integration of the looking patterns of the two individuals also takes place with such rapidity: as Stern (1977) has put it, mother and infant interact in a split-second world, where social signals are perceived and responded to more rapidly than we realise. The speed of interpersonal synchronization is in fact so great that a stimulus-response model could not account for all interactive sequences. It seems rather that the temporal integration one sees within a dyad may be used on a shared programme – Stern (1977) uses the analogy of a waltz, where both partners know the steps and thus move in synchrony, though they are also able to react to each other's cues in stimulus-response fashion in order to reset their general direction.
>
> (Schaffer 1984: 54–5)

By five months, and perhaps by three months, infants can distinguish and react differently to happy, sad and angry vocal expressions, and to facial expressions a little later, at five to seven months (Walker-Andrews 1988). Facial expressions are now changing from physiological responses elicited by physical stimuli, to more organised responses produced by psychological stimuli, which are at least partly under voluntary control.

The expression of emotion is at first very similar to an automatic reflex response – startle is an example. Gradually, it comes under voluntary control, and is used in the service of more complex social plans. This is first shown in the instrumental use of crying and smiling, but withholding such expressions when there is no one to see or hear, and equally to exaggerating them when there is, as is found at 12 months. Thus the use of emotional expressions to communicate with other people seems to be a very basic feature.

Vocalisations occur most when mother is out of touching distance though still in sight, but infants also vocalise a lot when alone. They also do this a lot in response to speech by adults, and adult speech elicits vocalisations rather than just acting as reinforcement.

At this age there is increased capacity to recognise emotions, and children react differently and appropriately to different facial expressions by their mothers (Harris 1989). By two months there is real interaction between mother and infant. Murray and Trevarthen (1985) found that infants at this age were happy to interact with their mothers over CCTV, but not at all happy to watch an earlier clip of mother's behaviour. Other experiments have found that if mother remains unresponsive to the child for a period it will look away, curl up, and look distressed and helpless; infants want to interact. Cohn and Tronick (1988) coded mother's and baby's behaviour in one-second units, and found that each was responsive to the other's behaviour, though the mother was more responsive. The earliest sequences often contain simultaneous vocalisation rather than turn-taking, especially during periods of high arousal and fun (Stern 1977). Evidence has recently been obtained, in a detailed study of three infants and their mothers, of the appearance of turn-taking as early as 12–18 weeks (Ginsberg and Kilbourne 1988).

Social behaviour at 5 to 12 months

By this age, children are very responsive to their mothers' emotional expressions. When she displays joy, they do so too, look at her more and engage in more play (Termine and Izard 1988). An important development at this age is increased interest in toys and other objects, partly because the child is now more able both to see and to manipulate them. The infant now looks less at mother, more at objects, but is able to follow her direction of gaze, so that both are attending to the same thing; this capacity increases over the period two to 14 months (Scaife and Bruner 1975). At nine to 12 months infants can also follow pointing; by 12 months many can point themselves, and by 14 months they look back at mother to make sure that she is following. When both are attending to the same object mother often labels it, an important part of early language learning; similar labelling occurs when the child is playing with an object. These are all aspects of 'topic sharing' (Schaffer 1984).

From about six months, turn-taking improves: the infant becomes silent while mother is speaking, she responds to his vocalisations as if they were contributions to a dialogue, and by 12 months quite good turn-taking is established (Snow 1977). Interaction sequences with mother are first established by games like 'peek-a-boo' and 'round and round the garden like a teddy bear'; by 12 months the child is not just a recipient but can initiate the sequences. These games may be how children learn turn-taking, reciprocity, and the other skills needed for social interaction (Bruner 1977). The child is now able to engage in spontaneous play to some extent, as a joint enterprise, accepting others as persons and realising that they too are attending to the same objects; this has been interpreted as a capacity for 'intersubjectivity', that is, awareness of the minds of others (Trevarthen 1980). However, we shall see later that cooperative play with peers becomes more common from age three.

Social behaviour at 18 months

The child now integrates vocalising and looking; that is, he looks during or after his own utterance; this is an essential part of adult interaction, since the 'terminal gaze' is used to collect feedback, and also acts as a signal that an utterance is ending (see pp. 179ff.). We have seen that infants of 14 months check that mother is following when they point.

Communication at 18 months is shifting from non-verbal to verbal, and it is generally believed that there is continuity between earlier gestures and vocalisations and the use of words. At this age utterances are very short; mother's are longer, and are in 'motherese'. Exactly how language is learnt is still a mystery, but it looks as if imitation and reinforcement are not sufficient to teach such a complex system unless some unlearnt capacities are present already.

Children of this age are growing in their understanding of social behaviour – what Schaffer (1984) has called 'meta-sociability'. The child realises that while he and others are independent agents, it is possible for them to cooperate in joint enterprises to their mutual satisfaction; he can take the initiative in bringing about an interpersonal activity, and is not purely egocentric.

Relations with parents

Several lines of research have shown the importance of the early relationship with mothers for the later emergence of cooperation, and other aspects of sociability. From the age of about seven months, infants begin to show a preference for one person, who is usually the mother, have a great desire to be near her, and are distressed at separation and absence. Lytton (in Grusec and Lytton 1988) measured attachment by non-verbal behaviour, seeking physical contact, and by verbally seeking attention and help. Attachment reached a peak between 13–20 months and declined from age two and a half. This is a universal pattern for human infants, and impossible to prevent. Bowlby observed that animals have a very similar pattern of behaviour, and proposed that there is an innate behaviour system, derived from evolution, for infants to send signals, such as crying and clinging, which attach the infant to its care-giver, thus ensuring care and protection (Bowlby 1971). The alternative theory that attachment is caused by food reward became less plausible after Harlow's experiments in which baby monkeys preferred bodily contact with artificial 'mothers' with terry-cloth skin, to wire 'mothers' who provided milk.

The next move was Ainsworth *et al.*'s discovery (1978) of three kinds of attachment using her 'strange situations' test, where the child is left alone or with a stranger. 'Secure' attachment is where the child is distressed at mother's absence and seeks her proximity when she returns. In the other types of attachment, children avoid her or resist contact when she comes back. It has been found that secure attachment occurs more if mothers are warm, sensitive and responsive rather than angry or tense. Securely attached infants are able to explore the environment freely when their mother is there – she is a 'secure base'. Punishment or other maltreatment does not prevent attachment, but leads to less secure attachment. And attachment of infants to parents does not always go with attachment of parents to infant.

Later research has found that while secure attachment depends on maternal warmth, this is partly in response to the infant's personality, partly to the mother's own personality. Secure attachment is also affected by the mother being happily married, having a supportive husband, and it can be enhanced by parent training courses (Clarke-Stewart 1988).

The most important finding for our present purpose is that attachment is a cause of cooperative behaviour. At 12–18 months, securely attached children have been found to be more cooperative, more socially competent, and to show more positive affect (Sroufe *et al.* 1983). Infants who are more securely attached cooperate more with unfamiliar peers, and interact with a greater number of peers (Clarke-Stewart 1983). By 30 months, children can keep in touch with their mothers by visual rather than physical contact, and feel comfortable at a greater distance from them. Many studies have found a relationship between maternal warmth and children being friendly and socially outgoing. Research on the origins of extraversion shows that extraverts (in adopted homes, so this is independent of genetics) had close relations with their mothers at an early age (see p. 204). Another way of conceptualising this warmth/love dimension is in terms of 'responsiveness'; that is, the parent's behaviour is closely meshed with and responsive to the child's behaviour. This is different from rewardingness; it gives experience and practice at closely synchronised interaction, and it gives the child greater control over parental behaviour.

Fathers are also important. It has been found that helpfulness, leadership and involvement with others were greater in three- to five-year-olds who had more physical play with their parents, especially with their fathers. Evidence was found that this was due to learning accurate encoding and decoding skills for non-verbal signals (Parke 1989).

Another aspect of parental behaviour is also relevant to the development of cooperation. A number of studies found that children from 'democratic' homes were more socially outgoing, became leaders in nursery school, and showed more affection and spontaneity. By democratic was meant that the child shares in decision-making, parents are not coercive, and rules are discussed in advance, compared with authoritarian homes. Baumrind (1980) however conceptualised a third type of home – 'authoritative', where parents direct children in a rational way, set standards and respect the child's autonomy and individuality. They are strong both in enforcing the rules and in encouraging independence. The children from authoritative homes were found at eight to nine years to be more friendly, cooperative, socially responsible, altruistic, and had a reciprocal attitude to others.

Cooperative play

Children spend a great deal of their time playing, much of it with siblings or other children, and a lot of it could be described as cooperative, as we shall see. Play is hard to define, but it has several characteristic features, such as being an end in itself, having goals which are self-imposed, and it often involves the means of doing something rather than any end product; it involves pretend rather than real fighting, for example, and there is freedom from externally imposed rules (Rubin *et al.* 1987).

The beginning of play

We have seen how mothers play simple games like peek-a-boo, and round and round the garden by the time the baby is 12 months. During the second year of life mothers encourage pretend play; for example, by Mad Hatter's tea parties, where 'tea' is poured from empty tea pots and 'drunk' (Deloache and Plaetzer 1985). Older siblings also encourage such fantasy play, and generate joint games; by 18 months infants will feed a doll from an empty bottle, and pretend to sleep; a little later they will pretend to telephone daddy. Where siblings cooperate over such play, mothers are more often spectators (Dunn 1988).

Rough and tumble play

This refers to play-fights and chasing, including wrestling or hitting, usually accompanied by shouting, in a high state of excitement. It is found in children in all cultures, and very similar behaviour is found in the young of monkeys, cats, wolves and other species. In human children it takes place from age three to adolescence, reaching a peak at four to seven, and then declining in frequency. There is a lot more rough and tumble play among boys, especially in wrestling and racing about, bodily contact and making a noise.

It is different from real aggression, in that it is not set off by conflicts, children usually don't get hurt, and they smile, or sometimes show a mischievous look, which has been likened to the monkey play-face. Further-more, rough and tumble play is mostly with friends, it is a form of sociability, and results in making friends rather than losing them. At age six this behaviour is wholly fun; in older children the fighting is rougher, and sometimes spills over into real aggression. The 'fighting' between football fans is mostly, but not entirely, of this harmless, mainly symbolic, character.

The result, and perhaps the biological purpose, is believed to be the acquisition of skills of fighting and hunting, which are less useful nowadays. It can also train in social skills, of leadership, negotiation, cooperation and forming alliances. Young children and some only children stay on the sidelines and watch; some will join in later when they have learnt how to do it, but some never do (Humphreys and Smith 1984).

Ritualised play

This is one of the simplest kinds of play between two children, based on controlled repetition. For example:

X's turn	*Y's turn*
Hello, my name is Mr Donkey	Hello, my name is Mr Elephant
Hello, my name is Mr Tiger	Hello, my name is Mr Lion

The round is repeated, with variations, until the game is exhausted, in one recorded case for 17 minutes.

Rituals are usually verbal, but can involve play with objects too; for example, taking turns to place different objects under a magnifying glass and proclaiming 'that's the biggest (hat) I saw in my life'. Older children engage in these rituals less, but they have more complicated ones.

Play rituals are clearly play, enjoyed for their own sake: there is no further goal. They are essentially social, need two to play, they require agreement on a particular ritual, and cooperation to pursue it. There can also be role reversal, a further aspect of cooperation.

The nature of early cooperation in play

Dunn (1988) describes the play of children during the first three years of life with their siblings, and concludes:

> Very young children do not only fight, argue, and laugh at the misfortunes and misdeeds of others; they also cooperate with others in play at an astonishingly early age, and with an appreciation of the other's goals and mood that is impressive and delightful to observe. It is an ability that depends on a sensitivity to the mood of the other, on a shared sense of the absurd and unexpected that presupposes a grasp of the expected, on a willingness to obey directions within the play context, to negotiate, concede to, and coordinate with another. And with the development of joint pretend play, it involves an intellectual leap into a shared world of pretend identities and roles.
>
> (Dunn 1988: 109)

Play between siblings is similar to that with non-siblings, except that cooperative play takes place at an earlier age. We will look briefly at the elements of cooperation observed by Dunn.

1 *Recognising and sharing mood and action.* One child copies the emotional state of the other, e.g. bouncing, laughing, repeated falling down, chanting.
2 *Recognising and cooperation in the other's goals.* One child joins spontaneously in playing with puppets, cars on track, etc. At age two infants cooperated 13 per cent of the time in behaviour or fantasy play, their older siblings 24 per cent.
3 *Compliance in the play context.* The children were also very willing to comply with directions from older siblings to cooperate – for example, in using the vacuum cleaner as a 'hosepipe', and later as a telephone, complete with conversation.
4 *Reversal of roles.* At 18 months, younger siblings were able to change roles in an established game, and by three years often initiated the role reversal.
5 *Cooperation in pretend.* By 24 months most of the children were able to take part in joint pretend play. This is a complex form of cooperation, since it involves sharing a complete imaginary social episode, with roles and rules.

6 *Development of negotiation*. During the third year there was more argument and negotiation, over choice of game, and how the roles should be played.

Social pretend play from three to seven

At this age, pretend play is one of the preferred forms of social interaction; it is what two or three children will normally do if placed in a playroom. A number of investigators have introduced children into a playroom, and analysed what happens. Forys and McCune-Nicolich (1984), for example, found that one child will suggest a theme, or announce a pretend identity – in a special voice to show that it is pretend. The others will fall in with this, perhaps with some negotiation of the details. For example, one child will suggest 'let's play doctor and patient', or 'cooking'; or he could announce 'I'm the doctor'. These roles can be relational (e.g. daddy), functional (e.g. driver), and more rarely occupational (e.g. police) or fantasy (e.g. superman). Often one role will lead to complementary roles for the others. And the roles will suggest the action plan, e.g. driving suggests a journey. This may be elaborated by the presence of suitable props, e.g. 'tools' suggest mending the car. Physical objects are readily relabelled, e.g. bricks as dynamite. Dolls and pets may be brought in and given their roles too, e.g. the dog is made to do 'show jumping' (observation by author).

Garvey (1974) found that children take turns in pretend play, that there is a series of repeated rounds, a kind of theme with variations. Sometimes this has a simple, repeated pattern:

	FIRST CHILD	SECOND CHILD
Round 1	I'm going to work (pause) No I'm not	You're already at work
Round 2	I'm going to school (pause) No I'm not	You're already at school
Round 3	I'm going to the party (pause) No I'm not	You're already at the party

Sometimes it is more complicated:

GIRL (3:3)

1. Say, 'Go to sleep now'

3. Why? (whining)

5. Why?

7. No, say 'because'
   (emphatically)

9. Why? Because why?

11. Why

13. No 'cause I bit somebody

15. Say, 'Go to sleep. Put your
    head down'
    (sternly)

17. No

19. No

21. My head's up (giggles)
22. I want my teddy bear
    (petulant voice)

24. Why?

26. Are you going to pack your
    teddy bear?

BOY (2:9)

2. Go sleep now

4. Baby . . .

6. Because

8. Because!
   (emphatically)

10. Not good. You bad

12. 'Cause you spill your
    milk

14. Yes, you did

16. Put your head down
    (sternly)

18. Yes

20. Yes. Okay, I will spank
    you. Bad boy
    (spanks her)

23. No, your teddy bear go
    away (sternly)

25. 'Cause he does
    (walks off with teddy bear)

However, pretend play is within a definite set of ideas and rules; roles must stay consistent, or the player will be corrected. Adults who try to join in may be put right for not knowing the conventions.

97

Pretend play shades into humour; here is one of Garvey's (1977) examples:

GIRL (4:9)	GIRL (4:7)
(writing letter)	(listening)

GIRL (4:9)

(writing letter)
Dear Uncle Poop, I would like
you to give me a roasted
meatball, some chicken pox . . .
and some tools.
Signed . . . Mrs Fingernail.
(smiles and looks up at partner)

Toop poop. (laughs) Hey, are
you Mrs Fingernail?

Yes, I'm Mrs Fingernail.
(in grand, dignified voice)

Poop, Mrs Fingernail
(giggles)

The relevance of humour to our concerns with cooperation is that it involves sharing the joke, whether it is to do with the lavatory, breaking the rules, incongruous events, or making fun of other people. Humour is also a major source of shared joy, during social behaviour between friends. This is a familiar feature of adult life too; it is interesting that it also takes place in early childhood.

Games with rules

These are games like tag, hide-and-seek, marbles, conkers, and blind man's buff, where there is competition to win, and there are rules to regulate the competition. Sometimes there is turn-taking as with marbles, sometimes there are special roles, often described as 'it' as in tag, and there is a certain amount of special vocabulary. These games are quite informal, often played in the street, but are traditional, in some cases centuries old, as the Opies have shown (1969).

Piaget (1932) proposed that children learn to cooperate during the period seven to 11, in the course of competitive games with peers, since they have the cognitive capacity to recognise and accept rules and to understand cooperation and competition. In later writings, as yet unavailable in English and therefore less well known, Piaget said that cooperative social relations between equals with reciprocity and social exchange is primary, and leads to the development of the cognitive structure of formal thinking; the external dialogue results in an inner dialogue; cooperation leads to reason. In his terms, the attainment of equilibrium (in cooperation) is needed for the equi-liberated structure of formal thinking (Kitchener 1981). However, the age for cooperation was still believed to be from seven onwards. And, indeed, six-and seven-year-old children start to argue about the rules of games. It has been found that games with rules are most popular at this age, reaching a peak of popularity at age 10. However, developmental psychologists have now shown that rules affect play at a much earlier age, even governing peek-a-boo, for example. Dunn (1988) found extensive evidence that rules affected play during the years one and a half to three, and showed that cooperation is learnt not only from interaction with peers but also with parents, and she proposes that 'children are motivated to understand the social rules and relationships of their cultural world *because they need to get things done in their family relationships*' (p. 189).

Games with rules are different from the kind of pretend play described earlier in that there is competition; the rules are traditional, not just made up on the spot or altered when players feel like it; and the roles are abstract ones with concepts like 'it' 'king', 'blind man', not those of 'monster', 'Mrs Fingernail', and so on. They are also different from games like football and ping-pong. These are introduced at school at five to six, and usually involve cooperation in teams; the games are more formal with a beginning and an end, and last longer. There is probably a developmental sequence here, each stage giving training for the next, formal games as played by adults being the final stage. Formal team games make demands for a high level of cooperation, and perhaps give a training in aspects of cooperation – sub-ordination of own desires to the team goal, division of labour, accepting a leadership hierarchy, as well as keeping to the rules.

Both evolutionary theory and sociology have emphasised the importance of reciprocity. But do children follow this principle? Studies by Staub (1978) found that 10-year-old children were no more likely to share a crayon with a child who had previously shared sweets, and Dreman and Greenbaum (1973) found that only 4 per cent of Israeli kindergarten children mentioned reciprocity as a reason for sharing sweets. There is plenty of evidence for reciprocity at the student age, so it looks as if this principle is wholly or mainly learnt, and that it is learned during adolescence.

Cooperation with peers

We shall see that attachment, the close relationship with mother or other caretaker, is necessary for social competence to develop. On the other hand, it was widely believed by psychologists that relationships such as cooperation are acquired from peer relationships, where two or more interactors are on equal terms. However, there is a lot of cooperation in relationships with parents too; they are not just one-sided affairs, as we have seen, so that the two kinds of relationship have some similarity (Maccoby and Martin 1983).

We have seen that communication occurs very early in life, and that this involves cooperation at the micro level. However, cooperation at a more molar level, such as building towers of bricks together, comes a little later – though not as late as Piaget and his followers thought. In a famous early study Parten (1932) devised a six-point scale of social participation, point six corresponding to cooperation. She found that social participation correlated 0.61 with age, and that cooperation was rare before age three, but then showed a sudden increase in frequency.

A number of very interesting experiments have been carried out on older children. Pepitone (1980) studied 918 children between five and 11, using a task of constructing a picture of a man from shapes of material. Under the cooperation condition both performance and group-oriented behaviour increased rapidly between five and 11, especially for working-class children. French (1977) used the task of building towers of bricks, the goal being to use as many bricks as possible without the tower falling down, with six- to eight-year-olds in groups of three. There was more division of labour under cooperation; one of the three might concentrate on straightening the bricks, and group performance improved with more experience of cooperation. However, there was no change between the ages of seven and nine. By the age 11, about 50 per cent of children's social activity is with peers (Barker and Wright 1955).

During childhood, on the other hand, there is still a lot of parallel play; that is, when children choose not to cooperate. The motivation for playing together is shown by what children say – 'It's fun', especially to play with other children of the same age; and compared to being with parents, 'Your friends don't tell you to wash your hands all the time, clean up your room, or apologise to your little brother' (Hetherington and Morris 1978).

What is the explanation for the increase in *cooperative* play. Piaget (1932) thought that it was due to increased cognitive powers, especially the capacity for reciprocity, role-taking, and the capacity to follow and negotiate rules. We have seen that there is the expected increase in cooperation between about six and eight, but that there is also cooperative play from the age of three, and play with siblings before this. A second source of cooperation is probably experience with the peer group. This is an important source of social competence, including the skills needed for cooperation. We have already seen how social play of various kinds involves taking turns, following and negotiating rules, seeing the point of view of others, taking different roles, and reciprocity. There are individual differences in such skills, which for example affect popularity. The most popular children are those who cooperate, are helpful, make friendly, positive approaches, are not aggressive, perceive situations accurately, and keep the rules rather than disrupting things.

How are cooperative and related social skills learnt from interaction with peers? Howes (1988) followed up children from the ages of one to five, and found that cooperativeness increased with age and followed from earlier experience, especially the amount of interaction earlier with a single member of the peer group, starting at the age of 12 months. The greatest increases in complementary, reciprocal, and other aspects of interaction take place within stable friendship pairs. We shall discuss the origins of extraversion later, and show that having siblings leads to a *lower* level of extraversion: it is social experience with peers outside the family that is important. This may be because cooperation and reciprocity between equals can take place. And friendships provide excellent settings for learning social skills. Sheer trial and error is probably one factor, helped by greater experience with other children in potential play situations. Reinforcement by other group members is important; for example, in reducing aggressiveness, and strengthening sex-roles. Imitation of other children has been found particularly important for helping behaviour. Conformity to social norms is enhanced by these processes, and cultural differences in cooperativeness are due to such social learning (see pp. 75ff.).

Children also learn how to cooperate in hierarchical structures. We have seen how siblings play in a stable, unequal relationship. In nursery school, where children quarrel over toys, a stable pecking order develops. This constitutes a stable social system, and reduces the amount of subsequent conflict. In middle childhood leaders emerge who are good at games, or good at organising things, since it is in the group's interest that they should do so. As we shall see later, boys' groups are larger and more hierarchical than those of girls, at all ages.

There has been extensive experimentation in school classrooms comparing various kinds of cooperative learning with the usual individual variety. If groups of four or so pupils work together, they learn more (individually) if there is a shared group reward, i.e. all members share the group reward, which is based on the sum of individual success, but individual efforts must be visible. In another method groups are formed, the work for a project is divided up, each member is responsible for a part, works with members of other groups doing the same part, and then teaches this to other members of his original group. This procedure yields better educational results than individual learning, regardless of whether the group is rewarded for individual or group products (Slavin 1983). Another version of this is the 'jig-saw classroom' to be described later (see p. 230). Peer tutoring is an alternative procedure, and is often very successful, especially for the tutors, especially if they are a little older than the 'pupils'.

However, we are more concerned here with the interpersonal effects of cooperative classroom experiences. A series of American studies, using several thousand school children, has found that under cooperative learning the children become more friendly to each other, and are more helpful, supportive, attentive, respectful, responsible, trusting and open to one another, creating what has been called 'social connectedness'. Under competitive conditions, on the other hand, there is more anxiety, fear of failure, hostility to other competitors, concern with preventing others from winning, and a concern with self and winning rather than intrinsic motiva-tion (Slavin 1983). However, it should perhaps be recognised that the world for which school children are being prepared is competitive in many ways, although it is certainly cooperative as well.

One kind of educational experience, is training in social skills or sensi-tivity of various kinds. An example is the Empathy Training Project devised by the Feshbachs (1982): this consists of exercises designed to increase cognitive and affective empathy, and it has been found to enhance empathy, and prosocial behaviour, and to reduce aggression. Many other 'early childhood programs', based on daycare centres for three- to four-year-olds, have been established and followed up in the USA. They all produce increased social competence, including more cooperative behaviour. There is evidence that the most important factor is greater experience with peers. There is usually a higher level of social competence, including cooperation with a familiar playmate, so more acquaintance leads to more experience at this level of performance, and it is found to generalise to new members of the group. There is evidence that experience with a greater number of children, and with a greater variety of children, are both important here, as may be experience with adults from outside the family, who are often more socially skilled than mothers.

Another general approach has been to modify the entire atmosphere of the school. Rutter *et al.* (1979) compared 12 London secondary schools. In some a greater number of children had official positions of some kind and, as a result, felt that they belonged, and felt some responsibility. Similar findings were obtained in comparisons of large and small schools: where there was 'overmanning', i.e. many jobs to be done by few people, as in small schools, again those involved felt more responsible for keeping things going (Wicker, 1973).

In Chapter 3 we described the education system of Russian collective schools, where a total regime of cooperation is used, with striking results. We also described how children are trained in cooperative ways in some highly cooperative primitive and Third World cultures.

Helping, sharing and empathy

There are two important kinds of cooperation commonly observed in children – helping and sharing, and it is widely believed that these depend primarily on a capacity for empathy. By help, or altruism, is particularly meant behaviour intended to relieve another's state of need or distress. This may take the form of touching, comforting or reassuring, or a variety of kinds of concrete help. By sharing is meant sharing toys, or sometimes food or money. Taking turns in using toys is an important kind of sharing. Curiously, young children are rather more willing to help, often spon-taneously, than to share. Empathy can be defined as 'sharing the perceived emotion of another – ''feeling with'' another' (Eisenberg and Strayer 1987). Sometimes it is defined in a more cognitive way – 'understanding the positive and negative experiences of another', often called 'perspective-taking', but this is found more in older children. There are several different ways of measuring empathy in children: in the picture-story method children are shown slides of another child while a story is told and are asked how they feel; questionnaires ask directly about being moved by others' emotional experiences; non-verbal reactions are observed while subjects watch videotapes; physiological measures are taken while watching a tape.

Many studies have been made of the relationship between empathy and helping behaviour. Since a number of theories of help and altruism assume that empathy is involved, this is an important issue. Batson et al. (1987) have shown in experiments with adults that arousing empathy increases the likelihood of help being given, even at a cost to self, like receiving electric shocks. A number of studies have investigated the correlation between individual measures of empathy and helping. On the helping side there is a certain amount of consistency between helping in different ways or on different occasions. However, the correlation with empathy is not entirely straightforward: it is weaker for children than for adults, and is strongest for the non-verbal measures. How about more cognitive measures, of being able to judge other's thoughts or feelings? Here too there is evidence for a reliable, though modest relationship (Grusec and Lytton 1988).

There is also evidence that, for older children at least, empathy leads to cooperation. Johnson (1975) found that nine- to 11-year-old children who behaved cooperatively at interaction tasks, judged the feelings and motives of other children more accurately; there was quite a strong relationship here: $r = 0.57$.

Empathy and helping behaviour are observed in children at an early age, so early that learning must play little role in this. Newborn infants, two-days-old, will cry in response to tapes of a child crying. However, this is probably not a response to another's distress, but more a kind of emotional contagion, perhaps based on similarity to own crying. But this may be the beginning of the empathic response. At two to three months babies interact a lot with their mothers, as we have seen, and it has been suggested that the goal is 'the mutual sharing of positive arousal during which infants manifest the excited engaged sociability that adults find rewarding', a state of 'positive affective synchrony' (Thompson 1987). They begin to interpret facial expressions in terms of emotions between six and 12 months, and check back on mother's emotional reactions when they are uncertain – a matter of self rather than other-concern.

The child is particularly responsive to mother's moods, since the two of them are in a kind of symbiotic biological relationship, and the child does not have a clear sense of differentiation of the self from others. Several lines of research show that the infants are not 'fundamentally egocentric organisms', but are 'highly responsive in non-egocentric ways to the socio-emotional expressions of others, and are motivated to use these expressions in their ongoing transactions with the surround' (Thompson 1987: 122). Trevarthen (1980) found evidence that by 12 months infants are aware of the thoughts of others since they point and try to direct another's attention, and appear to be seeking a state of 'intersubjectivity' or joint attention.

By the age of two they are certainly aware that another person may be in a different emotional state from themselves; for example, 'Mama, why is Tara mad at me?' (Bretherton *et al.* 1981). In the second year of life, helping moves beyond mere global distress, to actually doing something. Zahn-Waxler and Radke-Yarrow (1982) observed three groups of children, each twice, to span the age range from about 12 months to 24 months. The younger children usually did nothing to help, though they often showed distress themselves. But from about 18 months they were increasingly likely to comfort or help in some way, like seeking adult assistance. This is perhaps the earliest sign of real concern to relieve the distress of others. Dunn (1988) carried out two studies of siblings. She found that by 14–15 months infants recognised the distress of a younger sibling, or even an older sibling. In another study she compared the reactions of 40 children to the distress of a sibling at one-and-a-half, two and three years. Helping was not the only response to another child's distress: Dunn found that when the distress was not caused by the child it was most likely to ignore the other's distress or to simply watch, and if it had caused the distress itself, to make it worse, at all three ages.

In a number of studies nursery school children have been asked why they had helped or shared; by four they often referred to the needs of others. However, this was not the only reason that they gave; they also did these things simply as part of enjoyable social behaviour with friends (Dunn 1988). This was the conclusion of Rheingold (1982) who found an increasing amount of cooperation and help with parents between 18 and 30 months; for example, over household jobs. They did this to enjoy the companionship, and the use and recognition of skills.

We can add to this story by looking at the maternal origins of prosocial behaviour like helping, sharing and empathy. These can be seen as aspects of cooperation, in a broad sense, and are found to be less common on the part of highly competitive children (Barnett 1987). Secure attachment is an important source of empathy and emotional responsiveness to others. Parental warmth has also been found to be correlated with empathy, but the relationship between parental warmth or nurturance and child prosocial behaviour is a weak one, and evidently quite complex processes are involved (Radke-Yarrow *et al.* 1983).

Some further principles of social learning appear as origins of prosocial behaviour. Parents act as models in this domain as in others, and if parents are seen to be emotionally responsive and to respond sympathetically to the needs of others, their children will do the same. 'Inductive socialisation' is a further source of empathy and help; that is, where parents draw attention to another's distress, and encourage children to imagine themselves in the other's place.

Cooperation in different relationships

Introduction to part three

Most human social activity is conducted within some kind of social relationship. Each relationship involves cooperation, and the attainment of goals, though in very different ways. What is usually meant by a social relationship is a more or less enduring pattern of interaction between two people, although others may be closely involved, as in the family. There may also be some degree of attachment or bonding. It is important for relationships to be enduring so that people can rely on the other person continuing to play their part for some time; for example, a female needs her male to look after her and her children at least during the period of childrearing, for many species of animals, and for humans.

We have already seen examples of relationships in the animal kingdom. In many species mating pairs keep together for a long time, and this is very common with birds. For procreation, it of course takes two to do it, and the male often stays around to cooperate in feeding and protecting the young when they arrive. The relationship between mates is often established by means of male courtship displays and ecstatic joint rituals; for example, entwining necks and eventually copulating. In these species there is evidently strong attraction between mating pairs, and a degree of attachment or bonding. Sexual behaviour has been selected, for all species, in the evolutionary process because it is essential for gene survival. In the same way, for many species, attachment between mates has also been selected, because it increases the prospects of survival of the young.

Infants and mothers too are strongly attached in most species; there has evidently been selection of instinctive patterns of infant behaviour to seek proximity and protection from caretakers, and for mothers to provide it. Without both of these innate patterns of behaviour, infants could not be fed or protected from predators (Nash 1988). Infants of many species seem to have a powerful drive to seek proximity with their mothers, or other caretakers, and are distressed by separation. It may be a mistake to call this a cooperative relationship, since most of the help is in one direction. On the other hand, infants from the very beginning are able to play their part in the mother-infant relationship, they know how to feed, and in some cases how to cling on.

In some species, as we have seen, other kin help in looking after the young, and kinship is one of the two main sources of mutual help and cooperation. This is part of the more general process of cooperation being selected because it can contribute to inclusive fitness.

In the human species, there are a number of relationships which are found in every culture, despite tremendous variations in language, material culture, and the rest.

1 *Work* to satisfy material needs is done in all cultures, and this requires at least two basic social relationships – between workmates, and between supervisor and subordinates. In developing cultures, workmates may also be kin; in the modern world they may also be friends.
2 In all cultures there is *friendship* between non-kin. In some Third World cultures, friendship is a serious matter, involving major help, whereas in the modern world it is based more on leisure.
3 *Kinship* is the basis of most relationships in developing cultures, where there is an extended family, living together or near to each other. In the modern world we live in small nuclear families, consisting of one or two parents and their children, and there is little contact with other kin.
4 *Love* comes before marriage in many cultures, but the order of events may be different when marriages are arranged, as many are in India and Japan. Love is an intense relationship, a source of great joy, and is of great interest from our point of view.
5 In all cultures there is *marriage*. The main variation is that in some cultures a man can have more than one wife, and in the modern world the wife has become equal rather than subordinate, and marriage is becoming less permanent than before for many people.

There are other relationships, but those above are the main ones, and will suffice to explore the cooperative nature of relationships.

Why do we need all these relationships? It was suggested earlier that cooperation has three motivational roots – material rewards, interpersonal rewards, and enjoyable joint activities. This is confirmed by a study of the different kinds of satisfaction in relationships. Subjects were asked to rate their satisfaction on 15 scales with a number of relationships. This generated three factors, as shown in Figure 6A.1 (Argyle and Furnham 1983).

Factor 1, which accounted for most variance, was about instrumental and material help from the other person. Some relationships, like those with spouses and parents, produced strong rewards of this kind.
Factor 2 referred to social and emotional support, and was highest for spouse, friends, parents and siblings.

Figure 6A.1 Sources of satisfaction in different relationships

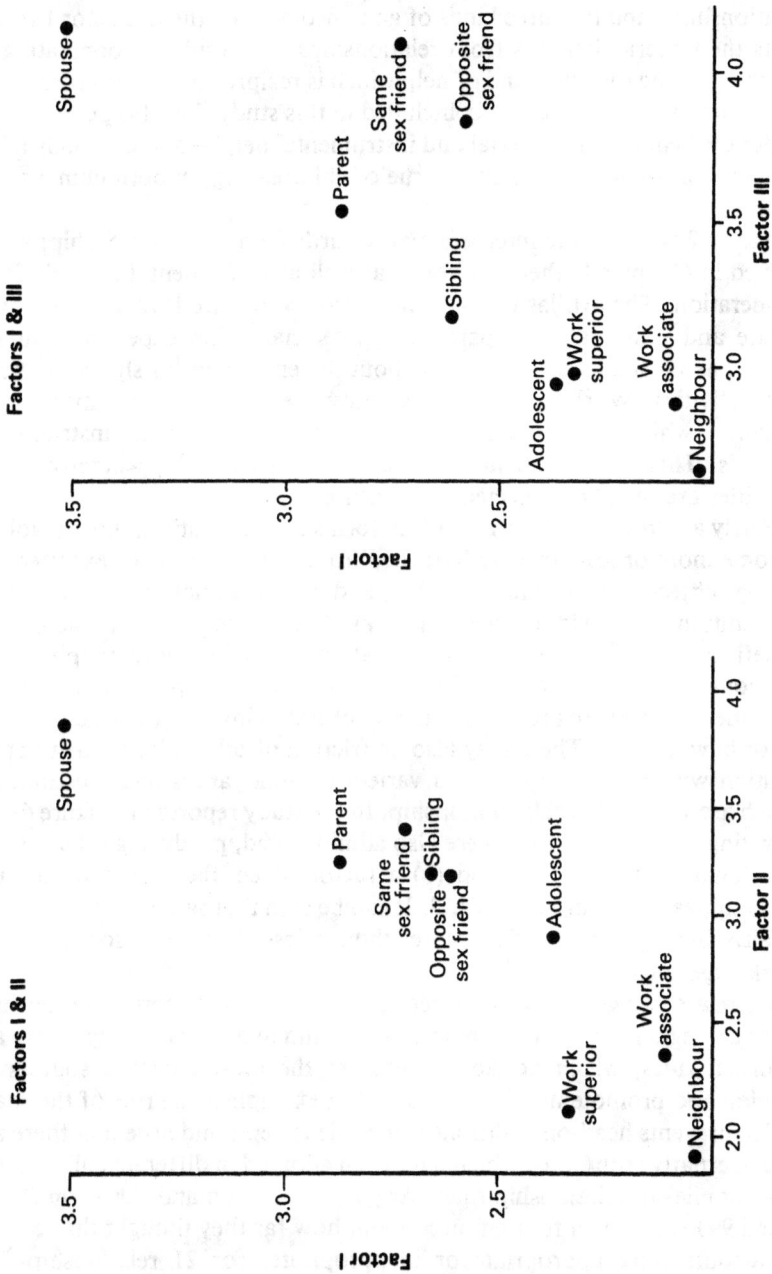

Factors I & II

Factors I & III

Source: Argyle and Furnham 1983

Factor 3 was about enjoyment of shared interests and activities. It was highest for spouse and same sex friends.

These three factors show the three sources of satisfaction provided by social relationships, and the three kinds of goal mediated by them. Factor 1 represents the material benefits from relationships, the result of cooperating to get things done together, and of help which is reciprocated. The procreation of children was not specifically included in this study, but this perhaps falls under the heading of 'material and instrumental help' – and definitely takes cooperation to do it; the same is true of childrearing, in both humans and animals.

Factor 2 is about the interpersonal rewards from the relationship; as we argued in Chapter 1, there are social as well as instrumental rewards from cooperation. The affiliative and other needs which are involved are partly innate and universal, and partly due to socialisation experiences in the family, as we shall see. Factor 3 is about the enjoyment of shared interests and activities. Working together is enjoyable, but there are many joint activities which have nothing to do with work, or with instrumental rewards. This is most obvious in the case of friendship, where the joint activities are mainly connected with leisure.

Partly as a result of these rewarding forms of cooperation, those involved become more or less strongly 'attached' to one another. They experience a strong subjective bond with the other, and want the relationship to endure. In addition to providing these three kinds of benefits, relationships are beneficial in other ways. They are great sources of joy and happiness, of freedom from stress and mental ill-health, and of good physical health. On the other hand, there are costs – mainly of not being free to decide what to do or how to do it. There may also be friction of other kinds, due to competition within the group, and a variety of annoyances and frustrations, which are specific to each relationship. In the study reported in Figure 6A.1, 15 rating scales for conflict were also administered, producing (a) a general emotional conflict factor, and (b) a factor of conflict based on mutual criticism, as shown in Figure 6A.2. It can be seen that same sex friends have a fairly high general conflict score, though less than those for spouse or work superior.

There are two general ways of reducing these costs. In some relationships there are legal rules about what is allowed, and in all relationships there are informal rules, which develop to prevent the most common sources of friction and promote need satisfaction. An example is the rule of the road, which prevents head-on collisions if the rule is kept; and note that there are two alternative solutions, which have been adopted in different cultures; the same applies to relationship rules. Argyle, Henderson and Furnham (1985) asked 993 subjects in four cultures about how far they thought that certain behaviours were appropriate or inappropriate, for 21 relationships. In

Figure 6A.2 Conflict in different relationships

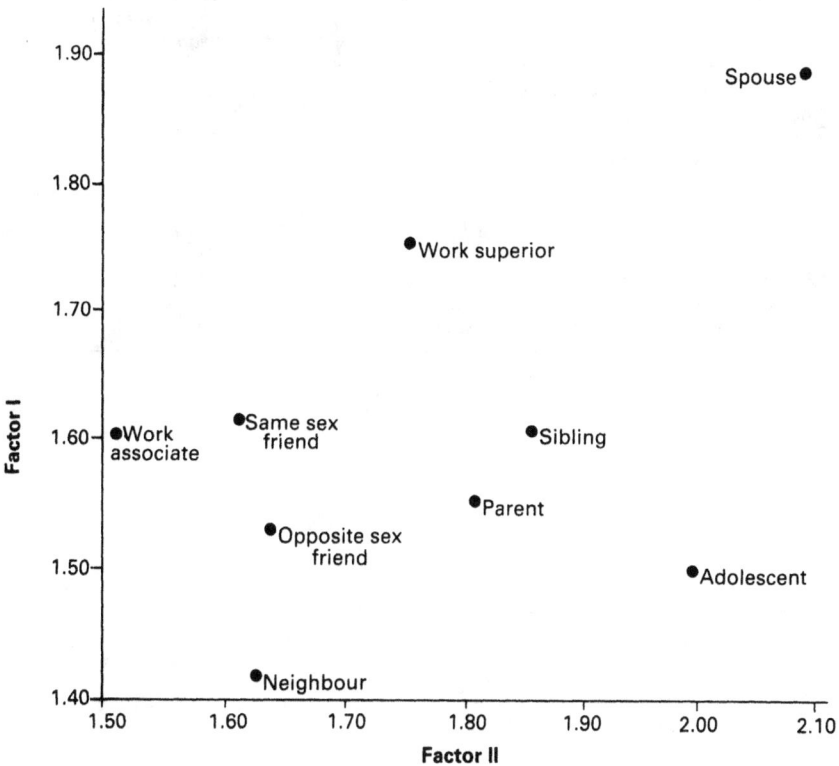

Source: Argyle and Furnham 1983

Britain a number of rules were thought to apply to all of them (Table 6A.1). Other rules were specific to each relationship and will be mentioned later.

A second solution to relationship problems is for individuals to become more socially skilled, so that they can establish and sustain their relationships more effectively, and have more say over decisions taken within them, including skill at finding the solution giving the maximum joint profit.

It is suggested that there are three basic kinds of relationships, which are found in all cultures, and where each is the basis of a particular form of cooperation: work, family and friends. My central thesis is that cooperation takes three forms as found in these three relationships.

Table 6A.1 General rules for relationships in Britain

	Number of relationships in which mean showed high endorsement
Should respect the other's privacy	22
Should not discuss that which is said in confidence with the other person	21
Should look the other person in the eye during conversation	21
Should not criticize the other person publicly	16
Should not indulge in sexual activity with the other person	15
Should seek to repay debts, favours or compliments no matter how small	14
Should stand up for the other person in their absence	12
Should share news of success with the other person	12
Should address the other person by their first name	11

Source: Argyle, Henderson and Furnham 1985

Chapter six

Cooperation in working groups

We saw that many species of animals cooperate over finding food, nest-building and defence. Ants are the most striking example with their large-scale organisation of work; meerkats are an example of the need for division of labour. For these species, cooperation over work is necessary for existence.

Among primitive societies, as we saw in Chapter 3, some are more cooperative than others, but in all there is some minimal level. Cooperation over work is necessary for several reasons: (a) some tasks are simply too big for one person, like dealing with large predators or heavy loads; (b) some tasks require division of labour, between individuals who have specialised skills for different parts of the job; (c) working in groups means that people can help and instruct one another; and (d) it provides company – that is, social satisfaction: the benefits of cooperation at work are not confined to material rewards.

The nature of cooperation at work and its links with rewards has taken quite different forms in different historical periods. (1) In very primitive societies groups of male kin went hunting, fishing or fighting together, in rather the same way as in groups of animals. There was a clear division of labour between the work done by men and by women: the wife looked after the children, did the cooking and housework, made clothes; the husband's job was outside, providing housing, food and protection, if necessary by fighting and organising others in the community. Cooperation led directly to provision of food, shelter and protection. (2) From about 8,000 BC onwards larger and more settled communities developed, there was more specialisation in the kinds of work done, so that food and other goods were bartered, or bought for money: work was less immediately related to immediate needs. (3) From 2,500 BC the ancient civilisations developed, in which a lot of the work was done by slaves, captured in wars, who were cooperating under duress, while the leaders were motivated in a new way, to achieve success in great enterprises. (4) Slavery was later replaced by feudalism, where the lower orders cooperated in a social system in which they received some rewards, such as protection and use of land, but believed that the hierarchical order was right and they accepted their place in it with its duties. (5) Mediaeval industry was partly based on the domestic system, where families cooperated over work for which they were paid, and partly on craft guilds, where skilled men worked for payment and promotion. (6) The Protestant Reformation saw the beginnings of the Protestant ethic, with small entrepreneurs who started firms, worked hard and made money, most of which was put back into the firm. (7) The Industrial Revolution consisted of the growth of large-scale manufacturing, using steampower; instead of working in small groups at home or in craft workshops, workers were now organised into large factories, doing often unpleasant work for payment and fear of dismissal and consequent starvation. The invention of assembly-line work made things worse by breaking jobs down into small and meaningless parts. (8) Recent industrial developments have brought about a lot of improvements: wage incentives are used less, and more people work for 'intrinsic' reasons – such as finding the work interesting and satisfying; better forms of supervision are used, making less use of coercion, more of persuasion and participation in decisions; use is made of small, cooperative workteams, who combine to complete units of work; organisations are less hierarchical, with fewer levels in the hierarchy, and more industrial democracy (Argyle 1989).

What exactly does cooperation at work consist of? There may be:

1 *Cooperation over a task*
(a) Parallel performance, e.g. independent assembly work, typing, research. There may be mutual help but this is unofficial.
(b) Sequential performance of different tasks, e.g. the workers on an assembly line. This needs coordination, and time is wasted while one worker waits for another.
(c) Cooperative performance of similar tasks, e.g. two-handed sawing, handling sheet steel in a press-shop.
(d) Cooperative and simultaneous performance of different but complementary tasks, e.g. pilot and navigator of an aeroplane.

In all these cases the worker receives input information from both the work of other persons and from task displays such as dials; events can be controlled either by influencing the other workers or by manipulating the controls of the task. The different feedbacks have to be considered together; for example, it may be necessary for different jobs to be synchronised.

2 *Supervisory relationships*
(e) Supervision.
(f) Inspection.
(g) One person is an assistant to others, e.g. nurse-doctor, technician-research worker.

In these cases one person does not actually do the work but has to make sure that someone else does it properly. Exactly what a supervisor has to do, and how he or she does it, depends greatly on the technology. If there is machine-pacing, as on an assembly line, the supervisor does not need to motivate subordinates to work harder. There may be inspection, but this, too, may be automatic as the supervisor may have equipment which gives clear information about the performance of the workers. The usual situation, however, is that a supervisor takes account of feedback both from task-display indicators *and* from observation of the subordinates' behaviour. The action which he or she takes is usually to try to influence the individual, although it may also involve changes to equipment.

3 *Other social relationships*. Other kinds of social skills are commonly found in socio-technical systems.

(h) Conveying objects or information.

(i) Discussion, by members of a cooperative problem-solving group.

(j) Negotiation, where there is some conflict of interest.

(k) Providing expert advice, without authority.

Some conversation is less directly concerned with the work – casual chat and gossip. Some social activity at work has nothing to do with work – games, jokes and teasing, gossip and discussion of personal life, not only in the lunch-hour, but while the work is being done. Homans (1950) suggested that this social activity formed a 'secondary system' which fed back into and influenced the primary system of work proper; for example, workers who enjoy playing games together may later cooperate over the work.

The causes of cooperation at work

The demands of the task

For primitive men faced with some large task, like building a house, it was the demands of this task which made them cooperate, since one man alone could not do it. The same applied to the mediaeval domestic system, where families did the work together at home. For many workteams in the modern world it must be equally clear that cooperation is necessary; for example, to run a restaurant, or a research team, or an airliner. There are two factors here – the need for the efforts of more than one person, and the need for people with different, complementary, skills or knowledge.

In modern industry it is equally true that one worker could not produce cars or nuclear power, but it is less obvious to those involved that they are cooperating to meet their own shared needs for the product. A modern factory requires many forms of cooperation, but some of this has been brought about in other ways. People may work quite independently on separate tasks, or they may be interdependent, so that one cannot do his work without the collaboration of others. This may be a matter of doing it together at the same time, as with the pilot and navigator of an aircraft, or have to wait for the other, as on assembly lines, or in other ways.

One important source of cooperation is the workflow system, where each person's work is linked to that of others. A good example of this is provided by the Longwall method of coalmining. There are three jobs here – cutting, filling and stonework. If the three are all done on each shift, there is more cooperation, resulting in fewer accidents and higher productivity than if they are done on different shifts. If miners doing the three jobs never meet, the stoneworkers, for example, may fail to leave the roof safe for the next shift (Trist *et al.* 1963).

Thomas (1957) created a laboratory analogue of different kinds of work arrangements, for making cardboard houses. In one design each person was dependent on the others in a five-person production line; in another different individuals did each of the five jobs independently. The interdependent condition produced more attraction to the group, more help, higher productivity and more responsibility for the group, but also more tension. Task interdependence has been used successfully to create cooperation in inter-group settings such as the 'jig-saw classroom' (see p. 230).

In almost all work groups there are different roles, such as doctor and nurse, and these are linked together in an interlocking system; that is, a doctor cannot perform his role without nurses, patients and others performing their roles. It is this interlocking which binds organisations together as cooperative systems. It creates pressure for those in each role to carry out performances which are complementary to those in the other roles. It is also the main cause of role conflict, where there are two or more others who have different expectations or demands of the occupant of a role. For example, doctors may experience different pressures from patients and research colleagues – since some patients should be in the control group for research purposes (Argyle 1989).

Affiliative needs

The primary motivation for cooperation at work is the need for the task to be performed. There is a second motive – people enjoy doing things together. However, the research literature is divided on the importance of work relationships. Some studies, like those shown in Figures 6A.1 and 6A.2 (p. 111 and 113) suggest that work relationships, especially with supervisors, result in more conflict than rewards, while the rewards which they do generate are only material ones. On the other side there are also studies showing that working relationships can be a great source of job satisfaction, and can buffer work stresses. A resolution of this controversy can be achieved by distinguishing between different kinds of relationship at work, as follows:

1 *Friends.* Some people at work become friends in the normal way, are seen outside work such as in leisure activities, and are invited home. Many friends are drawn from work in this way.

2 *Friends at work*. Others are seen a lot at work, at lunch or coffee breaks for example, but are never seen outside the workplace.

3 *Work colleagues*. Others are seen quite often in the course of work, and these encounters may be quite agreeable, but their company is not particularly sought for lunch or coffee.

4 *Disliked colleagues*. Other people at work are positively disliked, and contacts are kept to the minimum required for work, and sometimes less than that.

We studied 124 people at a fish-processing plant, asked them if they could think of an individual in each of these four categories, and to report on how often they did various things with them. The results are shown in Table 6.1. It can be seen that the closer the relationship with the other, the more likely they were to engage in work-related forms of cooperation, like working on a joint task, and also in purely social activities, like joking or teasing (Henderson and Argyle 1985).

Table 6.1 Percentage of workers who frequently engaged in work and social activities

| | With | | | |
	Social friend	Friend at work	Work colleague	Disliked colleague
Helping other with work	52%	32%	18%	8%
Discussing work	49%	52%	32%	17%
Chatting casually	72%	63%	26%	15%
Joking with the other	72%	54%	24%	13%
Teasing the other person	46%	32%	18%	20%
Discussing personal life	30%	19%	13%	11%
Discussing personal feelings	26%	10%	5%	5%
Asking for or giving personal advice	33%	19%	8%	6%

Source: Henderson and Argyle 1985

Cooperation can be generated by increasing group cohesiveness. This is the extent to which members of a group like one another, enjoy each other's company. There is usually a great deal of purely social activity at work, in the form of jokes, games and gossip, and this affects cooperation at work. The people who play games together also cooperate and help one another over the work. An experiment was carried out in which cohesive teams of bricklayers were created: they laid more bricks and wasted less materials than non-cohesive teams (Van Zelst 1952). In cohesive teams, the members help each other more, and they have an extra, social incentive for working.

The effect of cohesiveness on cooperation at work varies with the nature of the work. If people are working entirely independently it makes little difference; cohesiveness is most important where help and collaboration are needed. And too much cohesiveness can be counter-productive – if coffee breaks get longer and jokes and gossip become more important than the work.

How can cohesiveness be produced. Sheer proximity – for example, working in the same room – leads to more interaction and increased cohesiveness, provided that social interaction is possible. A group of clerical workers was installed inside a steel mesh cage; they worked hard but had a lot of time for fooling about, such as 'sniping' with elastic bands. When management stopped all this by better surveillance, productivity fell (Sundstrom 1986). A delightful example is 'banana time', one of several diversions invented by a bored group of workers studied by Roy (1959). At a certain time each day one man would steal and eat another's banana; at another time someone would open a window, thus creating a draught and a row. They said, 'If it weren't for the joking and fooling, you'd go nuts.' Cohesiveness is greater if group members are fairly homogeneous in age, social class and so on, and if their supervisor is good at generating positive relationships, and removing friction inside the group.

Cooperative incentives

It is possible to encourage cooperation by incentive systems. A classic study was carried out by Deutsch (1949). Groups of five students met for five weeks for 50 minutes to solve human relations and other problems. In the cooperative groups the students were given class grades based on the group solutions; each member received the same grade. In the competitive groups each student was given a grade based on their individual contribution to the work of their group compared with the others. As Deutsch and Gerard (1967) later described it, 'In the cooperative group a common goal was thus imposed on the group and the motives of individual members were made to coincide with the group goal. . . . One member could not detract from the group performance without defeating his individual purpose'. In the competitive groups 'one person could only achieve his individual purpose of attaining a high grade at the expense of someone else's good attainment' (pp. 609–10). This manipulation made substantial differences to behaviour in the groups, and in the quality of work produced. This general method has become the standard laboratory procedure for creating cooperative groups.

Group piecework is sometimes used in industry – again the whole group is rewarded equally for their productivity. It avoids friction inside groups and encourages cooperation and help. As an incentive, however, it is usually less effective than individual payment by results, and it has been found that the larger the group the weaker the effect (Marriott 1968). However, there are situations in which group piecework produces better results than individual piecework. Individual incentives in department stores, for example, lead to salesmen grabbing the best customers, hiding the goods, and neglecting stock and display work. Group piecework is appropriate for small, cohesive work groups, where workers are closely interdependent, such as the mining groups described above. However, in large groups of independent workers it simply acts as a weak incentive and results in hostility towards slow workers.

Group decisions

A number of early laboratory and field studies, inspired by Kurt Lewin, showed that if a group made a decision to adopt some change in behaviour, successful changes were achieved. For example, groups of American house-wives in World War II were persuaded to make group decisions to eat brown bread and other previously rejected food.

An important advantage of group decision-taking is that those who took part understand why the decision was taken and why alternative solutions were rejected; they are therefore more likely to accept the decision, and are more prepared to implement it. It is no use taking good decisions if others are unwilling to carry them out. Lawler and Hackman (1969) carried out a field study in which a bonus scheme was introduced to reduce absenteeism among janitors. The same scheme was developed with the participation of janitors in one part of the company and imposed on them in another part. With participation there was a much more positive response to the scheme; without participation it was regarded with anxiety and suspicion.

Why does it work? There are probably a number of factors. Taking part in a decision internalises a new norm or goal, and each individual now shares the group goal. The individual's own views have been expressed, and influenced the decision; he or she has been exposed to the reasons for the final decision, and appreciates how much the other members value it.

Groups and individuals will work harder if they are induced to set goals for themselves. A meta-analysis of 87 studies of a variety of jobs from logging crews to professors found that this was particularly effective if specific goals were set, if these were fairly difficult, and if there was feed-back, or knowledge of results, about how well they were doing. Workers can be persuaded to accept such goals if they are consulted and if they participate in group decisions (Tubbs 1986).

Salience of group membership

In a recent analysis of the psychology of social groups, Turner (1987) argues that the reality of a social group exists in the minds of the members when they categorise themselves as members – 'psychological group formation may be the necessary intervening process before objective interdependence leads to cooperative activity' (p. 34). The more strongly individuals identify with a group, that is the more group membership is a salient part of their self-image, the more they become 'depersonalised'; in other words, they 'come to perceive themselves more as the interchangeable exemplars of a social category than as unique personalities defined by their individual differences from others' (p. 50).

Hogg and Turner (1985) confirmed these ideas in an experiment in the inter-group tradition. Subjects were given information about other imaginary persons, suggesting either that they belonged to the same group or were very likeable. The in-group manipulation, but not the likeable manipulation, produced in-group favouritism; the second manipulation produced liking but not in-group favouritism – it did not lead to a feeling of group formation.

Depersonalisation is expected to lead directly to cooperation because 'the perception of identity between oneself and in-group members leads to a perceived identity of interests . . .', because 'the goals of the other group members are perceived as one's own', and 'in-group members are assumed to share one's own goals' (ibid. p. 65). Depersonalisation is brought about by shared attributes and experiences, and by shared clothes and other aspects of appearance. It is similar to the older concept of 'de-individuation'. Research has focused on the effects of de-individuation on anti-social behaviour, but it was also found that it produced weakened memory for who said what (Festinger *et al.* 1952).

The main attempts to study such identification with in-group members have been in connection with cross-cultural studies of collectivism. As we saw in Chapter 4, there are separate factors here of subordination of one's own needs to those of the group, concern for in-group members, and perceived distance from the in-group.

Cooperative rules

In our studies of informal social rules for different relationships we found sets of rules for different work relationships. The rules which were most strongly endorsed for workmates are given in Table 6.2. Rules 3, 4, 6 and 9 were directly concerned with maintaining cooperation over work. Many of the other rules are concerned with maintaining positive relations between workers, and preventing common causes of friction. Informal rules like this are probably developed to deal with common sources of difficulty in a relationship. We found for friendships that disruption of the relationship was often caused by one person breaking the rules (Argyle and Henderson 1985).

A problem with workmates is that usually we don't choose them, and as a result there are some that we don't like. There are rules for how to deal with this situation, and they are shown in Table 6.3.

Table 6.2 Rules for co-workers

1. Accept one's fair share of the work load.
2. Respect other's privacy.
3. Be cooperative with regard to the shared physical working conditions (e.g. light, temperature, noise).
4. Be willing to help when requested.
5. Keep confidences.
6. Work cooperatively despite feelings of dislike.
7. Don't denigrate to superiors.
8. Address the co-worker by first name.
9. Ask for help and advice when necessary.
10. Look the co-worker in the eye during conversations.
11. Don't be over-inquisitive about each other's private lives.
12. Repay debts, favours and compliments no matter how small.
13. Don't engage in sexual activity with the co-worker.
14. Stand up for the co-worker in his/her absence.
15. Don't criticise the co-worker publicly.

Source: Argyle and Henderson 1985

Table 6.3 Rules for people you don't get on with

Some of the general rules
1. should not discuss what is said in confidence.
2. should look the other person in the eye during conversation.
3. should respect the other person's privacy.
4. should seek to repay debts, favours or compliments, no matter how small.

Additional rules
5. strive to be fair in relations with one another.
6. should not ignore the other person.
7. should not invite the other to dine as a guest at a family celebration.
8. should not denigrate the other behind their back.
9. should not ask the other for material help.
10. should not display hypocritical liking for the other.

Source: Argyle and Henderson 1985

Cooperative skills

A number of social and related skills are needed for successful cooperation at work.

Supervisor-subordinate skills

We have seen the importance of participation in decisions. That means that subordinates should be consulted, and their views taken into account as much as possible. As Figure 6A.2 (p. 113) shows, there is often conflict between supervisors and subordinates. This is mainly because supervisors have greater power, and give directions, some of these unwelcome. Conflict between supervisors and subordinates can be minimised, and the job satisfaction of the latter increased, if supervisors show *consideration*, that is look after the needs of subordinates and deal with interpersonal problems in the group, and if they use *participation*, where subordinates are consulted, and allowed to have some say in how things are done. There is a third component of effective supervision – *initiating structure*: telling people what to do and how to do it. This is necessary for efficiency, but should be done tactfully, and with a light touch. The performance of a skill can be represented in general as in Figure 6.1: the performer pursues certain goals, his performance is corrected following feedback on its success or lack of success; perception of feedback is then translated into appropriate corrective action.

Figure 6.1 Motor skill model

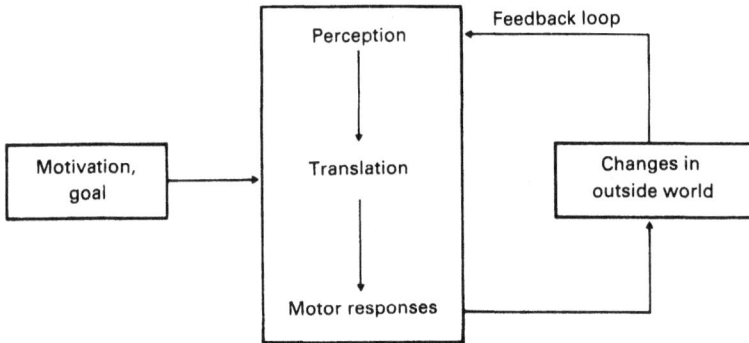

Source: Argyle 1983

This model can be used to describe the social skills of dealing with people, as well as the motor skills of dealing with equipment. In cooperative work one is dealing both with equipment *and* with people, *two* sets of feedback are received, and there are *two* ways of taking corrective action – by operating on the equipment, or by influencing the other person.

Supervisors can also be sensitive to friction between different subordinates, due to competition, unequal treatment, or other sources of difficulty.

Workmate skills

This brings us to the heart of cooperation, and to a number of issues which are explored elsewhere in this book. Cooperative workmates are sensitive to each other's thoughts and feelings, have skills of coordination, similar to those used in dancing, music and sport, and have a positive social interest in each other.

Rituals and ceremonies

Primitive societies are famous for their elaborate ceremonies, and these are believed to be important in maintaining social cohesion and cooperation. Modern working groups have their rituals too, and we saw an example above (see p. 120). The social psychology group at Oxford has kept up the following events for nearly 30 years: 'Monday morning mania' (i.e. coffee) in the author's room at 11 a.m.; Friday evening seminars, followed by a visit to the King's Arms; a Christmas party; and, in the summer, a group photograph and a barbecue. Oxford colleges have an elaborate calendar of dinners, garden parties, chapel services, and events like 'collections' connected with the academic year.

What a cooperative group is like

Cooperative groups are different from other groups in several important ways.

1 *Mutual help.* One of the key differences is that members help each other a lot. This was found in the Thomas experiment; in the Deutsch experiment there was more working together and coordination, as rated by observers, in the cooperative groups. Studies of high and low output industrial groups find that amount of help is an important factor. There is an obvious motivation to help in a cooperative group – it is not because of altruism but because it will promote the group goal; each member's rewards depend in part on the performance of others.

2 *Division of labour.* One of the reasons for cooperation over work is so that different individuals can specialise in whatever they are good at and like doing, and the group benefits from the combination of different skills or knowledge. When a group is given a cooperative incentive, some degree of division of labour develops, and the members make different contributions to the work, as happened in the Deutsch experiment.

3 *Interpersonal attraction.* We showed above that group cohesion can be a cause of cooperation. The reverse also applies: people like each other more in cooperative groups. Deutsch found that the cooperative groups were rated by observers as more friendly and less aggressive. Thomas found that his cooperative groups were more cohesive in the sense of being attracted to the group more. Industrial field studies have found that cooperative groups have lower absenteeism and labour turnover, as would be expected if the members were more attracted to the group. Part of the explanation is probably that members of cooperative groups help and thus reward each other. We shall suggest later that the experience of coordinated interaction, as much in work as in leisure, is a basic source of satisfaction (see pp. 157ff.). In addition, belonging to a cooperative group, and all the positive interaction that that entails, would be expected to satisfy needs for affiliation and intimacy, and to provide social support.

4 *Commitment to the group.* The feeling of commitment or loyalty to group or organisation has been much studied by occupational psychologists, and can be measured by attitudes scales. It is partly a matter of cognitive assessment of the rewards and costs of sticking to the group. However, it is also partly due to emotional commitment, based on non-instrumental attachment, and internalising the group's values. This kind of commitment is a powerful predictor of staying with the group (Argyle 1989).

5 *Internalised motivation.* A method of measuring motivation is by use of the 'Zeigarnik effect' – memory for an uncompleted task, which a person wanted to finish, is enhanced. Hornstein (1982) ran experiments in which subjects saw on video the hands of another person doing a number of puzzles. The relation with that person was manipulated using the Deutsch method, and he completed some tasks, not others. If the tasks were to be resumed later there was a Zeigarnik effect (i.e. uncompleted tasks recalled better) for 28 per cent of the cooperating subjects, and 40 per cent of subjects in the competitive condition. In other words, the uncompleted task tension had been partly discharged under cooperative conditions.

The performance of cooperative groups

Are cooperative groups more effective?

In the Deutsch experiment described earlier, the cooperative groups were faster at solving problems than the competitive groups, and their solutions to human relations problems were rated more highly by observers. There have been many other studies of the performance of cooperative and other groups at solving problems, other laboratory tasks, and academic achievement. The results of 122 studies have been put together in a meta-analysis by Johnson *et al.* (1981). The main results are as follows:

1 *Cooperation v. competition.* Cooperative groups did better, over 84 studies; the average person did 0.75 SD (standard deviation units) better under cooperation, for academic achievement, and for laboratory tasks, but not for rote performance.
2 *Competition between individuals and between groups* (i.e. with cooperation within the groups). The groups did better. For 44 studies the difference was 0.37 SD.
3 *Cooperative v. individual efforts.* Again cooperation did better – for 156 studies 0.75 SD better.

The advantages of cooperation were more marked under certain conditions – when the groups were small, when the tasks were interdependent, for problem-solving as opposed to rote tasks, when resource-sharing improved performance, and where division of labour was required. These figures are 'effect sizes', that is differences in standard deviation units, showing that the average person in the cooperative groups performed better than the average person in the competitive or individual groups. It was found that the cooperative groups did better for older subjects, and when the task required interdependence and the sharing of resources.

Field studies of group incentive schemes in industry produce slightly different results. If workers are doing quite independent jobs, group piece-work becomes more effective the smaller the group, and is greatest for individuals (Marriott 1968). On the other hand, if the group is engaged in some kind of joint activity where coordination is needed, organising them into autonomous, and integrated teams leads to increased productivity. Creating *cohesive* groups, where the members like one another, has been shown, with bricklayers and other work groups, to lead to greater productivity.

However, competition appears to be necessary to produce the greatest efforts at sports, and is widely used, apparently with success, in education, the arts and many other spheres of individual endeavour (Argyle 1989).

Studies of group problem-solving usually find that groups arrive at better solutions than most individual members, but often not as good as those of the best members. Webber (1974) studied groups of managers and compared the times taken, and the number of problems correctly solved, for individuals and groups (Table 6.4). It can be seen that individuals were faster than groups, but groups obtained higher scores. For the younger managers the group scores were better than the best individual scores in the group.

A number of explanations have been put forward to explain the success of cooperative groups:

1 *Motivation*. The reverse prediction might be made that individual competition would arouse greater motivation because individual efforts and their rewards are more closely related. Deutsch found no evidence for any difference in motivation; there was a non-significant trend for cooperative groups to be more motivated, perhaps because of pressure from other members of the group. However, the effects of cooperative motivation were greater in smaller groups, as would be expected.

2 *Coordination*. Deutsch found that observers rated the cooperative group members as working together and coordinating more. It is found that larger groups do less well, *per capita*, at tug-of-war pulling and similar tasks, partly because of coordination losses, i.e. not all pulling at the same time (Ingham *et al.* 1974).

3 *Help*. In cooperative groups there is more helping, in competitive groups more interference. We described problems in shops above (see pp. 120ff.). Cooperative group members see that their rewards depend partly

Table 6.4 How age/position level is related to success of group problem-solving

Subjects	Mean score (no. correct)	Mean time (min.)	Mean group effectiveness (group score minus mean of individuals in group)	Mean group excellence (group score minus best individual score in group)
Executives (mean age 47)				
40 individuals	13.4	4.0		
8 groups	15.8	9.0	+ 1.8	− 1.4
Middle managers (mean age 40)				
55 individuals	13.3	4.2		
11 groups	15.1	6.2	+ 1.7	− 2.9
Young managers (mean age 32)				
90 individuals	13.2	4.2		
18 groups	15.3	5.3	+ 2.3	− 3.1
MBA students (mean age 25)				
90 individuals	14.3	4.7		
18 groups	16.3	6.0	+ 3.7	0
BS students (mean age 20)				
40 individuals	11.5	5.5		
8 groups	17.5	6.0	+ 3.5	+ 1.5

Source: Webber 1974

on the activities of the others, and feel some responsibility for others' performance, and a positive attitude towards it. The behaviour of self and others is seen as interchangeable.

4 *Communication.* There is more communication in cooperative groups, fewer communication difficulties, and less trouble in understanding the others. Cooperative group members are more likely to accept the ideas and suggestions of others. There is more social influence in cooperative groups.

5 *Division of labour.* However, there is *less* homogeneity and greater division of labour in cooperative groups, each person specialising on what he does best. In problem-solving groups it is often possible to divide up the work in this way, and to take advantage of each member's expertise.

These five broad processes show the rather complex pattern of behaviour in cooperative working groups, and can explain why they have greater productivity under many conditions, and why the members like one another more.

Do cooperative groups provide benefits for individuals?

How far does cooperation at work cause satisfaction, joy or other benefits? It is found that job satisfaction is higher for people who belong to cohesive working groups, that is where the members get on well together and like one another; the factors leading to cohesiveness will be discussed later. Satisfaction is closely related with popularity: 0.82 in one study. It is greater in smaller groups, and when there is plenty of opportunity for social interaction – for example, not too much noise or distance between workers. In view of the close connection between cohesiveness and cooperation, for example, there is more mutual help in cohesive groups; it seems very likely that cooperation will also increase job satisfaction. And cooperative groups have lower rates of absenteeism and turnover. Workers often have a great deal of fun from non-work activities, from jokes, games, gossip and general fooling about, and this is an obvious source of joy.

Work relationships are also a powerful buffer against stresses at work: when a person has supportive relationships at work he is far less likely to become mentally disturbed or ill as the result of stress at work; he sees events as less stressful, because supportive workmates can actually help to deal with the problem. Figure 6.2 shows how the effect of stress on mental health is removed when there is good social support at work.

Later research has found that there are also modest main effects of social support; that is, it is effective whether the stress is high or low; and in either case it has more effect on anxiety and measures of subjective wellbeing, than on objective measures of health (Buunk *et al.* 1989).

The shared activities at work are often rewarding too: both the cooperative achievement of work goals, the work activities involved, and the purely social activity – jokes, games and gossip.

There can, however, be conflict between people at work, and here cooperation apparently fails. First, there can be competition as well as cooperation between individuals – for promotion, desirable jobs and so on, especially with disliked work colleages. We found that there are informal rules, devised to prevent such conflict – 'strive to be fair in dealings with one another', 'don't denigrate the other behind their back' and 'repay debts, favours and compliments' (see Table 6.2 on p. 123). Second, there can be conflict not between individuals, but between groups, such as management and unions, or between different departments. This is a more difficult problem, and we take it up in Chapter 10. Third, there is often conflict between supervisors and subordinates, as Figure 6.2 shows. Again this can be avoided by keeping to informal rules, but even more by supervisors using certain styles of supervision.

Figure 6.2 Buffering effects of co-worker support on relationships between perceived job stress and somatic complaints

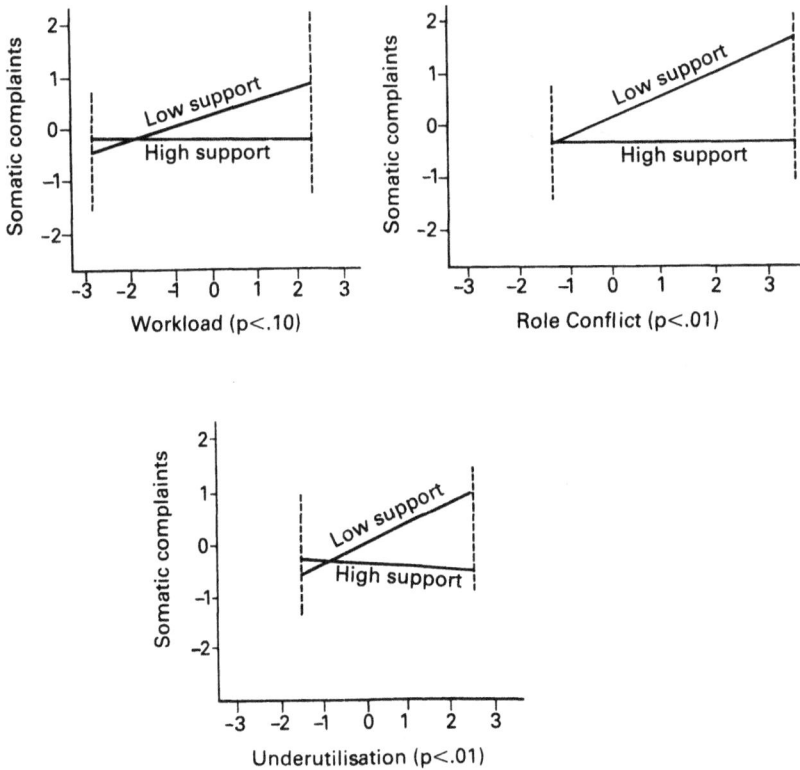

Workload (p<.10)

Role Conflict (p<.01)

Underutilisation (p<.01)

Source: House 1981

Cooperation in organisations

'Industrial democracy' is the general term to describe the extension of con-sultation and participation in decisions to all levels. We have seen that this form of cooperation is successful with working groups; can it also work on a larger scale?

There are a number of different variations of industrial democracy, which are described more fully elsewhere (Argyle 1989). The main ones are:

1 Trade union representation by elected shop stewards. This is a very weak form of industrial democracy and usually not very cooperative, often formalising conflict (Britain).

2 Joint consultation, with committees of representatives from all levels (Europe).
3 Workers' councils. The factory is run by a workers' council, all of whose members are elected, together with committees at lower levels (Yugoslavia).
4 Worker-directors. Here some of the top management committee are worker-directors, some of them nominated by unions (West Germany).
5 The Scanlon plan. Departmental production committees are elected and find ways of improving efficiency; most of the savings made are paid as a bonus (USA).
6 Quality circles. Voluntary groups meet once a week to analyse data and make suggestions for improved efficiency (Japan).

How far has industrial democracy developed? There are elaborate arrangements for it in all European countries, but the degree of involvement and amount of influence is felt to be quite small. Britain lags behind Yugoslavia, West Germany and Norway.

Do workers want it? Surveys show that 50–60 per cent would like more participation, especially in their immediate affairs, while a few want to take part in decisions affecting the company as a whole. Skilled workers are particularly keen, and the preferred scheme is for equal influence of management and workers (Wall and Lischeron 1977).

Does it work? A number of field experiments have studied the effect of introducing more participation. It has usually been found that job satisfaction increased, though not very much, and not with some groups of workers; for instance, unskilled ones, who don't seem very interested.

Increased participation is also linked to greater productivity, correlating as high as 0.27 SD in a meta-analysis of 25 studies (Miller and Monge 1986). One advantage is that it makes changes easier to introduce.

Chapter seven

Cooperation in the family

We saw in Chapter 4 that in virtually all societies, including the most individualistic, people live in families, where there is cooperation such as sharing food, sharing houses and other property, procreation and rearing of children, and mutual help of many kinds. In this chapter we will look in more detail at family life, to see what form this cooperation takes, the social bonds involved and how they are formed, the benefits if any in terms of joy or satisfaction, and how possible conflicts are dealt with by appropriate rules or skills.

Love and courtship

By romantic love is meant a strong feeling of sexual attraction towards another person, usually of the opposite sex, together with a need to be with them and to look after them. Compared with friendship, there is sexual desire, a stronger sense of caring, and exclusiveness. Pope defined romantic love as follows:

> A preoccupation with another person. A deeply felt desire to be with the loved one. A feeling of incompleteness without him or her. Thinking of the loved one often, whether together or apart. Separation frequently provokes feelings of genuine despair or else tantalising anticipation of reuniting. Reunion is seen as bringing feelings of euphoric ecstasy or peace and fulfilment.
>
> (Pope *et al.* 1980: 4)

It particularly happens to young people; American students between 19 and 24 report five to six romantic episodes, and to have been in love 1.25 times (Kephart 1967). If two people get married, the passionate state of romantic love slowly gives way to a different kind of love, 'compassionate love', consisting of deep attachment and strong affection, but with less sexual excitement (Argyle and Henderson 1985).

We saw that some species of animals have something similar to love.

Many kinds of birds, for example, have both an elaborate period of court-ship, and a life-long monogamous relationship. For the human species the position is more variable and cultures have handled the mating process in very different ways. The romantic, Hollywood, Mills and Boon, type of love affair, with free choice of a complete stranger, is found mainly in the modern world. Elsewhere, families have more control of the situation, and for most people in India and for many in Japan, marriages are arranged by families: love comes later. Another important cross-cultural variation is in attitudes to pre-marital sexual behaviour. In Britain there has been a 'sexual revolution' since before World War II, under the influence of America and Scandinavia and the availability of contraception. More recently, fear of Aids has reduced promiscuity. During the Middle Ages there was a shortage of upper-class women, since many went into convents. This led to the growth of chivalry and 'courtly love', pursued with elaborate rules and restrictions, and usually leading nowhere.

In our own time several kinds of love have been distinguished; between passionate and compassionate love, for example:

Passionate love is a wildly emotional state, a confusion of feelings; tenderness and sexuality, elation and pain, anxiety and relief, altruism and jealousy. Compassionate love, on the other hand, is a lower-key emotion. It's friendly affection and deep attachment to someone.

(Walster and Walster 1978: 2)

Other research has found further types, and shown that love has a number of components, though they tend to occur together.

People in love spend a lot of time together. What do they do? They do much the same things as friends – talking, eating, dancing, walking and so on, but they do it away from other people. There is a much higher level of self-disclosure and discussion of intimate topics. A study of 1,200 people (Swenson 1972) who described their frequency of engaging in 400 activities with those they loved, produced seven areas of activity specific to love:

1 verbal expression of affection
2 self disclosure: revealing intimate facts
3 non-material evidence of love: giving emotional and moral support, showing interest in other's activities and respect for their opinions
4 feelings expressed non-verbally: feeling happier, more secure, more relaxed when other is around
5 material evidence of love: giving gifts, performing physical chores
6 physical expression of love: hugging and kissing
7 willingness to tolerate less pleasant aspects of other: tolerating demands in order to maintain the relationship.

A lot of time is spent most agreeably in 'affectional activities' – a combination of sexual activity and intimate conversation, and this intimacy may include intercourse. Sex is one of *the* cooperative activities – it takes two to do it, it requires coordination and timing, and it is deeply rewarding, though no external rewards are involved. And it is based on one of the most fundamental biological imperatives – to perpetuate the species.

The conversation and deep self-disclosure reflect a desire to know the other person very well, to achieve a high level of intimacy. And there is a strong sense of caring for the other, a concern for his or her happiness and welfare. As the relationship develops, it changes in a number of ways:

1 spending more time in each other's company and being together in a wider variety of situations and settings
2 an increase in positive feelings towards each other; there is more liking, loving and trust
3 an increase in the expression of feelings, both positive and negative; with increased commitment, there is greater potential for the growth of both intimacy and conflict
4 mutual disclosure of more intimate aspects of the self, including attitudes and values about the partner and relationship commitment
5 an increased concern with the other's welfare; joy is caused by their joy, pain by their pain
6 a shared sense of unity and commitment; both partners increasingly view themselves as a unit, and are treated by third parties as a couple. Associated with this increased sense of shared identity, there is a concomitant reduction in uncertainty about the future of the relationship (Argyle and Henderson 1985).

Can love be interpreted in terms of an exchange of rewards? It certainly *is* very rewarding, and moreover through activities which it takes two to do. Berscheid and Walster (1974) thought that people are attracted to others who can satisfy their needs. However, there are several kinds of evidence which show that love is not simply based on reinforcement. Hatfield *et al.* (1979) proposed that people in love want the rewards of both parties to be equitable, that is, related to their contributions to the relationship. They found that individuals who reported equal benefits said they were happier about the relationship than were those who thought they were getting too much or too little. This is consistent with other evidence that concern for the other is very important in love.

The subjective experience of love includes deep concern for the other; Rubin's scale (1970) for measuring romantic love includes this as one of the three areas to be measured. This being so, it becomes difficult to decide who is being rewarded, if A's rewards also count for B, possibly more than for A. McAdams (1980) compared the imaginative stories written by people in love and not in love, on Rubin's scale. The largest differences were on positive affect union (physical or psychological) after being apart, escape to intimacy from a cold and non-communicative situation, harmony in relationships, and relationship transcending limits of time or space. In a study of 264 student couples, it was found that empathy, particularly taking the role of the other, predicted positive marital behaviour, like warmth and good communication, which in turn predicted the partner's degree of satisfaction (Davis and Oathout 1987). Other research has shown that caring is the activity most typical of love (Clark and Reis 1988). This all suggests that love is not about seeking rewards, but about seeking intimacy and communion. In any case, love is a very inefficient way of seeking rewards – 'Romantic relationships pose a particular problem for theories of people as cool-headed accountants seeking maximal rewards' (Kenrick and Trost 1989), since it is far too impulsive and emotional. The motivation involved is certainly sexual in part, but it also includes the intimacy motivation described above.

This is a form of motivation which is relevant both to love and to other close relationships. McClelland (1986) found that it could be aroused by showing a film about Mother Teresa, and that it increased the level of activity of the immune system, as measured by immunoglobin in saliva. Apparently, love may be good for our health.

What are the origins of the kinds of motivation and attachment found in love? Evolutionary theories suggest that monogamous mate bonding occurs in animals under certain environmental conditions, such as need for help in gathering food while the other guards the nest. Just as infants need to become imprinted or attached to parents, for their own good, so mates need to become attached for the children's good. Several theories of love have been sociobiological, suggesting that the biological function of love is to attract and retain mates, reproduce with them, and for the female to keep a mate who will look after her and the infants (Clark and Reis 1988). And while romantic, sexual love does the job for a limited time, it is later replaced by compassionate love (Wilson 1981). There is an interesting gender difference in matters of love. Women are 'cooler' than men, less likely to fall in love quickly. A British study found that 25 per cent of men fell in love with their present partner at first sight, and this was especially true of older men. An American study found that 43 per cent of women, but only 30 per cent of men were not sure whether they were in love by their twentieth date (Argyle and Henderson 1985). However, recent research has found that as choices are made for more permanent relationships, men become just as discriminating as women. The interesting sex difference is for more temporary relationships. Men are simply more promiscuous than women (Kenrick and Trost 1989). And when they do fall in love, women find this a more intense and rewarding experience (Dion and Dion 1985).

Buss (1989) carried out a massive social survey of mate preferences, with

10,047 subjects in 37 cultures. As predicted from evolutionary theory, there were a number of gender differences. Females valued the financial capacity of potential mates, such as ambition and industriousness. They also preferred somewhat older mates – there is a correlation between age and income. This reflects the primitive need for a mate who is a good provider and can look after wife and children. Males valued youth (just under 25) and physical attractiveness in women – perhaps reflecting their fertility. Males preferred chastity in 23 out of 37 cultures, perhaps to allay doubts over paternity. In another study, using American students, Buss (1988) found that males and females used different techniques for attracting mates, which reflect the different mating interests of the two sexes. Females did it by wearing provocative and sexy clothes, by attention to cosmetics and hair, and by flirting; men did it by displaying or boasting about their wealth and accomplishments and showing how strong and fit they were. Other techniques had little to do with evolution – displaying a sense of humour, being sympathetic to other's troubles, and showing good manners.

Attractiveness is partly based on certain features of face, figure, hair and so on, which are very widely found to be desirable, though these features do vary between cultures. And individuals have preferences for certain kinds of appearance, and as in the case of animals this seems to be based on similarity to either the opposite sex parent or to siblings.

Attachment between lovers is rather similar to that between infants and mothers, and indeed uses some of the same kinds of baby-talk and bodily contact. Perhaps one is derived from the other? Shaver and Hazan (1988) proposed that the three kinds of infantile attachment distinguished by Ainsworth *et al.* (1978) lead to similar styles of adult love attachment: secure, avoidant and anxious/ambivalent. Secure lovers are comfortable getting close to others, avoidant people feel nervous when others get too close, anxious or ambivalent people want to get close but are worried that their partner doesn't want it. They found that these three styles are stable over time and correlated with reported relations with parents. They found that 53 per cent of their subjects were secure, 26 per cent avoidant, and 20 per cent anxious/ambivalent. Love is like infant-mother attachment, but with the addition of sex and of reciprocal caring.

What benefits does love convey? The most obvious is intense joy. We asked a sample of subjects to rate a number of positive life events as sources of positive emotion: falling in love was rated the highest. This is not at all surprising: for once common sense was right. As well as joy, sex provides a great deal of excitement, which people have a strong need for; we have just seen that it also stimulates the immune system. But love should not be looked at only in terms of benefits: as we have seen there is great concern for the needs and welfare of the partner – love is a prime example of a 'communal' relationship. Experimental research on this kind of relationship has found that those involved do not keep count of their own rewards or costs, but more of the other's needs (Clark and Reis 1988); when they are able to help the other this produces a positive mood and increased self-esteem, which are not always found for exchange relationships (Williamson and Clark 1989).

On the other hand, lovers are well known for their quarrels. Often lovers fall out of love, despite the rewards, because they are unable to cope with the problems of such a very close relationship. Braiker and Kelley (1979) found that as couples progressed from casual dating to marriage the frequency of arguments and problems increased, although feelings of love also increased. For some couples there is a prolonged period of courtship lasting three to four years, with periods of conflict and separation. The cause of this conflict is that as two people get to know each other better, and do more things together, more differences emerge, which have to be discussed, worked through, and compromised over.

The informal rules of courtship throw more light on these conflicts. For couples in serious dating, the following rules were both believed in and kept (Argyle and Henderson 1985):

1 show unconditional positive regard
2 look after the other when ill
3 show an interest in other's daily activities
4 be faithful
5 ask for personal advice
6 show distress and anxiety in front of other.

Special social skills are required to engage successfully in courtship. Young men who were more successful in dating girls were found to be more fluent at saying the right things quickly, and agreed more; they smiled and nodded more. Other non-verbal signals which are important are gaze, pupil dilation (unfortunately not under conscious control), proximity, bodily contact and preening. Above all, physical attractiveness is most important; it correlated with frequency of dates in one American study 0.61 for women, 0.25 for men (Berscheid and Dion 1971). Attractiveness can be considered enhanced by attention to clothes, hair, cosmetics, diet and exercise, and facial expression (Argyle 1988).

Marriage

We have seen that in many species of animals mates stay together for years, sometimes monogamously, as in the case of most birds, often with several wives, as for most primates. If different species are compared, the larger the males compared with the females, the more mates they have, probably because size and strength lead to success in competing for females (Hinde 1987). Permanent bonding occurs under particular environmental conditions; for instance, one bird is needed to find food while the other guards the eggs in the nest. Both monogamy and polygamy are found in human cultures, not as the result of different evolutionary histories but from social evolution. There appears to be a pervasive sex difference – women have a greater concern for their children, with the result that they are less promiscuous, more interested in a mate who can be relied upon to look after them and their children. We saw above how in modern society women are more cautious about falling in love.

In primitive societies there is a clear division of labour between the roles of husband and wives. In modern society things have changed a lot: these are becoming more similar, though the wife still looks after infants, and does more of the housework.

What do married people actually do together? In earlier times, as we have seen, there was a great deal of work to do in and around the house. We carried out a study of modern couples in Britain and found that the activities now most characteristic of marriage were as shown in Table 7.1; the numbers are ratios of the frequency of doing each with spouse and in all relationships studied. Compared with friendship (Table 8.1, p. 153), the main difference is the amount of work to do, childrearing, preparing meals, housework and gardening.

Table 7.1 Frequency of choosing situations for spouse/frequency for all relationships (mean ratio 1.64:1)

Situations above this ratio	Frequency
Watch TV	2.61
Do domestic jobs together	2.48
Play chess or other indoor games	2.31
Go for a walk	2.28
Go shopping	2.15
Play tennis, squash	2.03
Informal meal together	1.93
Intimate conversation	1.92
Have argument, disagreement	1.84

Source: Argyle and Furnham 1982

There are several different aspects to cooperation in marriage:

1 *Sex.* Married couples usually share a bed, and have regular sexual intercourse. In addition to leading to the procreation of children, this is an important ingredient in binding couples together: sexual satisfaction is correlated with marital happiness.
2 *Childrearing* is one of the central tasks of marriage – feeding, caring for and training children.
3 *Division of labour.* In all societies wives in the past have done most of the housework, looking after children, cooking and clothes, while men went

out to work – fighting and hunting, building houses, doing wood and metal work. Either looked after crops. There has been a lot of pressure from women to equalise these sex roles, and there are now many dual-career families, though the wives still do more of the housework.

4 *Joint ownership of property*. When couples are married they usually share all their possessions, which does not happen in any other relationship; it is a special kind of cooperation. In modern and in primitive societies the main possession is often the home itself.

5 *Eating together* is an important part of family life, the wife usually preparing the meal. Meals are the main occasions on which the family meet, and eating is accompanied by talking.

6 *Talking*. The talk is about many things. Spouses report the main events of the day, work out a shared reaction to them, and in this way build a common view of the world. One partner may have problems and need information or advice. These may include more or less intimate personal problems, and then the other acts as a kind of counsellor or psychotherapist. There is also talk about family problems which need to be solved, large or small, and on which agreement and decision is necessary. Hence 'argument and disagreement' are characteristic material activities.

7 *Joint leisure*. Married couples share a lot of their leisure activities, and the more they do together the greater is their marital satisfaction. They typically watch TV together, share social life with friends and relatives, and may play games like tennis, or engage in various kinds of serious leisure.

8 *Looking after each other*. When people are ill, they are looked after at home, especially by the spouse.

Marriage produces a high degree of bonding, in most cases. This is shown by the number of years that most couples spend together, and the distress experienced after bereavement or separation, assumed by research workers to be the greatest source of stress, and resulting in an elevated rate of mental disorder and death from heart attacks (Stroebe and Stroebe 1987). When people get married they make some degree of commitment to stick to this relationship, for a long time, perhaps till death do them part. This is heightened by the wedding ceremony itself, with its public vows and ritual, the legal bonds, and the social support of those present. It is reflected in the high level of synchrony found between spouses while interacting. There is 'physiological linkage', where their physiological reactions are correlated, emotions like love and hostility are reciprocated (Clark and Reis 1988), and in happily married couples there is accurate communication of emotions (Noller 1984).

There are a number of other causes of the attachment between married couples. (1) It seems very likely that sex is part of the explanation; the very high rate of copulation at first, and regular intercourse later are powerful rewards for intimacy, and the relatively large penis and breasts of the human primate suggest that sex is important to us (Hinde 1987). (2) The close cooperation over both domestic tasks and leisure make the partner instrumental to a wide range of satisfactions. (3) Affection, esteem and social support are greater than for any other relationship. (4) Hours of talk and self-disclosure build up a shared cognitive world, a joint construction of social reality. (5) Investment of effort, time and money in joint enterprises, especially children and home, are partly lost if the marriage dissolves. (6) There are external supports; the shared home, children, friends and relatives provide a powerful and supportive framework in which the couple have a joint interest (Argyle and Henderson 1985).

Marriage produces strikingly positive benefits. We showed in Figure 6A.1 (p. 111) the results of a study which found that marriage produced much more satisfaction than any other relationship. An American survey found that the percentages of men and women who said they were 'very happy' was higher for the married than for the single or divorced (Table 7.2). Other studies have shown that mental health is affected in a similar way (Table 7.3). Although simply being married is good for mental health, the quality of the relationship is even more important; that is, the extent to which the spouse is a confidant and sympathetic listener and can provide social support (Brown and Harris 1978).

Table 7.2 Happiness of the married, single and divorced

	percentage 'very happy'	
	men	women
married	35.0	41.5
single	18.5	25.5
divorced	18.5	15.5

Source: Veroff et al. 1981

Table 7.3 Mental hospital admissions and marital status (England, 1981)

Marital status	Mental hospital admissions per 100,000
single	770
married	260
widowed	980
divorced	1437

Source: Cochrane 1988

Physical health follows a similar pattern. Furthermore, husbands and wives share many aspects of their lives – their leisure, their food, their good and bad habits; they are in a real sense 'one flesh'. As a result, they share a similar state of health and length of life, depending on the husband's occupation. This goes beyond cooperation to biological integration.

However, there can be a great deal of conflict in marriage. Argyle and Furnham (1983) found that more conflict is reported than in any other relationship, on average (Figure 6A.2, p. 113). We also found that some couples reported high levels of both satisfaction *and* conflict. We found that arguing was one of the activities most characteristic of marriage (Table 7.1). This can be very serious: an American national survey found that 28 per cent of married people had used physical violence of some kind against their partners, 16 per cent of them in the past year (Straus *et al.* 1980). In unhappy marriages rows occur daily, in happy marriages once a week or less.

The main areas of conflict are money (wife spending too much, husband not earning enough), sex (not enough, unfaithfulness), nagging (mainly by wives), how to handle the children, disagreement over which TV programme to watch, too much drinking (mainly by husbands), not enough affection (by husbands). These are some of the main friction points in modern marriage, which can lead to unhappiness and eventually divorce. They are problems created by two different individuals living at very close quarters, and having to cooperate closely over many spheres of life.

One solution has been the emergence of informal rules, closely linked to the main problems. We found widespread support for a set of marital rules, and also found that people in happy marriages reported keeping these rules more. Our rules are as listed in Table 7.4: it is a longer list than for any other relationship.

We can get some ideas about the skills needed in marriage by looking at the kinds of behaviour found in happy marriages. The main ones are:

1 pleasing verbal acts, e.g. compliments, and few negative ones, e.g. criticisms and complaints
2 pleasing non-verbal acts, e.g. kisses, bodily contact, presents, helpful behaviour
3 enjoyable sex life
4 a lot of time spent together, e.g. in leisure activities
5 agreement over finances
6 a problem-solving approach to matters to be decided
7 acting as a sympathetic confidant to the other.

Marital therapy has concentrated on rewardingness and handling conflicts:

1 Increasing rewardingness, finding what rewards the other most, and making special efforts to increase them.
2 Improved communication, expressing positive feelings clearly, putting suggestions tactfully and constructively.

3 Better ways of handling disagreements, seeking cooperative solutions, being prepared to compromise and give way, not becoming angry.
4 Contracting, if he does this she does that. For example she agrees to more sex if he will engage in more conversation, he goes dancing if she goes to football.

Follow-up studies of marital therapy along these lines have shown positive effects, both long-term and short-term (Argyle and Henderson 1985).

Table 7.4 Rules for both spouses

1. Show emotional support.
2. Share news of success.
3. Be faithful.
4. Create a harmonious home atmosphere.
5. Respect the other partner's privacy.
6. Address the partner by first name.
7. Keep confidences.
8. Engage in sexual activity with the other partner.
9. Give birthday cards and presents.
10. Stand up for the other person in his/her absence.
11. Talk to the partner about sex and death.
12. Disclose personal feelings and problems to the partner.
13. Inform the partner about one's personal schedule.
14. Be tolerant of each other's friends.
15. Don't criticise the partner publicly.
16. Ask for personal advice.
17. Talk to the partner about religion and politics.
18. Look the partner in the eye during conversation.
19. Discuss personal financial matters with the other partner.
20. Touch the other person intentionally.
21. Engage in joking or teasing with the partner.
22. Show affection for one another in public.
23. Ask the partner for material help.
24. Show distress or anxiety in front of the partner.
25. Repay debts and favours, and compliments.

Additional rules for the husband

1. Look after the family when the wife is unwell.
2. Show an interest in the wife's daily activities.
3. Be responsible for household repairs and maintenance.
4. Offer to pay for the partner when going out together.

Additional rules for the wife

1. Show anger in front of the partner.
2. Don't nag.

Source: Argyle and Henderson 1985

Kin

We have seen in Chapter 3 the great importance of kinship for animals: it is the main source of cooperation and help, and indeed of all social relationships. The more shared genes, the more cooperation and help. This leads to helping at the nest, giving alarm calls, sharing food, working together, grooming and play. In human primitive societies, kinship is also very important: people live together in large family groups, and know how they are related to everyone else in the village; kinship is the main form of social organisation.

The way in which these kinship systems have emerged can be explained in terms of their functions. They are examples of group problem-solving, over long periods of time. The simplest is the rule of descent from one parent, found in agricultural societies. The direct result is the formation of large, strong kinship groups who can band together for mutual protection and support. However, this is usually combined with the rule of exogamy – marrying into other family groups – which has the effect of creating bonds, mainly female ones, between the different clans.

In Western countries kinship is much less prominent, but nevertheless many kinship links are kept up. People feel closest to kin, in the following order: parents and adult children; brothers and sisters (siblings); grandparents; aunts and uncles; cousins; in-laws (Argyle and Henderson 1985).

A survey in Toronto found that 50 per cent of the strongest ties outside the home were kin (Troll *et al.* 1979). We shall see that the first two kin relationships on the list above – between parents and adult children, and between siblings, are kept up most strongly, and that kin are very useful in old age. In this section we shall concentrate on these two relationships. What do these close kin do together, when adults, and how far do they cooperate in modern society?

1 *Living together.* In primitive societies there are usually rules about living near the husband's family. In modern society there are no such rules, and children are expected to leave home by the age of 18 or so. However, in working-class circles they often don't move very far, and a daughter may be in daily contact with her mother; many young people of all classes live in the same part of the country as their parents. Unmarried siblings may live together, while many people over 65, especially if widowed or divorced, live with their children, either a married daughter or an unmarried child (Argyle and Henderson 1985).

2 *Frequent contact.* There is a high rate of contact between parents and adult children. A British study of over 65s found that 69 per cent had seen a child 'today' or 'yesterday', and another 17 per cent in the previous week. Frequency of contact is affected by distance, and is replaced by telephone when the distance is too great. Siblings also keep in touch, though less frequently, and often at the parental home. The strongest bonds here are

between sisters, who may meet often, and provide a lot of advice and social support, especially when their husbands are not very good at listening to emotional problems. More remote kin, like cousins, nephews and grandparents, are seen much less often.

3 *Shared activities.* These contacts normally take the form of visits to each other's homes, where a meal is eaten, a general interest in each other's welfare expressed and family news passed on. Sometimes there is some kind of celebration – of birthdays, anniversaries or Christmas. Family meetings are occasions for affection and social support rather than any specific work or leisure activity. An exception is joint holidays – an occasion for shared leisure.

4 *Provision of help.* More major help is provided for kin than in any other relationship. A lot of this help is domestic, provided by women, for a wife who is ill, or having a baby, or looking after elderly parents. Table 7.5 shows the results of a study of three generations in Minneapolis. It can be seen that 50 per cent of parents help their children with childcare, 47 per cent with household work, 41 per cent with money; and that help flows in both directions, though more from older to younger. Financial help may include, in Britain, helping with school fees. There may also be help with finding a job and choosing a career. About 25 per cent of people are influenced by kin in this way.

Table 7.5 Help given and received by kin (USA)

		Parents	Married children	Grandparents
Economic	given	41	34	26
	received	17	49	34
Household management	given	47	33	21
	received	23	25	52
Child care	given	50	34	16
	received	23	78	0
Illness	given	21	47	32
	received	21	18	61

Source: Hill *et al.* 1970

Siblings also help one another, on a much smaller scale, though some pairs of siblings form a close relationship, and some are involved together in family businesses.

5 *Inheritance of property.* In earlier historical periods inheritance played an important part in life. Usually the oldest son inherited land or property and became the new head of the family. Now property is divided more equally – but nearly all is left to the children, or to other close kin. Among middle-class families in London in 1968 a third had inherited money or houses from parents (Firth *et al.* 1969), and this percentage is probably larger now.

Kin relationships are definitely cooperative, but in a special way, compared with friends.

1 People often live with kin, or very close to them.
2 Kin are less voluntary, though there is some choice in keeping up with siblings, and more choice in the case of cousins. There is a feeling of obligation to keep up close relationships.
3 Kin relationships last longer, indeed for ever, while friendships can be quite short, and often end when one person moves.
4 Kin are a source of major help, whereas friends are not.
5 Quite different activities are shared – leisure, eating and drinking (with friends), chat, keeping in touch, and tangible help (with kin).

Primary kin relations show a high degree of bonding, in that these relationships usually last indefinitely, especially parent-child relations, despite separation by distance, quite unlike friendship. It is not necessary for them to be sustained by regular reinforcement, though this may strengthen them. How does this bonding become established? It seems very likely that inclusive fitness theory can explain at least part of it, especially the long-term attachment, and the provision of major help. Another possibility is that something like imprinting in birds takes place in the intimacy of the family. There are various theories about how this could occur, but it seems to be connected with the intense and coordinated interaction in the family. Cousins we can take or leave; 'favourite cousins' are the ones who were also childhood playmates (Adams 1968). Finally, cultural rules must be at least partly responsible for kinship behaviour, since different kin are recognised and cared for in different cultures. In Africa, for example, second and third cousins are treated as 'brothers'. In some tribes women move to the husband's village and look after people who are unrelated to her.

What kind of benefits does kinship produce? We saw in Figure 6A.1 that parents and siblings are major sources of satisfaction, especially in material and instrumental help, and we saw above some of the forms this takes. This is very important in Third World cultures where the kinship network replaces social security, and other public sources of help in developed cultures. We have seen the material help provided in our own country. More important perhaps is the social and emotional support, especially that received by women, who often depend on their mothers or sisters for this.

There are also conflicts between kin, and especially between siblings. During childhood there is a lot of rivalry, and in later life they compare their achievements; in one study 71 per cent of adults had rivalrous feelings towards their siblings. There can be discord over inheritance, and sharing the duty of looking after elderly parents. Nevertheless, the unbreakable bond persists, and is especially strong between sisters.

Parents and children

The production of children, and looking after them until they can look after themselves, is one of the central tasks of family life, in which the parents cooperate closely. This happens in all human societies, and in many species of animals; in the others the mother carries out this task alone or helped by her kin. Although this looks like a one-way operation of parents looking after children, rather than cooperation, as we saw in Chapter 5 infants are born with the capacity to interact with caretakers, and soon establish both patterns of interaction and close attachments to them; in later life they may look after their parents, and the direction of help is reversed.

In Third World countries families are large, they live in groups round courtyards, so there are more adults and more children together. Some of these play an important role in childrearing, such as grandparents and sometimes the mother's brother. In the modern world families are much smaller, partly as a result of industrialisation, which needed families to be mobile. The nuclear family consists mainly of parents and their children, sometimes with an elderly grandparent. This pattern is changing again since there is a growing number (about 9 per cent in Britain) of single-parent families, mostly mothers and their children. This is either because they did not get married in the first place, or as a result of divorce. There are also many families with stepchildren, following re-marriage.

What do parents and children do together?

1 *Feeding.* This is one of the main things that parents do for their children. Infants are first fed at the breast, though only 51 per cent were breastfed at all in 1975, and only half of those for more than a month. Feeding, whether by breast or bottle, takes up a great deal of time in the early months. Valuable information on this and other parent-child behaviour was provided by three surveys by the Newsons in Nottingham when their sample of 700 children were one, four and seven years of age (1963, 1968 and 1976) By the age of four children are having normal meals, but a lot of them have feeding problems – not eating what they are given or leaving food on the plate – and efforts are made to enforce proper behaviour at meals. During middle childhood mealtimes are an enjoyable family occasion; during adolescence they may be the only time parents and children meet, and can be the occasion for major rows.

2 *Supervision and discipline.* Children have to be trained, partly for their own safety and welfare, partly to conform to the demands of society. They need to be dressed and undressed, bathed, praised and punished. Physical punishment is used a lot for young children, especially in working-class homes. Older children are controlled more by verbal methods, persuasion, explanation, threats and so on. They have to be taken and fetched from school and other activities, and girls are looked after more closely in this way than boys.

146

3 *Conversation*. We saw in Chapter 3 how mothers talk to infants and develop early dialogue. In most families parents and children talk a great deal, and parents also read to the children. Children ask many questions to which they may or may not receive adequate answers; and they like to report what has happened at school and on other outings. In early adolescence the amount of conversation falls off, as children prefer to talk to their peer group. They become expert at non-communication:

Parent: 'Where have you been?'
Adolescent: 'Out.'
Parent: 'What did you do?'
Adolescent: 'Nothing.'

4 *Showing affection and enjoying each other's company*. Mothers of infants spend a great deal of time in physical contact with them; later this occurs particularly at bathtime, bedtime, and while reading to them. There is a high level of bodily contact with parents during the early years, and children still cling to their mothers or keep close to them when in strange places or when meeting strange people. Older children, up to adolescence at least, enjoy being with their parents. Daughters are at home more, and mothers enjoy doing their hair and dressing them up. Boys, on the other hand, are more likely to share interests with their fathers, and spend time together, for example playing trains or going to football. During adolescence children spend much less time with their parents, and a lot more with the peer group.

5 *Helping*. Parents do a great deal for infants and four-year-olds, but the children cannot do much in return. By the age of seven most children are expected to tidy up their toys, either alone or with mother. Only 18 per cent of children do regular household chores, such as washing up, more boys than girls, and more in middle-class homes. A further 53 per cent earn money from their parents for doing jobs. Adolescents may be helpful, and in Third World families they have to be; in the modern world they are often quite unhelpful.

The attachment between parents and their children is one of the most powerful social bonds, in some ways the strongest of all. We have already seen that his attachment often lasts until the death of the parents. We saw earlier how similar attachments in the animal kingdom are based on genetic similarity, a drive for 'inclusive fitness', and this may be part of the explanation of human concern for children. However, children become attached to the person who spends most time looking after them, and this may not be one of the parents. Babies usually develop an attachment to their mother, especially during the period seven to ten months, when they object to being separated from her, want her to be near, and try very hard to get her attention. From about seven months they want their mother rather than anyone else (Schaffer and Emerson 1964). Attachment is established during the first three years of life, and is strongest when the caretaker feeds the child, plays, and engages in social stimulation, involving bodily contact, looking and smiling.

After a long period of early attachment and dependency, children establish their independence, often with a lot of conflict between them and their parents. However, once this independence has been achieved the attachment remains, though the relationship has changed.

The parent-child relationship confers great benefits to both sides. It could be looked at as a cooperative relationship where the main joint goal is the production of happy and competent young people, or it could be looked at as cooperation where enjoyment of the relationship is an end in itself. For the parents the benefits are:

1 *Health*. Being a parent seems to be good for health, especially for parents between 35 and 50 who have a considerably lower mortality rate than childless couples (Kobrin and Hendershot 1977).
2 *Happiness*. This is more complicated. There is no question that children are a great source of joy, and generate a lot of fun. They are also hard work and can produce a lot of stress. Marital happiness is actually depressed by the presence of children aged one to three and by adolescents (Walker 1977). However, several studies show that despite the strains of parenthood, most people say that this is overall a rewarding experience, and they believe it brings couples together (Argyle and Henderson 1985).
3 *Satisfaction*. Children are felt to be satisfying in several ways (Hoffman and Manis 1982):
   providing love and companionship (63 per cent)
   stimulation and fun, pleasure at watching them grow (58 per cent)
   self-fulfilment, purpose in life (34 per cent)
   feeling more adult and mature (22 per cent)

The children, of course, gain a great deal more than this, since they are totally dependent on their parents, not only for bringing them into existence, but for continually feeding, housing, clothing and protecting them, over a number of years. They also receive a lot of physical affection, are given pocket money, and played with for some hours a day. In a study of 199 children aged 11–13 it was found that the parents were regarded as the greatest source of emotional rewards – especially affection, reliable alliance, enhancement of worth, as well as instrumental help. Perhaps surprisingly, grandparents came next (Furman and Buhrmester 1985).

Childrearing is difficult and calls for a high level of social skills. The most important component is acceptance and warmth. Accepting parents love their children and spend a lot of time with them; their interaction with the children is warm and rewarding, rather than critical or hostile, and they have a high opinion of the children. A second important component is the use of discipline which is neither too permissive, nor too strict, and which uses explanation, pointing out the consequences of behaviour for others.

Styles of childrearing vary along other dimensions, and in this way pass on the kinds of personality and behaviour that are valued in the culture. Children may be brought up to be aggressive, achievement oriented, individualistic, or cooperative. In this way the family is cooperating with the community to maintain its way of life.

There is quite a lot of conflict between parents and children, especially during adolescence, when the relationship may have a temporary breakdown. The child feels increasing urges to break out of a childish, dependent form of attachment to the parents, to one of greater independence and equality. This is less of a problem in primitive cultures where nothing changes very much, but more of a problem in our own where historical changes create a 'generation gap' between the ideas and interests of parents and children. There is often some degree of rebellion, if only to establish that the child is a separate individual in his or her own right, and this rebellion is supported by the peer group, which becomes a rival source of influence and identity to the family.

In primitive societies the transition from childhood to adult status is marked by dramatic ceremonies – 'rites of passage'. As for marriage and graduation, these ceremonies make public the change in status of those concerned, and give them social and dramatic support for a change in their condition. In modern societies there are no such ceremonies for adolescents. For parents in western society, handling adolescent children requires a lot of skill. It has been found that 'democratic' styles of supervision are successful, where adolescent children contribute freely to discussion of matters relevant to them and may make their own decisions. However, the final decision has to be approved by the parents. This style is better than permissive, egalitarian, or authoritarian styles, in that it is seen as more fair, less rejecting, and results in greater independence and confidence for the child. Parents need to set limits, but to bear in mind that things might have changed since they were young. Warm, rewarding, parental behaviour again has a variety of favourable consequences, including the better achievement of an independent identity, self-confidence and self-esteem.

In comparing the families of normal adolescents with those of disturbed adolescents, it has been found that there is more joking and laughter, more cooperation, more information-sharing and more agreement in normal families, though they can also disagree in a friendly way (Elder 1968).

Another way of looking at the skills of handling adolescents is in terms of the rules which parents generally believe should be followed. These are shown in Table 7.6.

Table 7.6 Rules for parents of adolescent children

1. Respect the child's privacy.
2. Give guidance to the child and an example.
3. Show affection for the child.
4. Encourage the child's ideas.
5. Respect the child's own views.
6. Show emotional support.
7. Don't engage in sexual activity with the child.
8. Keep confidences.
9. Don't be overly possessive.
10. Treat the child as a responsible adult.
11. Share news of success.
12. Look the child in the eye during conversation.
13. Address the child by first name.
14. Give birthday cards and presents.
15. Stand up for the child in his/her absence.
16. Talk to the child about sex and death.
17. Talk to the child about religion and politics.
18. Be responsible for rules of respectable behaviour.
19. Seek to repay debts, favours and compliments.
20. Don't be critical of the child's choice of friends.

Source: Argyle and Henderson 1985

Chapter eight

Friendship

At work people cooperate to carry out tasks which one person could not do alone, and to share the rewards, for example from housebuilding and hunting. In the family there is cooperation of quite different kinds, over the production of children, joint ownership of property, shared eating, and mutual care. Cooperation between friends takes different forms again, largely based on the enjoyment of the relationship, and of various forms of joint leisure, which have no external goals, and no obvious biological purpose. Friends spend a lot of time together, eating and drinking. This is enjoyable in itself, and while they are doing it they provide each other with a lot of help and social support.

Do animals have friends? Some species of primates form coalitions with non-kin based on reciprocity, for example to obtain help in finding a female. And young animals play a great deal, though mainly among kin. Friendship, in the form of attraction between non-kin, may be important in encouraging cooperation over a period of time. Between mates, sexual attraction may not last long enough to produce an enduring bond, and non-sexual attraction may take over (Wilson 1981). And within the larger group, non-sexual attraction may be important in preventing aggression and encouraging cooperation between non-kin, over 'work' like foraging for food, nestbuilding and defence against predators.

However, friendship is much more important for the human species. Friends are people who are liked, whose company is enjoyed, who share interests and activities, who are helpful and understanding, who can be trusted, with whom one feels comfortable, and who will be emotionally supportive. Friends are people who like each other, and enjoy doing certain things together. Friendship is entirely voluntary, unlike kinship, and there are no clear rules about who may be friends or what they should do together. In surveys people claim to have about five 'close friends' and about 15 'friends' on average, and in addition to have large numbers of acquaintances. Friends may form tight-knit groups, but often there is a network, with no boundaries, sometimes stretching round the world.

Friendship appears to be a universal human phenomenon – it is found in all cultures. In our own society there are some interesting class differences: working-class people often know people as members of groups, who are seen in particular locations such as church, pub or football, and rarely invite them home. For many working-class people no very clear distinction is made between friends and neighbours, and in the past at least there was quite a lot of material help, not only 'lending sugar', but lending money and giving other quite serious help.

Middle-class people pick up friends from work or leisure settings, but see them in more than one location – for example, on joint outings – and invite them home (Allan 1979). While friendships may be mainly conducted through leisure activities in the modern world, in some other cultures it is more serious and involves help in major life activities. In Australia in the early days, 'mates' were expected to stick by each other when things got difficult. There, and in some other cultures, friendship is a formal relationship, sometimes established by a ceremony, as in the case of 'blood brothers'. In these cultures friendship is not only for leisure; in the absence of welfare state and efficient government there is a great need for help from the friendship network. In Third World countries there is some overlap between friends and kin, since large numbers of kin are recognised.

Social psychologists have often looked at friendship in terms of an exchange of rewards, and there is plenty of evidence that we like people whom we find rewarding. But turn back to Figure 6A.1 on p. 111, and it can be seen that friends provide three kinds of satisfaction – not only material help, but also emotional support, and satisfaction through shared interests and activities. Close friendships are examples of what have been called 'communal' relationships, where positive acts like gifts are not linked to any reciprocity. Philosophers have argued that friends are an end in themselves, not a means to further ends, gifts to them are expressions of love, with no thought of gain (Badhwar 1987). As for the shared activities, this is another case where it takes more than one to do it – as with music, sport and most forms of leisure.

We will now look at the forms that cooperation takes in friendship by examining the main things that friends do together. Argyle and Furnham (1982) asked people to report the frequency with which they had engaged in a variety of activities in different relationships. The figures in Table 8.1 show the ratios of the rates for friends and for all relationships; that is, they show the activities which were most characteristic of friendship for this adult, Oxford sample. Friendship, for this sample, is mainly about eating, drinking, talking and joint leisure – all of them enjoyable activities. Talking and much joint leisure (like dancing and tennis) need at least two to do them, while it is a powerful convention to eat and drink with others, rather than alone.

Table 8.1 Distinctive activities shared with friends

Friends similar age	
mean ratio	1.26:1
Activities above this ratio	
Dancing	2.00
Tennis	1.67
Sherry party	1.63
Joint leisure	1.63
Pub	1.60
Intimate conversation	1.52
Walk	1.50

Source: Argyle and Furnham 1982

Cooperation in friendship

I shall show that friends cooperate closely over their leisure pursuits and other joint activities. This cooperation is strongly rewarded, in the first place by *joy*. In a recent survey in five European countries, subjects were asked the cause of a recent experience of joy: the most common cause, reported by 36 per cent was relationships (Scherer *et al*. 1986).

An American study with students, along similar lines but not specifying *past* experiences, also found that social relationships were a common source of joy – with family members, romantic partners, friends and sports teams. While task success – for example, at sports – was described as reward for hard work, romantic rewards were not actively worked for; there was much anticipation of pleasure here, and some anxiety. 'The accounts of joy episodes with friends generally describe either reunions with long-lost friends or gatherings at which friends talk, laugh, relax and feel close' (Schwartz and O'Connor 1984). This may be partly because of the enjoyable things that friends do together (see Table 8.1). It may be partly because friends look, smile and send other positive non-verbal signals, which is very rewarding. On the other hand, this can itself be seen as part of the intimacy which is being sought. Philosophers, among others, have noticed the close link between friendship and joy: 'pleasure or delight is intrinsic to perceiving and responding to someone as lovable by her very nature', and 'happiness is intrinsic to love' (Badhwar 1987).

Friendship is correlated with and is probably a cause of happiness. Friends are particularly important for the young, such as students, and for the old; family and work relationships in some ways substitute for friends during the years between, though as we have seen relationships at work include special kinds of friendship. Friendship also contributes to physical health: there is a lower death rate for those with friends, especially for those in their sixties (Berkman and Syme 1979). We shall see that intimacy motivation is associated with greater strength of the immune system. Extraversion works a little differently – it *interacts* with social support; that is, extraverts' health is greater when there is also social support (see p. 204). Friends provide one another with a great deal of social support and help, and this is one of the reasons for the beneficial effects just described.

The link between joy and friendship has another side to it, since joy results in increased sociability. A number of experiments have been carried out in which positive moods are induced in subjects: it is found that this produces greater sociability towards a confederate in a waiting room, more help, and more self-disclosure (Cunningham 1988).

The study of individual differences in friendship behaviour adds a little more to the story. Extraverts engage in more positive social behaviour of all kinds, including more positive non-verbal communication, and verbal utterances. They also experience greater joy during social encounters. This can be partly explained by their childhood experience, since they have a background of close maternal attachment, probably leading to positive expectations about social encounters (see pp. 201ff.).

We shall now discuss the most common friendship activity – talking, which is often accompanied by eating or drinking. After that we will consider help and social support, and finally cooperation in some of the main kinds of leisure.

Conversation

As Table 8.1 shows, friends spend a lot of their time together talking. This takes place over meals, over drinks in pubs, while drinking tea or coffee, while walking, in each other's homes, at cafés and restaurants, while on outings together, and while taking part in shared leisure activities. Indeed, it is an almost constant activity during the time friends are together. Young people from 15–25 in particular spend a great deal of time together, often every day, up to three hours a day, and more time later on the telephone talking to the same people – especially in North America where there is no extra charge for local calls. Women friends of all ages spend more time in talk than male friends. Men often prefer to *do* things together, like playing squash, and their talk tends to be about impersonal topics like sport and politics.

There are several kinds of conversation, and these involve cooperation of different kinds. However, all conversation between friends has a positive, friendly quality. In Chapter 9 we shall describe some of the verbal devices used to express positive attitudes – such as paying compliments, agreeing, pleasure talk, reaching for similarity, and humour.

1 *Sheer sociability.* Friends simply enjoy being together. The conversation can be casual and sporadic, including such topics as the weather, sport and political news. In the early stages of friendship they are finding out about each other, comparing notes, finding out how much they have in

common. With slightly larger groups there can be jokes, tall stories and a lot of euphoria.

2 *Gossip.* There is no doubt that a great deal of the talk between friends could be described as 'gossip'; that is, it is about other friends and acquaintances. Some of this could be described as 'news', and it is useful to share information about what is going on. This is another kind of cooperation when A and B discuss C, perhaps to work out how to help C, to laugh at C, or to try to understand C. We shall see below that there are strongly-felt rules about the conduct of gossip, especially about the keeping of confidences.

3 *A shared cognitive world.* Pairs of friends talk about common interests, shared experiences, politics and so on. As a result they develop similar ways of looking at events, a shared cognitive world of opinions, evaluations and explanations. They may end up, like married couples, by saying 'we think . . .', 'we feel that . . .', and so on. In this way they get social support for opinions and beliefs for which there is no objective evidence. This takes a deeper form for religious and other groups, as will be shown later (see pp. 163ff.). Friends engage in a great deal of self-disclosure, which increases with time, and is reciprocated. Some experiments have found that it is emotional self-expression, or disclosure, that is most important for intimacy, and this is a matter of non-verbal rather than verbal communication (Clark and Reis 1988). Friends may spend a lot of time discussing common interests, in psychology, Scottish dancing or the Church, for example.

4 *Providing information and solving problems.* Friends are a most useful source of information and advice; different people may be called on at different times. If you want to know something it is often easiest to use the social network. Sometimes shared rather than individual problems need to be solved, for example, by members of clubs or leisure groups, and groups are better at this than individuals, as we have seen.

5 *Providing social support* will be described below.

Eating and drinking

Friends spend a lot of their time together eating or drinking. Drinks can be alcoholic, tea or coffee, or soft drinks; eating can be at home, in cafés and restaurants, or at banquets. Friends talk while eating and drinking, and this seems to be a characteristic combination of activities for friends.

Table 8.1 showed that these are activities which people do particularly with their friends. Table 8.2 shows how often they do it. It can be seen that the most common of these events is visiting or entertaining at home, and going out for a drink. Men drink more than women, especially young men. And all of these activities decline with age, especially meals and drinks out. We will now look at the special kinds of cooperation involved.

Table 8.2 Frequency of eating and drinking with friends

	In last 4 weeks	
	men	women
going out for a drink	65	47
going out for a meal	47	47
visiting/entertaining friends or relations	90	93

Source: Social trends 1986

1 *Drinks out.* In Britain this is typically at pubs or clubs. Alcohol has the effect of relaxing people, who talk more freely and have more fun – two common goals of friends; in addition, this mood is shared. There are rules about paying for drinks in an equitable way. At drinks parties a concerted effort is made to achieve a mood of gaiety and perhaps abandon. We have found that there are definite rules for such occasions and these will be listed later.

2 *Non-alcoholic drinks.* Tea and coffee breaks at work are an occasion to relax, gossip, chat, tell jokes and engage in non-serious release from work. Tea and coffee are drunk probably as mild stimulants, perhaps also to provide a form of shared activity. We saw in Chapter 6 the importance of the informal contacts at work, in creating social cohesion, and the basis of collaboration over the work (see pp. 118ff.). Women friends often drink tea and coffee as an occasion for intimate conversation, self-disclosure and emotional support.

3 *Meals at home with guests.* Alcohol may promote intimacy by creating a relaxed mood, but eating together is commonly assumed to be more intimate. In some cultures people eat from the same dish, or help one another to food, and it seems that a bond is created by sharing the same food. There may be cooperation over preparing the meal, or by bringing a dish, or helping with the washing up. It is usually expected that there will be reciprocation by invitation to a similar meal. In some cultures guests are expected to bring a bottle of wine or other gift. In Japan the presentation of gifts, and their reciprocation, is an important side of life, controlled by elaborate rules. Meals with guests are the focus of a great deal of etiquette – large sections of etiquette books are about this, covering every aspect of behaviour at table. In Japan you may not pour your own drink out, in Boston at one time it was prescribed whom you should talk to during each course. As in music and dancing, the performers have to know their parts, and cooperate in the whole production, which is an end in itself.

Help and social support

Friends are a major source of social support, and this is important in preventing stress from generating mental ill-health. Two main kinds of social support are now distinguished: attachment in a close relationship is one, integration into a social group is another. The latter has been found to have a main effect on mental health; that is, it has a positive influence whether stress is present or not (Hobfoll 1988). Integration into a social group prevents isolation and loneliness, and keeps up self-esteem. Interaction with females is found to do more to relieve loneliness for both sexes; these meeeting are found to be pleasanter, more intimate, and more meaningful than those with men (Wheeler *et al.* 1983).

One of the main ways in which friendship produces these positive effects is by *helping* – material help, information, sympathy, or in other ways. We are much more likely to help friends and members of in-groups, partly because we empathise with them more readily; that is, we are aware of their feelings, and removing their distress becomes a positive goal. This does not appear to be due to concern for genes shared with them, nor is it based on reciprocity, as we shall see shortly. It may be based on group selection to favour in-group members, or it may derive from socialisation.

Leisure

We shall be concerned with activities that are shared with friends outside work – that is, leisure activities – though as we have seen many friends are initially drawn from work. It is usual to regard as leisure those activities which people do simply because they want to, for their own sake, for fun, entertainment, self-improvement, or for goals of their own choosing, but not for material gain. Work tends to be more serious, to demand efficient standards of performance, and obligations to others. Leisure is usually more playful, and while some people strive for prizes, usually the standard of performance is not very important.

We will now examine the forms that cooperation takes in the main leisure activities, starting with sport.

Sports and games

Young monkeys spend up to 80 per cent of their time in play, but give it up when they are older; human beings keep on playing as adults, though in increasingly complicated ways. The amount of time we spend in this way is shown in Table 8.3.

It can be seen that people spend a lot of time in outdoor and indoor sports. Forty-six per cent do these things sometimes, and they do it once or twice a week. There are substantial sex differences, not shown here: men do

Table 8.3 Sports and games

	Percentage participating in past 4 weeks	Average number of times in 4 weeks
OUTDOOR		
walking (2 miles +)	19.1	8
football	2.7 (M 7, F 0)	5
golf	2.7	5
athletics, and jogging	2.6	9
cycling	1.9	9
tennis	1.4	5
all outdoor, excluding walking	18	—
all outdoor, including walking	32	—
INDOOR		
(dancing	11	3)
swimming	9.5	3
snooker, billiards, pool	9.3	7
darts	5.8	6
keep fit, yoga	3.3	6
squash	2.4	4
gymnastics, athletics	1.9	9
all indoor	28	
all indoor and outdoor	46	
SPECTATORS		
football	3.1 (M 5, F 1)	3
other sports	6	4
at least one	11	5

Source: 1986 General Household Survey of Great Britain

a lot more sport than women. There are substantial age differences: sporting activities gradually decline with age. And there are class differences: for most sports middle-class people are more active than working-class, especially for squash, tennis, golf and swimming (Birch 1979; GHS 1986). People also spend a lot of time on indoor games, such as darts, snooker, cards and board games, mostly with friends.

There are many different kinds of games, and a number of classifications have been made (Avedon and Sutton-Smith 1971). Several kinds of cooperation, and competition can be found here.

1 *Competition between two individuals.* Tennis, squash, chess, and many other games are like this. They are basically competitive, but they are also cooperative in that it takes two for the game to be played at all, the players must keep to the game rules, and they must also play it in the same 'spirit'; for example, with an agreed degree of seriousness, or competitiveness. In

many games there is also a high degree of coordination, in responding rapidly to the other, so close in fact that observing a rally at tennis one might be excused for thinking it was cooperative.

2 *Competition between two teams.* Here there is close cooperation within the teams, including division of labour, and mutual help in pursuit of the same goals – literally. There is, however, less cooperation between teams in games like football, where each side is physically obstructing and attacking the other.

3 *Purely cooperative games.* There are a number of games like this, mainly played by children and adolescents, especially by girls at parties, or used for therapeutic purposes. Examples are see-saw, skipping, and kissing games (e.g. how long can you make it last). A lot of exercise is carried out in this way; for example, walking, climbing or jogging together.

4 *Apparently non-cooperative games.* A lot of games are quite aggressive, dangerous, risky and in other ways not cooperative. Boxing is a case in point, yet, as in tennis, there is cooperation to keep the rules, and also a very high degree of split-second coordination and anticipation of the opponent's punches (Hinde 1979). Rough-and-tumble play among boys doesn't look very cooperative either, yet as we saw earlier boys fight mainly with their friends, since it is a form of friendship activity. It must be admitted that playground fights can be more violent than this, and that children get bullied and sometimes injured. Here, evidently, cooperation has broken down (Sutton-Smith and Kelly-Byrne, 1984). Geertz (1973) described the 'game' of Balinese cock-fighting, in which fights are arranged between well-matched birds, and very large bets are placed, so that prestige, pride, poise and masculinity are at stake as well as wealth, a 'status bloodbath', and a very high level of tension is created. He called this 'deep play'.

5 *The spectators.* More people watch football, tennis and some other sports than actually play (see Table 8.3). Are they cooperating too? In several ways they are. They follow the action closely, turning their heads from side to side at tennis, and sharing bodily empathy with other sports performers. Football fans are closely identified with their teams, wear shirts or other symbols of these teams, and engage in mock battles with supporters of rival teams. This is evidently a very important part of their lives, and an important part of their identity (Marsh *et al.* 1978).

Music and dance

In primitive society these went together, but in the modern world there is a lot of music without dance, although much of the music was originally written for dancing. Music may involve singing in choirs, in church or elsewhere, playing in bands, chamber music groups or orchestras, or just listening to concerts, classical or pop. Dancing may be in couples, as in ballroom or disco dancing, or in larger groups, as in folk dancing, such as Scottish country dancing and other national forms.

Table 8.4 shows that 11 per cent of people in Britain had danced during the last four weeks, when interviewed in 1986, and they had typically done it three times. Performing amateur music was combined with amateur drama in this survey, and 4 per cent had done this, but they had done it no less than 11 times in four weeks on average. Certain sections of the population are most active here both in performing and attending – women and young people, and also middle-class people.

Table 8.4 Music and dancing

	In last 4 weeks	Number of times
Dancing	11	3
Amateur music and drama	4 (M 3, F 4)	11
Theatre, ballet, opera	5 (M 4, F 6)	1
Pop concerts	<1	2
Classical concerts	<1	2
Other musical entertainment	4	2

Source: *Social Trends* 1989

We will now examine the forms that cooperation takes here. There is a common theme. There is usually no external reward, the performance is simply a satisfying end in itself. This is less true when there is an audience, as there may be for amateur musical performances; for professional musicians there are external rewards, but then they are working.

Music

Music is found in all primitive societies, not primarily as an art form, but to express emotion, in ceremonies connected with religion and magic, war, healing or courtship (Crossley-Holland 1966). Experiments have shown that music conveys and arouses emotions very effectively. For example, Hampton (1945) asked for listeners' reactions to a number of compositions for which the composer's intentions are known. Thus, Part 5 of the second movement of Beethoven's *Eroica Symphony* was correctly identified as expressing 'sadness, despair or grief' by 93 per cent of subjects. A similar study was carried out by Semeonoff (1940) with compositions intended to convey visual images. Thus Sibelius's *Finlandia* was correctly judged as describing a 'wild and rugged' scene by 81 per cent of listeners, and the 'elephant' from the *Carnival of the Animals* by Saint-Sëans was correctly identified by 46 per cent.

Music has been described as 'the language of emotion': it expresses emotions in a way that is pleasing and satisfying. Langer (1953: 40) suggested that 'art is the creation of forms symbolic of human feeling', and that music is especially capable of representing the inner emotional life of energy, conflict, tension and its reduction, growth and spontaneity. Rogge (cited by Farnsworth 1969) found that musical pieces could be matched to descriptive verbal passages with the same sequence of arousal and resolution of tensions. Jazz rhythms are probably exciting because syncopation deviates from expectations, and creates tension.

Music in Europe has become greatly elaborated, and is widely performed and listened to. In earlier times people sang while marching, working, and on other occasions. Now they often sing in choirs, without need for special occasions, as a leisure activity. The performance itself is the goal, pleasing because of the sounds produced and the pleasure of cooperating to produce them. There are usually different parts, but each part is sung by a number of singers together. There is cooperation to put it all together, with correct timing, as directed by the conductor, and the musical accompaniment. Church services usually have music from choirs, and this plays an important part in arousing religious feeling.

Playing in bands and orchestras is different from the other forms of music and dancing in that a high level of skill, needing a lot of training and practice is required, which takes us into the realm of 'serious leisure'. The cooperation involves much more division of labour, each person playing his own instrument, with his own part. However, the cooperative goal is essentially the same; to produce joint performances of pieces of music, which are deeply satisfying ends in themselves.

When there is an audience, they share the emotions expressed by the performers. They often follow the music closely and share each emotion as it comes, and may make small bodily movements. Members of the audience may share a sense of identity, since quite different audiences attend, for example, pop concerts and opera. It was found that regular followers of 'music viva' (that is, chamber music) in Sydney felt that they belonged to a special social and aesthetic élite (Sue Kippax, lecture at Oxford).

Dancing

Music has an intricate connection with dancing, which is probably one of the origins of music. Music which has a strong rhythm, loudness, percussion, and produces a physical response makes listeners want to march or dance. Dancing is another art based on non-verbal expression, of emotions, relationships with others and, above all, of ecstasy and vitality.

Dancing is universal in primitive society, on the same occasions as music. The music makes people want to dance. Vernon (1930) pointed out that:

Many also hear and think of music muscularly. They raise their heads or contract some other muscle when the music rises, or they perceive it in terms of their hands at the pianoforte or other instruments. Thus several of my audience noted that their fingers tried to follow those of the pianists, others felt that they wanted to dance in strong rhythmic music.

Folk dancing is found all over the world, often associated with special occasions, festivals, or times of the year, like May. Here whole groups are involved, though often paired off in couples. In Scottish country dancing, for example, there are usually sets of eight, consisting of four couples. Here there are complicated figures, with 'division of labour', where different dancers are doing different though complementary things, and giving mutual help, to turn or to guide beginners, for instance. The goal is partly achieving a close relationship but more producing a skilled performance of the dance: the performance itself is the product.

The roots of heterosexual dancing may be seen perhaps in the courtship displays of some birds – though without music. Dancing is a regular part of human courtship in primitive, as well as in modern societies, and in many versions it permits close bodily contact, emotional arousal and enjoyable joint activity. Even when courtship is not taking place there is an unavoidable sexual element. Dancing involves coordination and synchrony, and behaviour which is oriented towards the other; the synchrony is guaranteed by the music and skilled performance of the relevant steps.

The essence of cooperation in all forms of music and dance appears to be the arousal of shared emotions, by a closely coordinated sequence of steps or notes. In addition, both performers and audience gain a sense of shared identity.

Clubs and other leisure groups

Much of the social life of friends takes place in clubs of different kinds, and in meetings of informal groups and networks, which may or may not have regular meeting places. The extent of this activity is shown in Table 8.5.

Table 8.5 Clubs and other groups

	In last 4 weeks	Numbers of times
Clubs and societies	12.3	3.6
Leisure classes	3.1	2.4
Bingo	9.3	5.6
Church weekly	about 13% attended church	
Voluntary work	9.6	5.6

Source: Social Trends 1989

There have been a number of other surveys of club membership. MORI (1982) carried out a very interesting study of neigbours and loneliness, and asked about where people met those they knew best (Table 8.6). This survey underlines the great importance of clubs as sources of friends.

We have already discussed music and dancing, which could also be included under clubs. The cooperation in clubs takes several forms:

Table 8.6 Where people meet

People known best

	men	women
People at local pub or club	23	10
Members of church	7	12
Members of sporting club	11	5
Members of club associated with hobby or interest	10	7
Members of voluntary organisation	2	3

Source: MORI 1982

1 *Group identity.* A person's self-image, or identity, is based partly on his or her individual characteristics, but also on membership of groups. Belonging to a church, a political party, a sporting or leisure club can add a major component of the self-image. This is particularly true for those who become officers of clubs – president, secretary or committee member. Identity is proclaimed by means of appearance for some groups, especially deviant youth groups like punks and skinheads. Sociologists have tried to explain the symbolism used here.

The Teddy Boy sub-culture can be 'read' as the theft of an upper-class style to celebrate heavy working-class masculinity; the skinheads' rolled-up jeans, cropped hair, industrial boots and preoccupation with 'trouble' can be understood as an attempt to recover and assert the virtues of the traditional working-class community; the mods' cool style with neat suits and pointed shoes can be interpreted as expropriating the consumption ethic, and extracting individuals from their true class locations.

(Roberts 1983: 121)

2 *Serious leisure and the development of skills.* The most deeply satisfying forms of leisure require some degree of dedication to the development of skills or knowledge, as in rock-climbing, amateur archaeology and, of course, amateur music and drama. Csikszentmihalyi (1975) found that the most satisfying elements were enjoyment of the experience and use of skills, the activity itself (the pattern, the action, the world it provides), and development of personal skills. Similar conclusions came from a sociological study of amateurs in drama, archaeology and baseball, who were found to be deeply devoted to a disciplined and demanding form of activity which was the very opposite of relaxing (Stebbins 1979). In addition to the expressive satisfaction obtained, there was gratification from the close social ties established, and in the social identity created. The development of skills is usually a group activity, as it requires coaching, shared techniques and shared standards of excellence.

3 *Ritual and ceremony.* Many groups engage in rituals, which can be

defined as standardised patterns of social behaviour which are mainly symbolic rather than instrumental. By ceremonies are usually meant rituals other than religious ones. Rituals achieve various collective purposes, and close cooperation is needed for the ritual work to be successfully accomplished. Rites of passage include greetings, weddings, graduation and other occasions when a change of status or relationship is being brought about. They are often performed by a priest or other official, assisted by many members of the group. Assemblies, at school, college dinners, drill parades, banquets or family gatherings are intended to maintain social cohesion, and often to sustain role divisions such as the power of authorities.

4 *Religion.* Church services are intended to influence the deity (in primitive religions at least), and to confirm and strengthen beliefs and good behaviour. This is helped by sharing in the singing of emotional music, and the use of impressive costumes and settings. A shared subjective world is built up and maintained, of beliefs and ways of interpreting the world, together with a shared style of life and agreed moral ideals. Religious beliefs give a meaning and purpose, but they have to be shared. Since there is no physical proof that the beliefs are true, social support from other believers is important. Church services provide deep emotional satisfaction and enhance commitment, but they need the cooperation of the others to do this.

In Britain about 13 per cent of the population go to church regularly, but many more watch TV services. Here it is possible to participate at a distance, with the very well attended and well conducted services which are shown.

The motivational basis of friendship

One theory of friendship is that interpersonal attraction is based on reinforcement; a more elaborate version, exchange theory, holds that people stay in a relationship if the balance of rewards over costs is as great as can be expected, based on past experience, and the alternative friendships which might be available (Chadwick-Jones 1976). There is a lot of evidence that rewards are important in friendship: popular people are those who are high in rewardingness, lonely and unpopular people are those who are low; social skills training may include training to deliver more rewards. The rewards which people expect to receive from friends are partly material – concrete help, presents, meals and so on, but most of them are not. As Figure 8.1 shows, esteem and affection are more important in the case of friendship than work.

Let us look at the goals which people appear to be seeking in leisure and the other friendship activities which have just been described. Four kinds of cooperation can be seen here.

Figure 8.1 The importance of goals and resources in work, friendship and love relationships

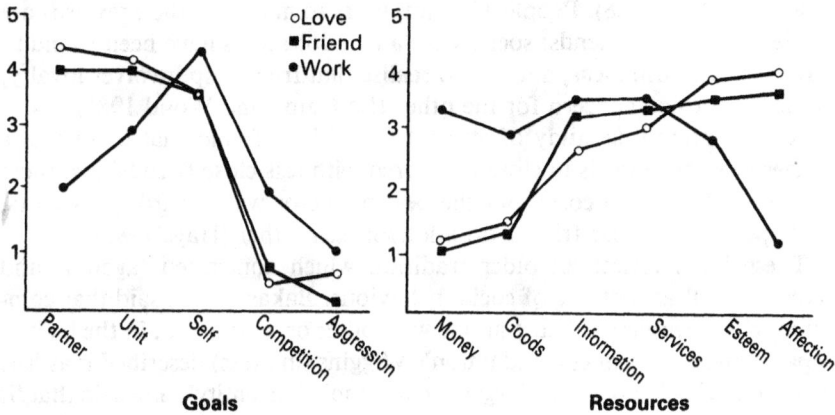

Source: Kayser et al. 1984

1 *Shared external goals*. This is not typical of friendship activities, though it applies to sports teams, and leisure groups putting on performances like plays or concerts. Friends also help one another, for example, by material help or information, and this is usually reciprocated.
2 *Relationships as goals*. Friends seek close relationships with one another, as a goal in itself, though this can also be described as meeting intimacy needs. Intimate conversation is one of the activities which are effective here. Belonging to groups also adds to identity and self-esteem.
3 *Activities as goals*. Many of the things which friends do together are ends in themselves, like sport, music and dancing. Most of them take more than one person to perform them at all. They usually require close coordination or synchrony. Even those that are 'competitive' involve keeping to the rules and coordination of behaviour.
4 *Shared subjective states*. Many friendship activities generate a shared emotional or bodily state – drinking and eating, music and dancing. Other activities produce shared opinions and beliefs, from conversation to rituals like church services.

It looks as if people are not seeking an exchange of rewards in friendship, and exchange and reinforcement theories have been criticised as inadequate explanations of friendship. Perhaps the most important point is that friends are concerned not only with their own rewards, but also with those of the other. It is found that in close or 'communal' relationships people feel that any positive acts should not be linked to any reciprocation, so that they can be seen as altruistic and spontaneous signs of affection. In close friendships people do not keep track of their inputs, or feel exploited if help is not reciprocated. Instead they are concerned with the other's needs. It is in work relationships that people are concerned about exchange or equity (Clark and Reis 1988). People who simply try to maximise their rewards are liable to lose their friends: socially isolated adolescents have been found to have such childish ideas, and fail to realise that friendship involves loyalty, commitment and concern for the other (La Gaipa and Wood 1981).

A very interesting study of student friendships found that there was a higher level of rewards in close compared with less close friendships, there was no difference in costs, but the best predictor was rewards *plus* costs, perhaps because close friends do a lot for each other (Hays 1985).

These ideas reflect an older tradition which contrasted 'agency' and 'communion' as patterns of social behaviour. Bakan (1966) said that communion is 'the sense of being at one with other organisms . . . in the lack of separation . . ., openness, and union'. Wiggins (in press) described it as 'the condition of being part of a larger social or spiritual entity', and said that 'it is manifested in strivings for intimacy, union and solidarity with that larger entity'. Adler had a similar concept, which he called 'social interest'. Writers in this tradition thought that agency and communion often operated in combination, and research in the social skills tradition confirms this. Not only are two indendent dimensions of social performance always found, but many social skills require the combination of task (that is, agency) and social (that is, communion) factors (see Figure 8.2).

Figure 8.2 Two dimensions – agency and communion

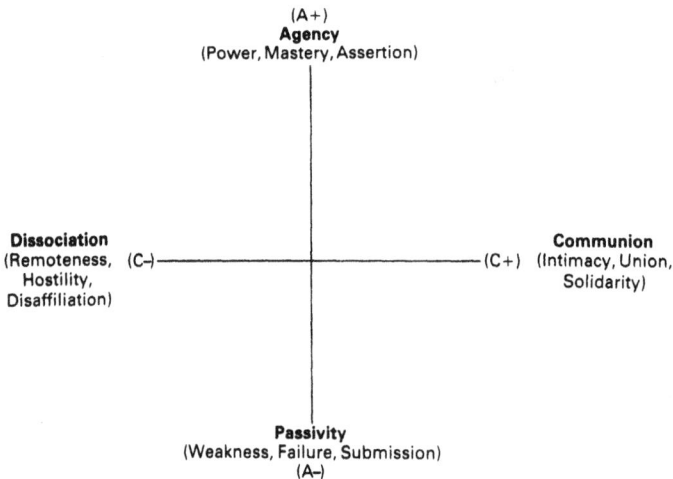

Source: Wiggins (in press)

However, here we are concerned with relationships which are dominated by communion considerations. McAdams (1988) has succeeded in developing a measurement of part of communion, in his 'need for intimacy', by means of a projection test. Crandall (1980) devised a questionnaire measure of Adler's 'social interest'. Both of these will be described in Chapter 10.

If friendship behaviour is motivated in this way, it would be expected to produce rewards of some kind. The most striking reward is joy, as we have seen.

Rules for friendship

In our earliest study of rules (Argyle *et al.* 1979) we found a number of rules which it was thought should be followed in all social situations:

1 should be polite
2 should try to make it a pleasant encounter
3 should not try to make the other(s) feel small
4 should not embarrass others
5 should be friendly.

At parties it was believed that a number of extra rules should be followed:

1 should try to keep to cheerful topics of conversation
2 should avoid disagreements
3 should dress smartly
4 should display positive affection towards the other.

Later we investigated rules which applied especially to friends, and came up with quite a long list. In order to check that these rules really were of some importance, we carried out a study of lapsed friends. Here we found that friendships had often been lost because one person or the other broke some of these rules, and especially the 'third party' rules – not keeping confidences, being jealous of other relationships, not standing up for friends in their absence and so on (Table 8.7).

For sports, and every other leisure activity there are more rules to keep. These are elaborate and written down in the case of sport. They are elaborate and not always written down in the case of formal meals, church services, and other ceremonial occasions. It is important not only to conform to these rules, but to do so in the right spirit – at games not being too aggressive or competitive, not taking advantage of the other, or using 'gamesmanship' ploys such as 'kindly say clearly whether the ball was in or out' (when it was out) (Potter 1947).

Table 8.7 Friendship rules and break-up of friendships

	Moderately or very important in breaking up friendship	Slightly important in breaking up friendship
Being jealous or critical of your other relationships	57%	22%
Discussing with others what was said in confidence with him/her	56%	19%
Not volunteering help in time of need	44%	23%
Not trusting or confiding in you	44%	22%
Criticising you in public	44%	21%
Not showing positive regard for you	42%	34%
Not standing up for you in your absence	39%	28%
Not being tolerant of your other friends	38%	30%
Not showing emotional support	37%	25%
Nagging you	30%	25%

Source: Argyle and Henderson 1985

Cooperative skills needed for friendship and leisure

Comparing popular with unpopular people shows the key skills needed to make and keep friends.

1 *Rewardingness.* We have seen that this is not the only source of inter-personal attraction, but it is nevertheless a very important one. In the verbal sphere this may include the use of compliments, taking an interest in the other, being interesting or amusing, being helpful.
2 *Positive non-verbal signals.* Smiling, looking, proximity, gestures directed toward the other; mutual gaze in particular creates a powerful feeling of unity.
3 *Concern for the other.* A common form of social skills failure is ego-centricity, and too little interest in the other. Good listeners, and sympathetic listeners, are greatly appreciated. 'Politeness' consists to a large degree in maximising the benefits to the other, rather than self, and praising others rather than self (Leech 1983).
4 *Self-disclosure.* Unless there is sufficient self-disclosure – talk about intimate, emotional and personal matters – a relationship will not progress to friendship.

Influencing people. Achieving more control over decisions requires quite different social skills.

1 skilful delivery of requests and proposals, e.g. showing how the other will benefit
2 non-verbal assertive signals, in the voice, face and posture

3 sufficient warmth and rewardingness
4 consultation, so that the other's wishes are actually met, and cooperation develops.

Leisure activities often require some further skills. Special motor skills are needed for music, dancing and sport, for example. These are partly social skills in that they involve close coordination, timing and anticipation, more than in any other kind of social behaviour. Boxing is an interesting case since reactions to the other's blows appear to take place faster than the usual reaction time. In team games there must be true cooperation and generosity, not hogging the ball, for example. In cricket so much value is placed on the manner of play that 'it isn't cricket' means failing in this respect. Music and dance also call for special cooperative social skills. The synchrony of performance is partly kept externally, by the conductor in the case of music, and by the music in the case of dancing. There is also performance of complementary skills, different parts which fit together to make up the whole performance.

Part four

Personality and social interaction

Chapter nine

Communication and conversation

We turn now to a more basic level of cooperation, which is needed for any communication or social interaction to occur at all – even in encounters which in other respects are competitive or non-cooperative. In order for A to communicate with B, A must send signals which B can understand, and B must be able and willing to attend to them and decode them. This is equally true of verbal and non-verbal signals, though the two are intricately linked in the process of ongoing social interaction. Interaction requires further kinds of cooperation, in order to produce a sequence of social signals that make up an acceptable conversation and enable those envolved to achieve their goals.

Non-verbal communication (NVC)

The main non-verbal signals are:

facial expression
gaze (and pupil dilation)
gestures, and other bodily movements
posture
bodily contact
spatial behaviour
clothes, and other aspects of appearance
non-verbal vocalisations
smell

Non-verbal communication, or bodily communication, takes place whenever one person influences another by means of facial expression, tone of voise, or any of the other channels listed above. The basic paradigm is as follows:

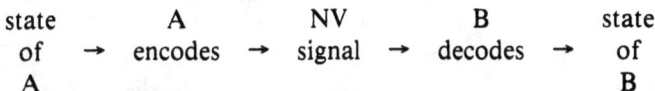

state		A		NV		B		state
of	→	encodes	→	signal	→	decodes	→	of
A								B

Sometimes a message is sent deliberately, as in the case of some gestures; often the sender is unaware of what he is sending, as in the case of pupil dilation or blink rate. Sometimes the receiver is not aware either, but may still be influenced, for example, by small head-nods or shifts of gaze. NVC conveys several different kinds of messages, which we will consider separately.

Emotions

Animals communicate their emotional states, especially by facial expressions (for primates) and vocalisations. The evolutionary origins of human expressions can be traced to some extent; for example, showing the teeth in anger is a ritualised 'intention movement' derived from biting. It has been assumed that the development of expressive 'read-out' areas like the face occurred because it was biologically advantageous for the sender to send and the receiver to receive. In line with more recent ideas on evolution, such as inclusive fitness, perhaps it was advantageous both to sender and close kin to be able to send and receive these signals. Somehow these systems of communication have evolved, and human beings have a complete physiological system whereby facial muscles for example are controlled by the facial nerve, which in turn is activated from the hypothalamus-limbic area, when emotions are aroused. This whole innate communication system can be seen as an evolution-derived device for facilitating social interaction and cooperation.

However, it is quite easy for human beings to produce facial or other emotional expressions which are different from the emotions which they are actually feeling. The reason is that there is a second neurological link between face and brain, this time from the motor cortex, from which voluntary and learnt facial expressions are derived (Rinn 1984). In every culture there are 'display rules' for controlling emotional expressions, to promote social harmony. In Japan it is not acceptable to display negative facial expressions at all.

Perhaps the forms of primitive emotional communication produced by evolution did not create enough social harmony and cooperation, so that an additional set of rules had to be added in each culture. In the west children know by age 10 not to display negative expressions when given an unsuitable toy, for example (Saarni 1979). Such control is partly a matter of self-interest, but also of concern for the feelings of others and general social harmony.

Emotional expressions were described above as 'read-outs' of inner emotional states, and we have now seen that they are partly controlled as well. Even spontaneous states are directed at other people, as deliberate social signals. Much stronger facial expressions are shown, for example, in the presence of others. And in a study in a bowling alley it was found that people were much more likely to smile at their friends when they had hit or missed than at the skittles (Table 9.1).

Table 9.1 Smiling at the bowling alley (%)

	Hit	Missed
at people	42	28
at skittles	4	3

Source: Kraut and Johnston 1979

Some NV channels are better controlled than others: the face is most controlled, voice and lower body least. When an emotion is being concealed, there is often some degree of 'leakage' via these less well controlled channels. One of several interesting gender differences in NVC is that women attend more than men to faces, men more to voices – a leakier channel. Women therefore are 'polite decoders', in the sense that they receive what others want them to receive, while men look for evidence of deception (Hall 1984). Women who behave like men in this respect are unpopular. This is a way in which women are usually more cooperative and trusting than men.

Interpersonal attitudes

Animals find mates, rear their children, make friends, frighten off their enemies, establish dominance hierarchies, and cooperate in groups, entirely by means of bodily signals. The human race has developed language, but it is used primarily for communicating information about other persons, objects and ideas, rather than about the feelings of one person towards his listener. There is a complete NV signalling system, which makes this network of cooperative relationships possible. The main attitudes here are like–dislike, sexual attraction, and dominance–submission. The signals for human liking are similar to those found in animals, and are decoded fairly accurately. If A likes B, he smiles, looks, approaches closer, may touch, has a friendly tone of voice, and often an open-arm posture. Disliking, however, is not expressed nearly so clearly because there are cultural rules preventing this. There may be some leakage here into less well controlled channels like tone of voice and posture. As with expression of emotion there are display rules, in the interest of sustaining group harmony – but at the cost of not knowing about negative attitudes.

Gaze, and especially mutual gaze, plays an important role here. When A looks at B, this carries the message that A is interested in B, wishes to communicate with or interact with B. Mutual gaze carries messages of mutual attentiveness, a special kind of intimacy and openness.

Sexual attraction is expressed partly by the same signals as liking, plus some extra ones – a high level of mutual gaze, pupil dilation, touching, an erect posture with increased muscle tone, women groom hair and clothes, visible arousal like blinking and perspiring, inviting gestures like protruding breasts and pelvis rolling. Again there are display rules inhibiting making too much use of these signals in most situations.

Dominance is communicated by occupying high status spaces like the judge's seat, height, not smiling, asymmetrical touching, pointing at the other, loud and expressive voice, and postures like hands on hips and expanded chest.

Information about interpersonal attitudes can be sent either verbally or by the non-verbal signals listed above. We and others have found that non-verbal signals have a greater impact than initially matched verbal ones. This may be because people think the NV ones are more spontaneous and less controlled, which is broadly true. Or perhaps it is because NV signals have an immediate biological impact where words have a primarily cognitive effect. However, we shall describe later ways of putting these attitudes into words (see pp. 189ff.).

People who are socially isolated, who can't make friends or sustain relationships, can be trained to send stronger signals for liking – smiling, looking and the rest (see p. 246).

Establishing and maintaining social relationships is done in animals entirely and in humans mainly by a sequence of NV signals. Friendly moves may be reciprocated, for example, and so may sexual signals, leading to a closer relationship, expressed by closer proximity, bodily contact and so on. Battles for dominance are settled, both by fighting, in most animals, and by a series of dominance or threat signals, until one or the other submits.

NV accompaniments of speech

We turn now to a faster-moving, more intricate aspect of NVC – the signals which add to the meanings of utterances, provide feedback from listeners and, as we shall see later, manage the synchronising of utterances. Nothing like this is found in animals, since they don't speak. And language in children develops out of earlier NV signals like pointing and gestures, and it continues to include important NV components.

When a person is speaking, he accompanies the words with several kinds of NV messages. Gestures are used to illustrate and supplement the words; for example, about shapes, sizes and movements; these gestures are often given during pauses, at the beginning of the words being illustrated. Emphasis is given by hand or head movements, while tone of voice and facial expression may provide additional information.

The NV accompaniments, especially vocal qualities, can modify the meaning of an utterance in several ways. Vocal emphasis, by loudness or pitch, can show which of several alternative meanings is intended, as in 'they are *hunting* dogs'. Noller (1984) asked spouses to deliver verbally ambiguous utterances in three non-verbal styles; for example: 'I'm feeling cold, aren't you?' to mean 'Please shut the door', 'Are you also, as a matter of fact, feeling cold?', and 'Please come and warm me with your body'. Husbands in unhappy marriages were poor encoders, especially of positive feelings. A rising pitch indicates a question, short pauses mean emphasis, longer ones grammatical breaks. More complex patterns of vocal cues indicate a joke, a threat, or other meanings.

Speakers look intermittently at their listeners, but especially at grammatical breaks, and at the ends of long utterances. These are the points at which feedback is needed, to show whether the listener understood, agreed and so on (Kendon 1967). The speaker looks at the listener's eyes and face, and seeks a brief period of mutual gaze at these points. There is a three-way linkage here between speaker's vocalisation and gaze and listener's face, which seems to be at the heart of cooperation to interact. Speakers also use gaze to some extent as a signal to add emphasis, and to point. Speakers look to collect feedback, listeners to receive additional, facial and gestural, information to supplement what is being said by the other, and as we shall see later, these carefully-timed glances help in the synchronising of utterances. Gaze is primarily a channel, but opening this channel acts as a signal to the other person: a long gaze by a speaker means that the utterance is about to end. The general meaning of gaze is interest in the other person, and this is even more informative if they are not yet interacting, but may do so. The precise meaning of gaze, the nature of the other person's interest, is given by his facial expression, and by the nature of the situation. Mutual gaze has a special quality, it creates a feeling of mutual openness, of intimacy, and is too arousing to bear for long; mutual glances averaged 1.3 seconds in our experiments (Argyle and Cox 1976).

Listeners also send a lot of NV signals, partly to indicate attentiveness, partly to indicate their reactions to what is being said. They look a lot more than speakers, and this indicates attentiveness, and willingness to hear more. Glances at particular points act as reinforcers and encourage the speaker to produce more of the same. Glances are often combined with facial expressions to give feedback signals, such as a smile for agreement, lowered brows for puzzlement.

Listeners often nod their heads, and occasionally shake them. They display a lot of facial expression, to indicate agreement or disagreement, surprise, disbelief, puzzlement and other reactions. Their posture can show interest or boredom. And they send short vocalisations, like 'good' and 'really?', or help the speaker by finishing the sentence for him or supplying missing words. Such help is more common than interruptions, which are usually mistaken anticipations of the ending of utterances. And listeners look a lot more than speakers, but to collect information rather than to send signals. It is not so much that listeners are helping speakers, rather that both are cooperating in the creation of a joint product – communication.

The use of NV signals and gaze in close coordination with speech develops very early in life. We described earlier how primitive turn-taking is found between mothers and infants of 12 months, and how by 24 months infants are looking at the ends of their utterances – they have achieved the integration of gaze and speech (see pp. 90ff.).

The 'gestural dance'

When two people are talking, they need to be at the right distance and angle to see and hear each other. They take turns to speak – with great accuracy, as we shall see. When a speaker starts to speak, his hands start moving, and when he stops speaking his hands are returned to rest. As he starts to speak he looks away, to avoid distracting input of information while he is planning the utterance; at major grammatical breaks, and at the ends of utterances he looks up.

A number of investigators have studied postural congruence – that is, where two people take up mirror-image postures. When people like each other, or are in rapport they are more likely to do this. Ellis and Beattie (1986) report that male-female pairs on the beach adopted such postures 53 per cent of the time, while for male-male pairs this was 28 per cent, both well above chance. And when a confederate deliberately copied the postures and bodily movements of real subjects, the latter evaluated the confederate more favourably, believed that he thought like they did, and said that they identified with him (Dabbs 1969). Maxwell and Cook (1985) found that not only were congruent postures seen as signs of liking, but that subjects who were asked to sit in chairs which produced congruent postures liked one another more. This is all very interesting evidence pointing to the importance of coordination at a fairly micro level.

There is a different kind of cooperation of gestures and facial expressions which are closely linked to speech, as we saw earlier. While the speaker illustrates his words with gestures and facial expressions, the listener provides feedback, mainly from head-nods and other facial expressions, indicating understanding, surprise or other reactions. Sometimes gestures and other bodily movements are copied, 'movement mirroring' as Kendon (1970) called it.

The integration of bodily movements of two interactors may go further than this, and some investigators have reported synchrony between such movements at $\frac{1}{24}$ or $\frac{1}{48}$ seconds, corresponding to small speech units, like phomenes. The clearest empirical support for this is perhaps the finding that speakers match each other on pause lengths, within and between utterances, length of utterance, and loudness. On the other hand, they often compensate to keep the level of intimacy constant, by the opposite kind of shift on gaze level, proximity, and other variables (Capella 1981). However McDowall (1978) failed to find above chance synchrony in a careful statistical analysis of the bodily movements of six interactors, filmed at eight frames per second. It is quite possible that these people did not know each other well enough for the gestural dance to occur, or that it only works in groups of two, not six. It may be hypothesised that the degree of synchrony is greater in close or cooperative relationships. Lanzetta and Englis (1989) took physiological recordings of subjects' faces: in a cooperative condition, the other's smiles produced a slower heart-rate, facial muscles expressing pleasure, and lower GSR (galvanic skin response), competition the reverse, on a timescale of 4−6 seconds. Using a quite different approach, it is found that mothers seen with one of their own children are judged to be in closer rapport, using the degree of observed synchrony, than when with another child (Tickle-Degnen and Rosenthal 1987). Meanwhile, the conclusion must be that there is a lot of cooperation of bodily movements at the time-scale of whole utterances, and of phonemic clauses, but that this is less evident at finer time-scales (Rosenfeld 1978).

Turn-taking

When two or more people are conversing they take it in turns to speak, and usually manage to achieve a fairly smooth 'synchronised' sequence of utterances, without too many interruptions or silences. How good is this synchrony in fact? One index is the length of switching pauses. These are on average 500 milliseconds − half a second − though many are much less than this. When the pause is 200 milliseconds or less, a length which is noticed by about 50 per cent of observers, it is known as a 'smooth transition'. Interruptions are relatively rare (and mainly by men), and often due to starting too soon, or are not intended to halt the speaker (like 'good'), or help the speaker with his utterance. At Oxford we found that interruptions in the middle of phrases are definitely disapproved of, those at ends of clauses less so, while those at the ends of sentences are acceptable.

Human beings have been conversing successfully (in most cases) for thousands of years, but not one of them has known, until very recently, how this synchrony is achieved. The first synchronising cue to be discovered was the terminal gaze. Kendon (1967) found that speakers ended 62 per cent of their utterances with a prolonged gaze at the other; when they did so the listener spoke at once without a pause in 71 per cent of cases, but this happened in only 29 per cent of cases if there was no terminal gaze. Later research has found that terminal gaze is effective as a non-verbal full-stop signal only if there is a fairly low level of gaze.

Another non-verbal cue is the use of gestures. People use their hands while speaking, and return them to rest at the ends of utterances; a hand kept in mid-gesture is a powerful 'interrupt-suppressing signal'. And listeners who want to speak try to claim the floor by head-nods, hand-raising or other bodily activity. It was expected by those of us involved in this area of research that synchrony would be impaired over the telephone, since neither gaze nor gestures can be seen. To our surprise there are *fewer* interruptions and pauses over the telephone. The explanation is probably that people feel more able to interrupt when they can be seen, and are able to send reassuring, positive non-verbal signals at the same time.

Another important synchronising signal is change of pitch at the end of an utterance. If ends of sentences in mid-utterance are compared with those at the ends of utterances, it is found that those at the ends have a falling pitch (unless they are questions), the final syllable starting at a lower pitch, with a reduced amplitude and final lengthening or drawl (Cutler and Pearson, cited by Ellis and Beattie 1986). Beattie (1983) studied TV interviews in which Mrs Thatcher was interrupted a lot; he found that subjects who listened to audiotapes of these interviews thought she had finished the utterance in many of these disputed cases, because she used a falling pitch in these cases.

Turn-taking is also achieved by the verbal contents – listeners can tell when the end of the utterance is coming. Slugoski (1985) carried out an ingeniously controlled experiment in which conversations of four utterances were recorded, ending on an utterance which varied in whether or not there was falling pitch, and whether or not the sentence was completed. Subjects pressed a button when they thought the last utterance had ended. Sentence completion led to faster button-pressing than did falling pitch. Sacks *et al.* (1974) proposed that pairs of utterances fit together, so that one 'projects' the next. We shall discuss this further under 'adjacency pairs'.

It was stated earlier that young children are taught turn-taking by their mothers, even before they can speak, but that there is a primitive mechanism to build on, whereby sound of another's voice suppresses speech.

Verbal communication

Linguists have traditionally treated language as a series of words with meanings, ordered by grammatical rules. And so it is. Sociolinguists, however, pointed out that language is much more than this: it is used to communicate, between people who are pursuing various goals in relation to one another, in a social context. Sociologists go further and see language as a set of social representations which are shared by members of society. Written language and monologues are derivatives: conversation is the primary form of language. As we showed earlier, words are accompanied by non-verbal signals, which modify and add to their meaning. On the purely verbal side there are several fundamental ways in which the relationship and setting play a crucial part.

The design of speech acts

An utterance is a piece of behaviour. Austin (1962) drew attention to utterances such as promising, ordering, apologising, judging guilty, declaring garden parties open, and making bets, which he called 'performative utterances'; they are neither true nor false, but they affect what is going to happen. He went on to argue that all utterances do things in this way and can be looked at as items of social behaviour which are intended to influence the hearer in some way. They are all 'speech acts'. He distinguished between the 'perlocutionary' force of a speech act – its effect on the hearer – and the 'illocutionary' force – the nature of the act as a question, order, bet, etc.

However, utterances are special kinds of social behaviour, because of the way in which words and grammar create meanings. As Grice (1968) observed, if A produces an utterance for B, this is because A wishes B to receive it, and because A has some intentions towards B which can be recognised by B. If A tells B he is hungry, he wants B to recognise his intention in saying this. 'Utterances therefore are inherently relational' (Clark 1985).

Utterances have to be carefully planned, so that they will be understood by the listener, be received in the intended manner – as a joke or an order, for instance, and lead to the intended results – he laughs or he does something. This means imagining the other's point of view, 'taking the role of the other', 'intersubjectivity'. As Rommetveit (1974) put it, 'encoding involves anticipatory decoding'. Experiments have shown that most speakers do this most of the time. For example, people say things quite differently depending on whether they are speaking to an expert or an ignoramus, a child or a dog, and depending on what they think the other person knows already and is able to understand (Krauss 1987). Lawyers use far fewer technical legal expressions when examining witnesses, than when arguing with other lawyers in courtrooms; defendants use far less criminal jargon and swear less when in court than when being interviewed by their lawyers in Sweden (Aronsson *et al.* 1987). If garage mechanics are asked a question about adjusting a car engine, they move rapidly down the hierarchy of technicality, if it becomes clear that the questioner doesn't understand (Wintermantel and Siegenstetter 1988). This accommodation to listeners is greater if the listener is of higher status or of limited intelligence.

Many mental patients are deficient in seeing other people's point of view; Blakar (1985) found that schizophrenics couldn't cope with a problem-solving task where each person had a map, but where these maps in fact were slightly different. Other people too sometimes fail in this respect; an American lady at a party, when I asked her where exactly her home town was, looked at me as if I was a total idiot and said 'Why, it's just over the state line', which left me none the wiser. O'Keefe and Delia (1985) suggest that there is a developmental sequence of types of utterance of increasing competence. Taking the role of the other is the penultimate stage, and the final one is where a speaker tries to incorporate the thoughts of both himself and the listener, combining and reconciling the different aims of each.

Shared language and information

Two people cannot communicate unless they have some shared language. First, they need some shared vocabulary, that is a number of words with same or similar meanings. A lot of the interaction between mother and child, during the period 18–24 months, consists of the child learning the labels for objects. By the age of six most children know over 14,000 words, that is, they have picked up about nine a day. They learn the concept of 'ball', for example, by finding the range of objects to which this word applies: they often include too wide a range at first; that is, there is 'over extension'. And they first form concepts on functional grounds, so that a ball is something that can be bounced or thrown (Carroll 1986).

Interactors also need some shared information or common ground that can be taken for granted, and that each assumes the other possesses. Many utterances add new information to old; like 'the coffee machine has conked out again'. This shared ground is cumulative, it builds up during the course of a conversation, as in a tutorial or a school lesson. Between people who know each other well or who belong to the same group or community, or who work together, there is extensive common ground (Clark 1985).

Conversationalists often need to refer to particular persons or objects; how do they do this? It depends on common ground, on being able to identify which person, dog, house or whatever is being referred to. Krauss and Weinheimer (1964) gave pairs of subjects a number of shapes to discuss in a communication task: the shapes most often referred to were gradually given shortened names, roughly describing their shapes. The better two people know one another the easier it is for them to identify individual people, objects or places, either by names, or by shorthand description (Clark 1985).

Shared context is important in helping people to convey clear messages. Many utterances are ambiguous without a context, since many words have more than one meaning, like 'Where is the bank?' Some conversations would be incomprehensible unless one knew the shared context, for instance (Levinson 1983):

A: I have a fourteen-year-old son
B: Well that's all right

A: I also have a dog
B: Oh I'm sorry.

This makes sense if you know that A is trying to rent a flat. In these cases a great deal is left out of the actual utterance – but the listener can understand it because he shares knowledge about the nature of the situation.

We all possess a great deal of background knowledge, which we share with other people when we enter social situations. One way of analysing this knowledge is in terms of 'frames' which consist of memories for stereotyped situations, with 'slots' for its main components. Another way of looking at shared background knowledge is in terms of 'scripts', which describe standard sequences of events – for example, when going to a restaurant – and which could be used to instruct a computer in what to say and how to understand the answers, when ordering and paying for a meal at a restaurant (Schank and Abelson 1977).

Two speakers need to share a 'definition of the situation', as sociologists call it. By this is meant the basic nature and purpose of a situation, and the roles of each person in it. This can be indicated by the nature of furnishings and decoration, which can hint that a relaxed social event is about to take place, or serious work, or a police interrogation. Symbolic interactionists have emphasised that interactors negotiate a shared definition, but we have argued that this is usually given already; for example, it is usually clear that it is a game of tennis, not a church service or a riot (Argyle, Furnham and Graham 1981).

Two speakers often 'accommodate' to each other; that is, they change their speech styles to be more similar. This can be in respect of the language spoken, as in French– and English–Canadian encounters; of accent, as between people of different social classes; of speech, loudness and length of utterance. All these kinds of convergence have been found to occur. An interesting example comes from the study of conversations between Americans and Japanese. The Japanese give many more back-channel responses, grunts and head-nods, probably because they speak in shorter sentences, so that there are more pauses, where back-channel responses would be appropriate. When American and Japanese speak to each other, there is accommodation on both sides – the Americans use more, the Japanese fewer back-channels (see Figure 9.1). When males and females meet they accommodate to one another in certain ways, such as length of pauses; they over-accommodate on utterance length, but actually diverge in some other ways; for instance, women laugh a lot more (Bilous and Krauss 1988). A study was made of a girl in a travel agency in conversation with 51 different clients. She accommodated to class-related aspects of their speech such as sounding the initial 'h', so that she sounded h's 3.7 per cent of the time at one extreme, and 29.3 per cent at the other, and her speech styles correlated 0.76 to 0.90 with those of her clients (Coupland 1984).

Figure 9.1 Frequency of back-channel signals displayed by American and Japanese listeners in intra- and cross-cultural encounters

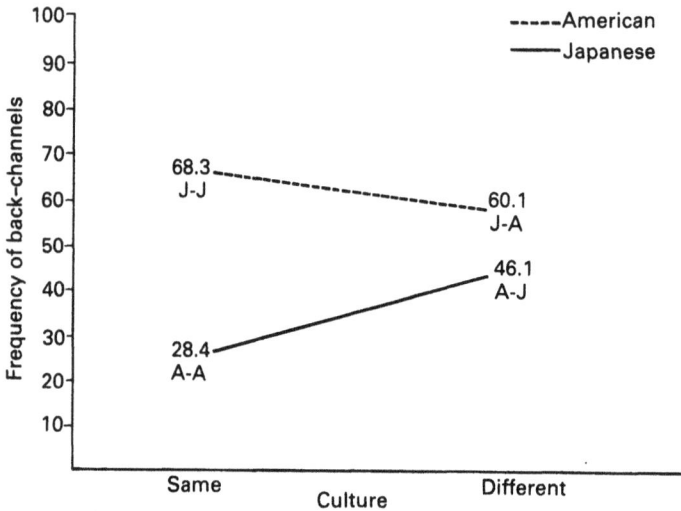

Source: White 1989

There may be a rule to the effect that one should do it because it makes understanding easier. It is more likely to take place on the part of a speaker who is keen to be accepted or liked by the other, and as a result accent shifts are more likely towards a higher status than the reverse. When speakers do accommodate to one another, they like each other more (Gallois and Callan 1988). Accommodation is less likely to occur if a speaker is not able to speak French, for example, or to speak in a Welsh accent. And there may be strong norms about speech styles, which prevent males and females accommodating very much to each other (Giles and Powesland 1975).

Conversational maxims

Our talk exchanges do not normally consist of a succession of disconnected remarks, and would not be rational if they did. They are characteristically, to some degree at least, cooperative effects and each participant recognises in them, to some extent, a common purpose or set of purposes, or at least a mutually-accepted direction.

(Grice 1975)

If we knew how to do this, it would be possible to give advice or training to bad conversationalists – those individuals who find it difficult to keep a conversation going.

Grice goes on to suggest his 'cooperative principle':

Make your conversational contribution such as is required, at the stage at which it occurs, by the accepted purpose or direction of the talk exchange in which you are engaged.

He adds a number of more specific maxims: provide no more or less information than is needed, be relevant, tell the truth and be clear. No empirical evidence has been provided in support of these maxims, though it is quite likely that most people would agree with them if asked, even though they often break them. A major class of such breakages is due to politeness, and these will be discussed in the following section.

Probably real language use involves a lot of failure to keep to the rules, though they may still be seen as desirable. And there is probably quite a lot of cultural variation in such rules. Perhaps the strongest evidence in support of them comes from experiments showing that listeners assume that speakers are following the rules, and interpret cases of irony, for example, accordingly. If A says 'What a delightful day' (when it isn't), the assumption that A means to tell the truth leads to taking this as a case of irony. If A says 'I'm out of petrol', and B replies 'There's a garage round the corner', A will assume that this is a relevant response, and that the garage probably sells petrol and is open (Clark 1985; Leech 1983). Furthermore, people on the whole provide listeners with information that is needed, rather than telling them what they know already (Turnbull and Slugoski 1988).

Eder (1988) reports how two people may collaborate when describing the same event to others, the second to speak may finish the other's sentence, repeat or expand what was said, or make comments which add to its importance or believability, and display a shared view of the event. This is a good example of *relevance*, one of Grice's rules. While relevance describes a single utterance in relation to the previous ones, *coherence* describes the whole conversation – the extent to which it 'hangs together', and the utterances are about the same topic. There are a number of ways of generating relevance and coherence – expanding on what has been said, explaining or evaluating it, generalising from it, giving an example, referring back to the same elements, using some of the same words (McLaughlin 1984).

An important limitation of Grice's rules is that speakers are often not entirely open, helpful or frank. Teenagers, when asked by their parents where they have been and what they have been doing, provide a familiar example (see p. 197). Politicians, subjected to hostile questions on TV, are often very evasive, or answer a quite different question. In committee work, diplomacy, cases of industrial and military secrets, and many other work settings, people often do not feel free to make relevant and helpful conversational contributions. In these cases there is cooperation between those talking in keeping up a sensible conversation, but not in providing the information that the others really need, though this may be seen as cooperation within a larger group.

We have been trying to re-train bad conversationalists for many years, and have found that their problems are of a rather different kind. Here are some examples of common difficulties, and the maxims which might be invoked to deal with them.

1 Not talking enough and, in particular, not initiating any conversational topics. Such individuals may kill the conversation by giving a brief reply to questions, but initiating nothing further in return. *Maxim*: Be responsible for keeping the conversation going.
2 Not taking an interest in the other person or in what they have to say. We mentioned this earlier under 'intersubjectivity'. *Maxim*: Take a serious interest in other people and their utterances.
3 Being cold or unfriendly. This falls partly under non-verbal communication, though friendliness can also be put into words; for example, by discussing personal topics, looking for common interests and experiences, expressing approval and paying compliments. *Maxim*: Be friendly and rewarding (Argyle 1983).
4 Being impolite or tactless. This will be discussed in the next section.

Politeness

For a conversation to proceed smoothly, and without giving offence, it is necessary for the participants to be polite. Following Grice's rules does not necessarily help much here. Indeed it can be seen that speakers often break Grice's rules, in order to avoid offence in some way. For example:

A: Geoff has just borrowed your car.
B: Well I like *that!*

or

A: We'll all miss Bill and Agatha, won't we?
B: Well, we'll all miss *Bill.*

Here speaker B is avoiding saying that we won't miss Agatha, and thereby breaks one of Grice's maxims (Leech 1983). If conversationalists did keep to Grice's rules all the time it would make for very boring, formal kinds of conversation – no jokes, metaphors, amusing exaggerations or irrelevancies. But, above all, these conversations would be regarded as very impolite.

Theories of politeness have tried to explain why deviation from Grice's rules is regarded as more appropriate than keeping them. Brown and Levinson (1978) thought that the basic principle of politeness was avoidance of damaging the face or self-esteem of the other. This is particularly likely to happen in the case of requests and criticism, so indirect forms are regarded as more polite, though this varies with the social relationship. Slugoski and Turnbull (1988) found experimental support for these ideas: counter-to-fact insults to liked partners were interpreted non-literally, that is as irony. Counter-to-fact compliments, to disliked partners, were also interpreted ironically. A weakness of most of this research, however, is the absence of non-verbal data, which would help to signal irony.

Lakoff (1973) suggested that three basic principles of politeness are needed:

1 Don't impose on the other, i.e. respect their privacy, don't ask personal questions.
2 Give options, i.e. let them make their own decisions.
3 Be friendly, don't damage their self esteem.

Leech (1983) suggested some further rules:

1 Emphasise benefits and minimise the costs to the other.
2 Maximise praise of the other, minimise praise of self.
3 Exaggerate agreement, and minimise disagreement.

Goffman (1967) had proposed that 'face-work' is needed in social encounters, that interactors must cooperate in reducing threats to each other's face, to guard against incidents which threaten face. A lot of face-work is concerned with protecting one's own face, but here we are talking about looking after the self-esteem of others. If there has been a damaging incident, some remedial or repair work is needed, usually in the form of an apology. This consists of expressing regrets, giving an explanation, and promising to do better in future. Another example is 'playing dumb', that is pretending to be less intelligent or knowledgeable than is really the case: 26.5 per cent of an American national sample admitted to having done this (Gove et al. 1980).

In a study which pre-dates the publication of most of these rules, we asked subjects to rate the importance of 20 rules for each of eight situations. The results are shown in Table 9.2. The rules in the top cluster were thought to apply to all the situations mentioned, and can be regarded as rules of general politeness. The last cluster consists of further rules for parties, where evidently a further degree of politeness is needed; the party rules did not apply to the others clusters of situations, which were work or informal social situations. This suggests that there may be some rules which are universal, others that apply only to certain classes of situations. Slugoski (1983) found that in sociable, relationship-oriented situations, compared with task-situations, additional politeness rules were important, in the sense

Table 9.2 Clusters of rules for situations

3.472	
3.118	
2.764	
2.411	
2.057	
1.703	
1.350	
0.996	
0.642	
0.288	
− 0.065	

Should be polite — 1
Should try to make it a pleasant encounter — 5
Should not try to make the other(s) feel small — 8
Should not embarrass others — 20
Should be friendly — 11
No one should make long speeches — 2
Should not comment on the other's behaviour or appearance — 4
Should not discuss personal matters — 9
Should avoid personal chat or gossip — 16
An utterance should be about the same topic as the previous one — 17
Should not touch the other person — 19
Questions should lead to relevant answers — 3
Only one person should talk at a time — 10
Should listen carefully to the person in charge — 15
Should do whatever the other person says — 6
Should only speak when spoken to — 12
Should try to keep to cheerful topics of conversation — 7
Should avoid disagreements — 14
Should dress smartly — 13
Each should display positive affection towards the other — 18

Source: Argyle *et al.* 1979

that when they were kept the encounter was judged to have been successful. The extra rules in the sociable situations were about being honest (one of Grice's rules) and being revealing. Being friendly was important for both kinds of situation.

Sociable conversation

We have just seen that additional politeness rules are thought to apply to situations where the focus is on establishing and enjoying social relationships. A lot of pleasant chat and gossip between friends and in the family is like this. We said earlier that non-verbal communication is very important here – the use of smiling, gaze, proximity and a friendly tone of voice. However, as Ellis and Beattie (1986) point out, it can be done primarily by words, as in the following example, though it would be regarded as very odd if the non-verbal style failed to match the words.

> *Scene*: train moving through the English countryside: in the compartment
> sit one man and one woman, both young.
> Man: Beautiful weather isn't it?
> Woman: Yes, not bad for this time of year.
> Man: Are you going far?
> Woman: To Edinburgh.
> Man: Oh, my brother lives there.
> Woman: Oh, whereabouts?
> Man: Castle Street.
> Woman: Oh, I know it well. I used to have a boyfriend who lived there.
> But we don't go out any more. Small world isn't it?
> Man: You've got a nice Scottish accent.
> Woman: Thank you.
> Man: What's your name?
> Woman: Zoe – Zoe Purvis.
> Man: Hello Zoe, mine's Ben.

This illustrates most of the verbal methods used to establish and enjoy relationships. The same types of utterances are used a lot by extraverts (see p. 203).

1 *Questions*, especially questions taking a serious personal interest in the other, and suggesting some self-disclosure. They must not be too intimate, or the politeness rule of respecting privacy will be broken (see Lakoff's first rule). The level of intimacy depends on the stage which the relationship has reached.
2 *Self-disclosure*. The reply should be at a sufficient level of self-disclosure, matching and perhaps going a little beyond what has been disclosed by the other.

3 *Paying compliments*. This is one of the main forms of verbal rewarding-ness, and often includes, in English, the word 'nice', as in the example above. This overlaps with the politeness rule about maximising praise of the other.

4 *Agreeing*. The purpose of these conversations is not to solve problems but to further the relationship, so if possible one should agree with what has been said (see the third rule from Leech).

5 *Reaching for similarity*. Speakers try to find things which they have in common – people and places, opinions and beliefs, interests and know-ledge.

6 *Pleasure talk*. Talking about pleasant events, keeping to cheerful topics of conversation. This kind of conversation has been found to enhance feelings of joy, reduce depression (Argyle 1987).

7 *Use of names and pronouns*. The other is addressed by name, preferably first name. The word 'we' is used to signal shared activities, feelings, group membership, cooperation.

8 *Humour*. It has often been suggested that humour leads to interpersonal attraction (Chapman and Foot 1977). Kane *et al.* (1977) said: 'With regard to humour, a cheerful demeanour is an invitation to interaction. Ready humour indicates a spontaneity and joy in relating to others . . . and conveys the goodwill and benevolence of the source.' Experiments have found that people who use humour are seen as more likeable. There are several possible reasons for these effects of humour. (a) Humour breaks down social barriers and status differences; for example, when used by teachers. (b) It increases group cohesion; for example, when directed towards an out-group. (c) It reduces anxiety or other tensions, and increases joy; the encounter is then more rewarding. (d) Sharing in humour is a case of close coordination and sharing of both thoughts and emotions.

Linguists have identified 'high' and 'low' speech styles in several languages. The low style is used more by uneducated people, and by everybody in informal, sociable situations. It is less fluent and grammatical, has a simpler construction, a smaller vocabulary, more verbs, adverbs and pronouns, meanings depend on context. In Britain Bernstein (1959) described the two styles as the elaborate and restricted codes. He argued that the restricted code is used in face-to-face groups and is concerned with immediate behaviour in these groups, rather than with impersonal and unambiguous transmisssion of information. He thought that the restricted code reflected the nature of working-class conversations at work, while the elaborated code was suited to managerial and professional work.

Adjacency pairs

This is one of the main building blocks of conversation, showing the way in which one utterance is linked to the next. The most familiar pair is question-answer: the second utterance is closely related to the first, and its meaning is incomplete without knowing about the previous utterance. For example, 'about 90 miles' conveys no information at all unless we know that it is a reply to some question. The first utterance of the pair has some compelling power to 'project' a relevant response. Question-answer is the most common type, but there are a number of others such as request-comply (or refuse), summon-answer, offer-accept (or refuse), thanks-acknowledge, greetings and partings (Clark 1985).

There is a kind of inner logic about these adjacency pairs, which gives the first utterance the power to project the second. The sequence is also found to occur with a high statistical probability, if sequence analysis is carried out, and 'Markov chains' – the probability that act X is followed by act Y – are studied. They can be studied experimentally, to see what happens if the expected kind of response is or is not given. Davis and Perkowitz (1979) studied 'responsiveness', that is, making relevant responses to the last speaker, and showing that one is interested in the topic of conversation, and in the speaker himself. When listeners were responsive in these ways the speaker liked them more and was more interested in them.

This aspect of verbal communication can be seen as taking place as a matter of empirical fact, as having an inner logic, as a social rule, or as a social skill producing positive results.

More complex conversational sequences

We know the rules of grammar, for putting words together in the right order to make sentences. Are there similar rules for putting utterances together in the right order to make conversations? If there are, it is very difficult to formulate them, though a start has been made with Grice's cooperative principle, for example. However, people have no difficulty putting together conversations which have been typed out, chopped up, and put together in the wrong order. For example, they have no difficulty in unscrambling the following kind of conversation (Clarke 1983):

No, bloody awful.
Well, what's been happening at home?
Did you have a good day at the office, dear?
Nothing much.
Hello.

We said that the question-answer sequence is a common building block of conversation. Often a question leads to a straightforward and relevant answer, but this is not the only possibility. The reply may be another question, which often results in an insertion routine, as in

A: Are you coming tonight?
   [B: Can I bring a guest?
   [A: Sure.
B: I'll be there.

A question may be open or closed; an open-ended question usually results in a fairly long answer, especially if non-verbal encouragement is given. Indeed the combination of open-ended questions and non-verbal reinforcement is the best way to make someone else talk more. A person who replies to a question often adds something else, that is makes a double move. In fact it is usually necessary to do so to keep the conversation going. Finally the person who has asked the question may refuse to answer, or give an unhelpful answer of some kind. We shall describe later how this is dealt with.

We developed the analysis of situations further, with a functional model, in which all the different features of situations can be explained in terms of their contributions to the realisation of situational goals (Argyle, Furnham and Graham 1981). Every situation has a characteristic repertoire of moves, verbal and otherwise, all of which can be seen as the steps needed to attain the goals. We found that the repertoires of behaviour for an interview, teaching, and seeing the doctor are rather different. There are also characteristic sequences of these elements – different routes to the situational goals. Consider the example of teaching: there are certain types of utterances commonly used by teachers and pupils. There can be a variety of sequences, from simple question-answer cycles, to more elaborate ones where pupils are encouraged to initiate (see Figure 9.2). In the study of behaviour in the classroom it has been pointed out that the cycles are not really repeated, since different questions and answers are involved.

Other situations have distinctive rules and sequences of interaction. In Law Courts much of the action consists of questions and answers, and those involved have to stand while speaking. In psychotherapy the therapist asks a lot of carefully non-threatening questions, to which the patient often replies by pieces of narrative. At university tutorials it is common for the student to read parts of an essay and for the tutor to interrupt. In what has been described as the 'Balliol method', the student reads the first sentence of his essay, and the tutor spends the rest of the tutorial explaining what was wrong with it.

Conversations usually start with a greeting. This involves a physical approach and exchange of non-verbal signals. Kendon and Ferber (1973) found that the following sequence was typical at an out-of-doors children's party:

Figure 9.2 Cycles of interaction in the classroom

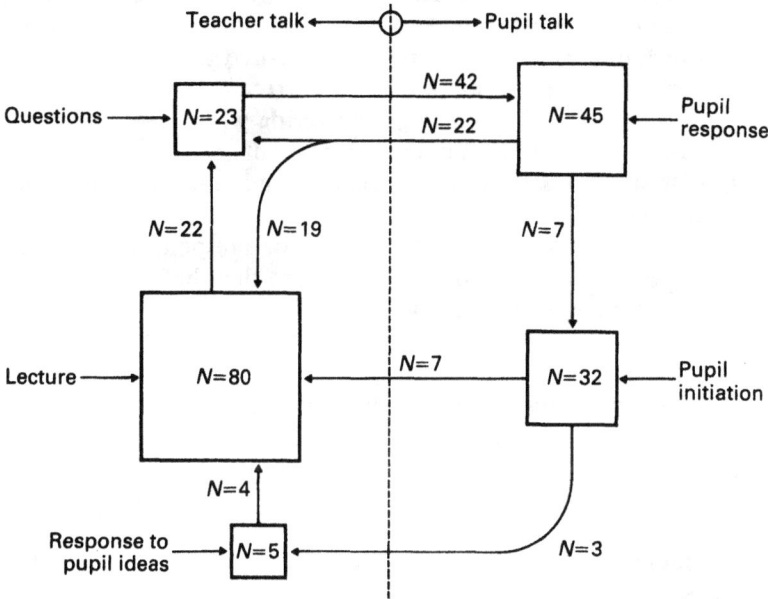

Source: Flanders 1970

1 A waves, smiles, looks and says something like 'Hi'. B probably responds, and there is a brief mutual gaze.
2 A moves nearer to B, looks away, grooms himself, frees his right hand.
3 A and B shake hands, or make other bodily contact, second smile, second mutual gaze, second verbal greeting.
4 A and B stand at an angle, and conversation begins.

What has to be accomplished in a greeting is establishing contact, signalling that those involved are willing to enter into an encounter, and initiating a topic of conversation or other activity. The greeting sequence, with its exchange of 'Hello, how are you?' etc., is able to perform the ritual work of making two people accessible to one another, so that the conversation can begin.

Partings have to achieve the opposite, that is agree that the meeting is over, and prepare for a period of separation. One speaker says something like 'I'm afraid I'll have to go in a minute', which the other may or may not agree to. They then reassure one another that the parting is only temporary, and look forward to meeting again. They may summarise the conversation that is ending, or say how much they enjoyed it (Clark 1985).

Conversation involves cooperative skills

Each participant in a conversation is like the performer of a motor skill, like someone trying to drive a car from A to B. Each person is trying to achieve some goal, which usually consists of responses desired from the other. He does this by trying certain moves and taking corrective action if he is not successful, rather like a driver turning the steering wheel (see Figure 6.1, p. 124). This is the essence of the motor skill model of social behaviour. The model fits best situations such as interviewing and teaching, where one person is in charge.

In a social survey interview it is very common for a respondent to give an inadequate answer, or to refuse to answer at all, so that the interviewer has to take some corrective action (Brenner 1981).

I_1: Asks question.
R_1: Gives inadequate answer or does not understand question.
I_2: Clarifies and repeats question.
R_2: Gives adequate answer.

or

I_1: Asks question.
R_1: Refuses to answer.
I_2: Explains purpose and importance of survey; repeats question.
R_2: Gives adequate answer.

So far we have looked at the social skills of one interactor. However, both are usually pursuing their goals simultaneously, and must synchronise by keeping to the acceptable rules of sequence. Here is a case of this happening in an interview between a college admissions tutor and an applicant.

I_1: How well did you do at physics at school?
R_1: Not very well, I was better at chemistry.
I_2: What were your A-level results?
R_2: I got a C in physics, but an A in chemistry.
I_3: That's very good.

This is an example of cooperative conversation in the sense that unlike conversations with schizophrenics the rules of sequence were followed, although the speakers were pursuing different goals. And, unlike the adolescents, TV politicians, committee men and diplomats referred to earlier, they are cooperating in providing the information needed by the other: they were following Grice's rules.

Chapter ten

Individual differences in cooperativeness

Some people are more cooperative than others, according to ratings made by those who know them, their behaviour in laboratory tasks and games, and as shown by self-report questionnaires. The first evidence to be obtained was from game situations, like the Prisoners' Dilemma Game. A method devised by Liebrand and McClintock (1988) gives a measure of cooperation and three other approaches to dividing up rewards.

Cooperation is defined as maximising joint gains, own plus others' outcomes.

Competition is maximising the difference between own and other's outcomes.

Altruism is maximising other's outcomes, regardless of own.

Individualism is maximising own outcomes, regardless of the other's.

Subjects are offered pairs of outcomes, in terms of money, for self and an unknown other; the other would make a similar set of choices, and payment of subjects would be directly affected. Figure 10.1 shows an example of one of 24 choices to be made, as presented on computer. It can be seen that the left-hand choice is more cooperative, the right-hand one more competitive. Individualists would also prefer the lefthand choice, as would altruists. It was found that cooperators and competitors took longer to decide – they were taking account of both outcomes, and that cooperators were slowest when there were negative outcomes for others – they were concerned about the other.

Kelley and Stahelski (1970) found that subjects who normally played in a competitive way thought that most of their opponents were also playing competitively – because their own behaviour made this more likely to happen. Cooperators on the other hand could distinguish more accurately between opponents who cooperated and those who competed. These investigators conclude that competitive individuals have a cynical view of the world since they create an environment of untrustworthy opponents against whom they have to defend themselves. Cooperative individuals, however, are aware of the diversity of other people.

Figure 10.1 Example of one item of the computerised version of the ring measure

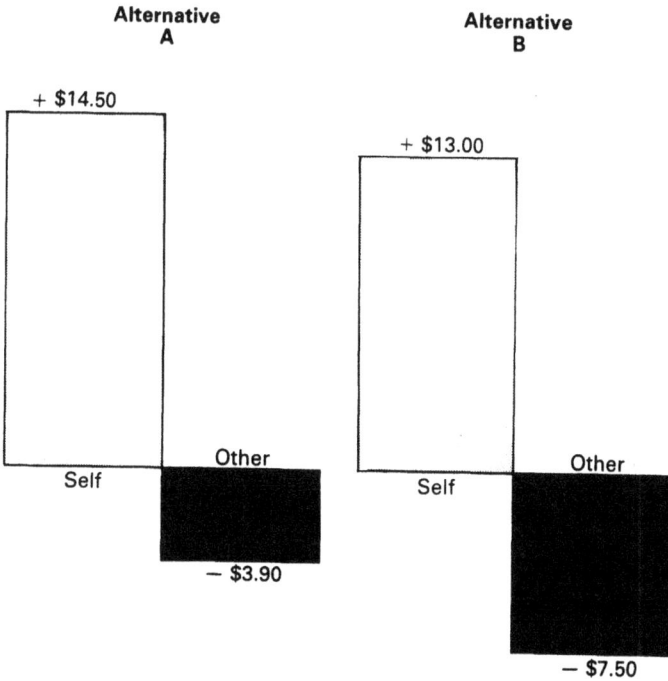

Which alternative do you prefer
A or B ?
Please type in A or B

Source: Liebrand and McClintock 1988

While such methods have a certain face validity, they are open to the objections to game-playing methods made earlier, that they are very different from any real-life cooperative situations.

Another approach to the study of personality is through ratings made by others. When this is done, five factors usually appear, whose main components are shown in Table 10.1. It can be seen that cooperative is part of the Agreeableness factor. And this factor is independent of Extraversion. This structure of ratings has often been replicated and appears even if the

Table 10.1 The five factors representing the 20 peer nomination scales

Factor name	Scale labels
Extraversion	talkative−silent
	frank, open−secretive
	adventurous−cautious
	sociable−reclusive
Agreeableness	good-natured−irritable
	not jealous−jealous
	mild, gentle−headstrong
	cooperative−negativistic
Conscientiousness	fussy, tidy−careless
	responsible−undependable
	scrupulous−unscrupulous
	persevering−quitting, fickle
Emotional stability	poised−nervous, tense
	calm−anxious
	composed−excitable
	non-hypochondriacal−hypochondriacal
Culture	artistically sensitive−artistically insensitive
	intellectual−unreflective, narrow
	polished, refined−crude, boorish
	imaginative−simple, direct

Source: Norman 1963

raters do not know those rated, or even if there are no target persons at all – the structure reflects a universal implicit personality theory, perhaps based on experience of many people in the past (Hampson 1988). At least in the minds of raters and self-raters cooperativeness is a central part of an important personality dimension.

Argyle and Lu (in press) have recently developed a questionnaire measure of cooperativeness, asking for self-reported cooperative preferences, skills, enjoyment and values, in the spheres of leisure, leadership, friends, family, education, clubs, work and committees. Some of the hypotheses about cooperation developed in this book are being tested with this measure.

Social interest

Crandall (1980) has designed a scale of 'social interest' based on an idea of Adler's. Social interest is thought of as being concerned about other people, and including cooperation, sharing and helping. It comes very close to being a measure of cooperativeness. The measure consists of 15 pairs of value-laden words, matched for social desirability, where one of each pair had been rated by a group of psychologists as fitting the definition of social interest. An example of one of the pairs is Intelligent and Considerate; in the test they are partly hidden by a number of buffer items.

Relation to cooperation

This scale correlates with several aspects of cooperative behaviour:

1 Cooperation in the Prisoners' Dilemma Game (r = 0.32)
2 Ratings by peers for Social Interest (not analysed by correlations)
3 Empathy (r = 0.40)
4 Volunteering for unpaid help
5 Hostility (r = − 0.50)
6 Self-centredness (− 0.44)

It has no correlation with extraversion.

Nuns, church-workers and charity volunteers had high scores; convicts, atheists and fashion models low scores.

It was found that high scorers were in better mental health, and were happier, more satisfied, and had a stronger feeling of purpose in life. This was predicted on the grounds that high social interest means less preoccupation with self, greater identification with others, and hence more social support, and that the main tasks or problems in life are social, and require social interest to solve them. The meaning of life needs a sense of community and brotherhood.

Origins

No research has been reported on the origins of social interest.

A scale for altruism was developed by Johnson *et al.* (1989), with sub-scales for the reported frequency of giving and receiving help, and the rated importance of help, which were quite strongly correlated with each other. The main correlate reported was with extraversion, and there were also some interesting cross-cultural differences (see p. 72).

Social competence

We saw above that people see cooperativeness as part of a broader factor of Agreeableness. I want to suggest that it is also part of a general dimension of social competence. Social competence, as commonly understood, is believed to include cooperation. Children, when rated as socially competent at play, are the ones who cooperate more frequently, are more rewarding to others and less aggressive (Dodge 1985).

In a previous book I defined social competence as 'the ability, the possession of the necessary skills, to produce the desired effects of other people in social situations' (Argyle 1983: 76). However, in this book we have noted the importance of communion, as compared with agency, in close relationships, and it seems that here people are not primarily concerned with their own needs, but rather with the relationship itself.

Socially skilled people are able to sustain social interactions and social relationships, without these breaking down. They may be primarily concerned with their own goals, but they will not be able to attain these unless they take account of the needs and points of view of the others. Skilled performance usually involves some integrative way of meeting the needs of both sides – or else the others will not stay in the relationship or agree to any desired course of action.

This is clearer if we look at those people who are definitely lacking in social competence. The most extreme case is probably schizophrenics. Here are some examples.

1 *The author with a patient*
  MA: I hear that the hospital football team did well on Saturday.
  Patient: (partly simultaneously) They've taken my railings away.

2 *A conversation with a schizophrenic*
  Dr: What shall I call you?
  Patient: I'm a very smart fellow. I don't twist in the, the same way twice, believe me. I'm a very different type of fellow.
  Dr: What shall I call you?
  Patient: You can call me by name. We have enough of them, and if we move that way we –
  Dr: What is your name?
  Patient: Well, let's say you might have thought you had something from before, but you haven't got it any more.
  Dr: I'm going to call you Dean.

(Laffal 1965)

It is not clear whether such patients are deliberately not engaging in the encounter, or whether they are simply pursuing their own thoughts, regardless of what others are saying. In either case there is a total lack of cooperation – often in not taking turns to speak, in talking about different topics, in not observing Grice's rules of sequence, or in producing meaningless utterances.

Neurotic patients are far better than this, but many of them are socially very unsuccessful. Many have great difficulty making friends of either sex, are very poor conversationalists, in that they can't keep a conversation going, are anxious and unhappy on social occasions, and are found very unrewarding by others. A number of processes are involved, but the central one may be their egocentricity, shown by a lack of interest in other people, frequent use of the word 'I', gestures directed towards their own body rather than communicating with others, and an inability to take the role of the other, to see anyone else's point of view (Argyle 1983). If this is correct, it suggests a new direction for therapy – practice and training in cooperation.

Other socially unskilled people apart from patients become socially isolated, have difficulty in sustaining relationships at work and elsewhere, find some social situations difficult and a source of anxiety. This can be very hard for them at work, if for example they can't deal with people in authority, or take part in committee meetings effectively. They may be given SST (social skills training) to improve their non-verbal communication, or the skills for particular situations. SST may also include training in taking the role of the other, either by explicit instruction, or experience of role reversal. However, the key factor that might produce the best results could be training to cooperate.

Many social skills involve leadership, persuasion, and so on. Do they require cooperation too? I believe that they do, and offer three examples to show this.

1 *Assertiveness*. This is often thought of in terms of making other people do something, and this is a widely held lay view. However, assertiveness trainers see it rather differently, and place much more emphasis on the rights of others and concern for the interests of other people. It is recognised that assertiveness situations often contain conflicts between the goals of the two parties, and that skill is needed to reconcile them, and to avoid damaging the relationship or hurting other people's feelings (Wilson 1989). Research on persuasion has shown that others can be influenced best if it is possible to appeal to their motivations.

2 *Leadership and supervision*. A great body of research in industrial, military, sports and other settings has shown that effective leaders should instruct, explain and motivate their subordinates. They should also look after the needs of subordinates. The combination of these two factors is essential, one is no good without the other: the leader indicates the path to be followed, and rewards his subordinates for following it. There is a third factor: leaders should allow their subordinates, as far as possible, to participate in decisions; this commits them to the goals agreed, and increases job satisfaction. Taking account of the ideas of subordinates also leads to better decisions being taken (Argyle 1989). This describes in a nutshell, the nature of cooperation between leaders and their subordinates.

3 *Negotiation*. Here the social skill performer is apparently on the opposite side to those he is dealing with. However, as we showed earlier, negotiators have to cooperate in keeping to the rules of the situation. Successful negotiators also collaborate, informally, to share information, engage in joint problem-solving and to see if an 'integrative' solution can be found, which would benefit both sides. For example, one side might make compensation for a concession (see p. 41). The way from conflict to maximum joint gains turns out to be cooperation, even though the goals of the two sides are apparently opposed.

Let us try to describe the cooperative component of social skills. It may have the following elements: (a) an interest in the other side; a desire to interact with, relate to them; (b) the capacity to empathise, or see the point of view of the other; and (c) the ability to discover lines of action which integrate the goals of both parties. The first two are assessed by dimensions like empathy, extraversion and the need for affiliation and intimacy, which are described below. However, the third component, integrating goals, has not yet been developed as a personality dimension, so a few words will be said about it now. Research into the social skills of children has been much concerned with the child's capacity to integrate two of its own goals, or the goals of itself and others. Suppose another child cheats in a game; a second child could cry, run away, hit the other, or it could suggest that the other has made an accidental mistake, and the turn should be run again. Or

> You're on a bike hike with five of your friends. One of the girls, who just moved into your neighborhood, is very slow and is holding the group up. The other girls you are with are all yelling at her and threatening to leave her behind.

One solution might be simply to slow down to be with her (Dodge, in press).

McPhail (1967) compiled a list of common social problem situations encountered by adolescents. He found that the number of socially skilled solutions, where the needs of both sides were considered, increased rapidly between the ages of 12 and 17. Research on child language has obtained similar results. By the ages 14–15 most children use arguments to persuade others, in which they show how it is in the other's interests to do what is suggested. They can recognise the different needs of the two parties, and are able to integrate them in a single course of action (Clark and Delia 1976). We have found that adults have quite clear ideas of the needs of themselves and others in everyday situations, and how they are related. Figure 10.2 shows how the nurse–patient relationship was seen: the nurse's goal of taking care of the patient's well-being leads to this, but her concern to look after herself is in conflict with it.

Extraversion

This is one of the most important personality traits, and it has some correlation with many aspects of behaviour. The core of extraversion is sociability – seeking out and enjoying social situations. An earlier version of Eysenck's measure, the EPI, included impulsiveness items, but in the later version, the EPQ, these have been moved into the Psychoticism dimension; the E scale is now all about sociability (Eysenck and Eysenck 1985), as are other measures of extraversion. Fox (1984) found that activities most distinctive of extraversion were liking to meet strangers, and liking parties. Furnham (1981) found that when they had a fairly free choice of activities extraverts chose social situations and situations involving physical activity. Extraversion is remarkably stable over time: Costa and McCrae (1988)

Figure 10.2 The structure of the nurse–patient situation

(c) Nursing

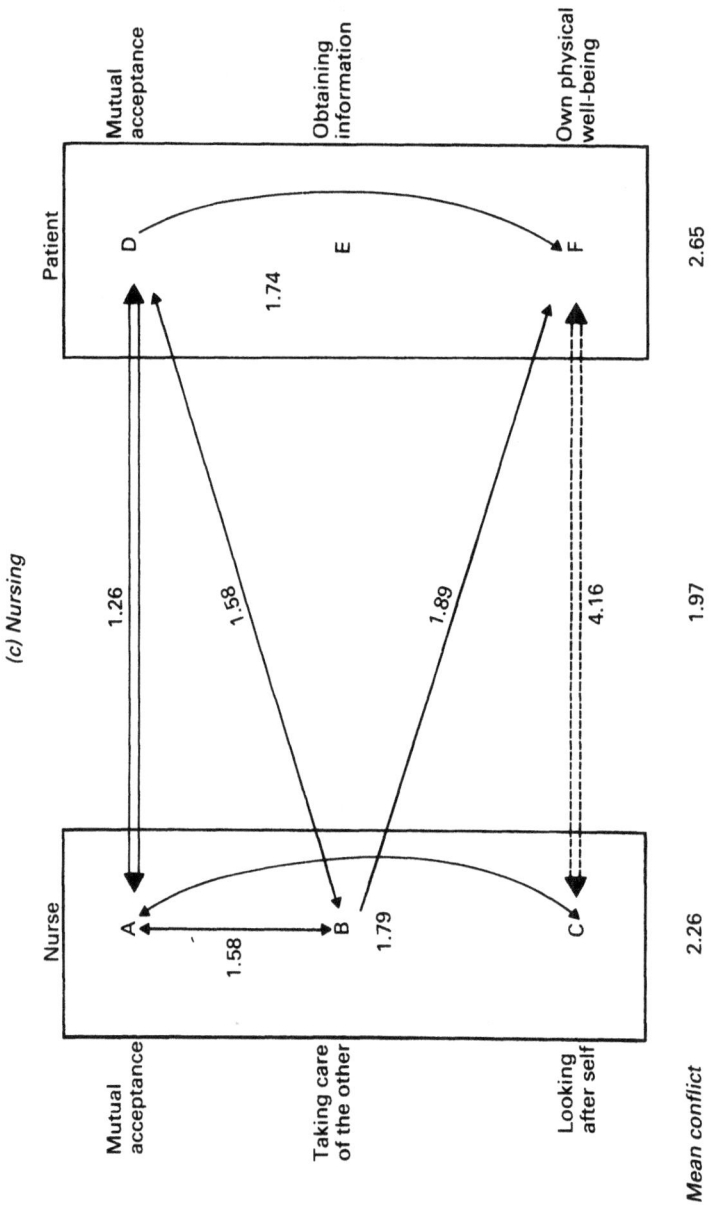

Source: Argyle et al. 1981

found test–retest reliability of 0.84 for males, 0.75 for females over six years, and other studies have found high stability from the age of five.

How cooperative are extraverts? They are certainly cooperative in their social behaviour and relationships in everyday social situations, and with friends. Thorne (1987) compared the social interaction between pairs of extraverts on the one hand and pairs of introverts. She found that the extraverts tried very hard to get to know one another, by asking questions, agreeing and paying compliments. She suggests that extraverts occupy 'the niche of catalyst of sociability', and have 'an underlying expectation that experience can and should be shared' (p. 725). I have run similar experiments, and have been amazed at the way the extraverts get to work on each other, and introverts' capacity to sit in total silence for up to five minutes.

In non-verbal communication, extraverts produce more smiling, gaze and proximity; they talk more, louder, faster and at higher pitch; they laugh more and show more accurate encoding and decoding (Argyle 1988).

Extraverts are more socially skilled: they are more likely to become leaders of groups, have more friends, receive more social support, have greater social influence. They approach social situations in a positive and cooperative way; for example, they expect that competitive games will be friendly, and they enjoy them more than introverts do (Graziano *et al.* 1985). A later study found that extraverts enjoy both cooperative and competitive situations, but they prefer cooperative ones. Table 10.2 shows how they rated imaginary cooperative and competitive game situations.

Table 10.2 Correlations between sociability* and ratings of cooperative and competitive situations

	Cooperative	Competitive
likeable	0.41	0.21
potentially rewarding	0.33	0.21
interesting	0.31	0.25
sociable	0.27	0.24
arousing	0.25	0.18
friendly	0.19	0.21
challenging	0.15	0.22
potentially punishing	− 0.19	− 0.25
anxiety producing	− 0.24	− 0.04
difficult	− 0.25	− 0.09

Source: Wolfe and Krasmer 1988

Note: * a sociability factor was extracted from the MPI (Maudsley Personality Inventory), probably very similar to E (Extraversion) on the EPQ (Eysenck Personality Questionnaire).

Finally, extraverts are happier, with a correlation of 0.40 or more, but especially in social situations. Argyle and Lu (in press) found that the happiness of extraverts could partly be explained in terms of their greater participation in social activities of two main kinds: teams sports and clubs, and parties/dancing/pubs/meeting new people. Later I shall suggest that cooperation leads both to positive social relationships and to positive affect; the findings about extraverts support this.

Origins

To begin with extraversion appears to be about 50 per cent inherited, as shown by the study of 12,898 pairs of twins in Sweden by Floderus-Myrhed and colleagues (1980). There is evidence about the physiological basis of extraversion. The best-supported theory is by Gray (1982). He proposed that differences in the hypothalamus and hippocampus make extraverts more sensitive to rewards; other people are the most important source of reward, which gives an explanation of why extraverts seek company, and are happier than introverts. This theory has some support from studies with drugs, and on the effects of brain lesions. There is also a link with the immune system: extraverts given a mild cold infection produced fewer cold symptoms $(r = -.38)$ (Totman *et al.* 1980). Studies of infants and their mothers find that individual differences in sociability are there from the start.

Kagan (1989) found that about 15 per cent of children in the second year of life are consistent sociable and 'affectively spontaneous', that this style of behaviour is preserved until seven and a half, and that it is correlated with physiological measures, such as lower and more variable heart rates and lower motor tension. However, relations with the mother are also important; we showed earlier the effects of early attachment on sociability and cooperativeness (see pp. 92ff.). Socialisation studies of adopted children show that relations with mother are more important than those with father, and the siblings are unimportant (Plomin 1986). This finding is similar to that of the effects of secure attachment in early cooperation and sociability. A British study of 4,000 11-year-olds found that extraversion was highest in children from small families, only children having the highest score, especially for girls (see Figure 10.3). Birth order made no difference. It might be expected that children from large families might become more extraverted as a result of their greater social experience at home. The opposite result may be because children from small families spend more time with strangers outside the family; being able to cope with strangers is very characteristic of extraverts.

Affiliative and intimacy motivation

These are aspects of personality which are conceptually very similar to extraversion, but have different ideas behind them, and are measured in a different way. The need for affiliation can be defined as the need to be with people, and to establish and maintain positive affective relationships with them. It has most often been measured by a projective test: subjects are

Figure 10.3 Extraversion scores as related to position in family and size of family

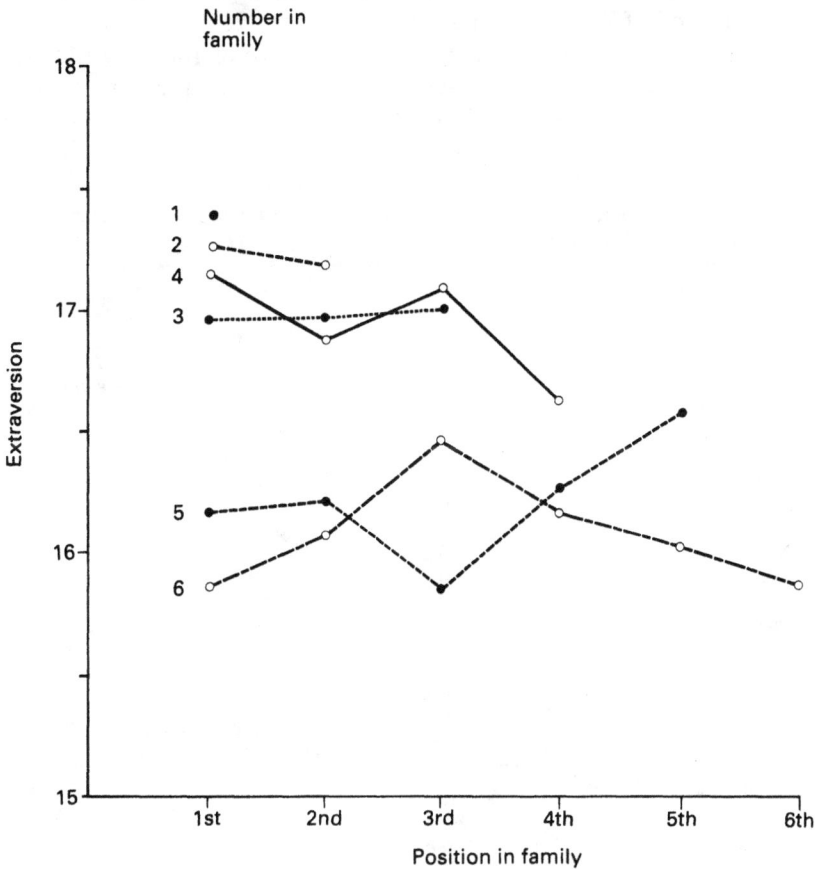

Source: Eysenck and Cookson 1970

asked to look at six cards from the Thematic Apperception Test (TAT), and to write five-minute stories for each; the stories are scored for themes about activities related to affiliation, including anticipation of it, and obstacles to it. Despite the problems of unreliability of scoring projective tests, this measure gives good predictions of affiliative behaviour; in one study subjects were called electronically on numerous random occasions, and those high on n.Aff. (need for affiliation) were more often talking or writing a letter to someone. There are questionnaire measures of n.Aff., but these do not predict affiliative behaviour as well as the projective measure (McClelland 1987).

However, it is found that individuals who are high in n.Aff., are very concerned to avoid competition and conflict, and to avoid rejection by others. They have sometimes been found to be unpopular, perhaps because they are anxious about rejection and are constantly seeking reassurance from others. This finding led to attempts to obtain a purer measure of the positive side of affiliative motivation as opposed to fear of rejection. McAdams (1980) did this, and developed a measure of Intimacy Motivation, the positive motivation to 'seek a warm, close and communicative exchange with others'. He used TAT stories again, and scored them for the presence of the themes in Table 10.3.

Table 10.3 Performance of the intimacy motive scoring system in differentiating between 'in-love' and control subjects

Scoring category	'In-love' arousal		
	Mean frequencies for two stories		Differences between arousal and control means
	In-love ($N = 36$)	Control ($N = 36$)	
+ A: Positive affect	1.08	0.69	0.39
Dlg: Dialogue	0.94	0.83	0.11
Psy: Psychological growth	0.31	0.19	0.11
CC: Commitment and concern	0.28	0.14	0.14
TS: Time space	0.61	0.33	0.28
U: Union	0.42	0.03	0.39
H: Harmony	0.33	0.08	0.25
Sr: Surrender	0.25	0.19	0.06
Esc: Escape to intimacy	0.42	0.08	0.33
COW: Connect. outside world	0.50	0.14	0.36
Total intimacy motive	5.14 ($SD = 2.96$)	2.72 ($SD = 2.39$)	2.42

Source: McAdams 1980

In other words, for high n.Int. (need for intimacy) individuals, the stories have characters who communicate with each other in a non-instrumental and reciprocal way, relationships promote the psychological growth or coping of one of the characters, and they surrender control in the process of relating to each other.

These two needs have quite a strong correlation with each other: McAdams and Bryant (1987) carried out a study of 1,208 subjects and found correlations of 0.55 for males, 0.58 for females. But as we shall see, they relate differently to various aspects of cooperation.

Links with cooperation

People who are high in n.Aff. (but not those high in n.Int.) rate themselves as cooperative ($r = 0.24$), unselfish, thoughtful and so on (McAdams 1980). Individuals who are high in n.Int. (but not those high in n.Aff.) are rated *by others* as cooperative, loving, less self-centred and less dominant. So which are really the more cooperative? To decide this we turn to measures of their actual behaviour.

People who are high in n.Aff. spend a lot of time with friends and join clubs; other people are evidently very important to them. The main evidence for their cooperativeness is that they dislike and avoid conflict and competition. Managers whose job is bringing different groups together have high scores. Individuals high on n.Int., on the other hand, also spend a lot of time with friends; in addition they are good listeners, engage in a lot of self-disclosure, engage in more reciprocal dialogue, surrender control, have greater physical proximity, and are more sensitive to faces (McClelland 1987). This could be summarized by saying that affiliative people are cooperative by avoiding competition and conflict, while those high on intimacy motivation cooperate at the level of synchrony and coordination.

Origins

Little is known about the genetic origins of this pair of drives, but their obvious resemblance to extraversion makes it probable that they too have a substantial genetic component. There is some evidence about the physiological processes connected with them. McClelland and colleagues found that subjects high in n.Aff. had stronger concentrations of the neurotransmitter dopamine. Films of close relationships increased dopamine levels, especially in the high n.Aff. subjects. Dopamine activates receptors in the hypothalamus and limbic area of the brain, and produces a positive affective response. Those high in affiliative motivation (and low in power motivation) were also found to have stronger immune systems, as measured by salivary immunoglobulin. Showing a film about Mother Teresa increased subjects' immune system levels, while a film about Hitler did not. This link with the immune system is very interesting, since it suggests that cooperative behaviour has become associated with biological fitness, in the course of evolution. Stone et al. (1987) found that fluctuations in salivary immunoglobulin correlated with positive mood. Marcus (1986), working with three to six-year-old children, found that longer cooperative play episodes took place when the children were rated as being in a happy mood. We saw earlier that externally-induced cooperation generated positive affect (pp. 125ff.). Social support/cooperation is thus linked both with joy and health.

On the socialisation side, it has been found that intimacy motivation is correlated with mothers' use of praise. We described earlier the research of Sroufe, showing that early secure attachment led to later sociability and cooperativeness (see p. 92). Parke (1989) found that parents influenced the friendship behaviour of their children in several ways. It was found that popular boys had parents who played a lot with them and elicited positive feelings during play, mothers who were verbally and fathers who were physically stimulating. Popular girls had physically playful and positive affect producing fathers. It was found that parents deliberately influenced the development of their children's relationships, by providing opportunities for play with peers, supervising this play – for example showing them how to play cooperatively.

Empathy

By empathy is meant an emotional response that is caused by another's emotional state, that is congruent with the other's emotional state or situation. It is much the same as the ability to decode non-verbal signals, and is a basic component of social skills (Eisenberg and Strayer 1987). It can be measured as a personality characteristic by self-report questionnaires, by reports of emotions felt while viewing videotapes, or by non-verbal or physiological reactions to emotional stimuli. The best known questionnaire measure is that by Mehrabian and Epstein (1972). The capacity for role-taking, or taking the role of the other, is a primarily cognitive ability to perceive correctly the point of view of others, and a number of cognitive tests have been used with children and adults.

Empathy and cooperation

The focus of empathy research has been on its links with helping and pro-social behaviour rather than with cooperation. Indeed, current thinking about helping behaviour makes empathy an essential part of the explanation (Batson *et al.* 1987). Many studies have shown that measures of individual empathy correlate with amount of helping behaviour and that arousing empathy makes help more likely to occur. For adults empathy is related to helping behaviour, with a variety of measures of empathy; the correlation is rather modest with questionnaire measures ($r = 0.17$), highest with physiological measures ($r = 0.36$). For children the effect is weaker, and best with facial/gestural measures (Eisenberg and Miller 1987). In view of the close connection between cooperation and helping behaviour, it seems very likely that empathy is involved in cooperation too, and this has been found, for example, in a study of 32 pre-school children (Marcus *et al.* 1985).

Other research has been concerned with the relation between cognitive perspective-taking and helping behaviour, and has consistently found a low positive correlation in children, of about 0.20. However, the correlation is higher for more assertive children (Underwood and Moore 1982).

The origins of empathy

There is evidence of empathy in animals; for example, rapid response to alarm calls, and affective responses to another animal's distress. Human infants at two to four days will cry in response to tapes of crying, and show other kinds of emotional contagion early in life. Emotional contagion is definitely present at 12 months, and becomes stronger with increasing age. There are consistent individual differences in empathy at age one to two, and these remain stable until later ages.

A number of socialisation variables have been found to be important for the development of empathy (Barnett 1987):

1 secure early attachment (see p. 92)
2 parental affection
3 empathic models, especially mothers who are emotionally responsive to other's distress, but also TV characters as models
4 use of inductive socialisation, drawing attention to victims' distress, encouraging the child to imagine itself in the victim's place
5 encouraging perception of similarity to others, showing how the child is similar to others in distress
6 discouraging excessive competition; competitive children are less empathic, but there is no evidence that reducing competitiveness enhanced empathy
7 encouraging self-esteem; empathy is greater in children with more self-esteem, and self-esteem is enhanced by experience of success, competence and recognition.

Collectivism

We discussed collectivism v. individualism earlier as a dimension for describing cultures. A similar dimension, sometimes called allocentrism v. idiocentrism, has been developed to describe *individuals*. Hui and Triandis (1986) suggested that collectivism consists of the following seven kinds of concern for others:

1 considering the implication of one's actions for the outcomes of group rather than self
2 sharing of material resources, such as money
3 sharing of non-material resources, such as time, affection and fun
4 greater acceptance of social influence
5 concern with group approval
6 sharing outcomes, e.g. being affected by another member's failure
7 feeling of involvement in others' lives and their decisions.

Seven questions were drafted to represent these processes. Eighty-one social scientists from many cultures described how they thought an individualist and a collectivist would behave in 10 relationships (see below), and no cultural differences appeared. However, concern with group approval and involvement in others' lives were less important than the other items, and sharing outcomes a little less important.

Triandis *et al.* (1988) developed questionnaire measures of collectivism, defined in this way, using large pools of relevant items. However, this did not produce a simple solution: individualism and collectivism are not the opposite of each other, but independent, so that it is possible to score high on both. Furthermore, each consists of several separate factors; collectivism includes factors for subordination of own goals to the goals of others, closeness to in-group, and concern for in-group. However, as Schwartz (1988) points out, this conceptualisation of collectivism is limited to concern for the in-group, not for the wider society, and it has been found that collectivists do less for the welfare of strangers. In fact 'collectivism' in these studies is definitely of the Chinese variety, emphasising devotion and attachment to the immediate circle of family and close friends.

Link with cooperation

Hui and Triandis (1986) asked their 81 social scientists how they thought individualists and collectivists would behave in seven situations (reflecting the seven processes) and 10 relationships. The results are shown in Figure 4.1 (p. 72). It was agreed that collectivists would show more concern, across all relationships, and much more concern would be shown in the closer relationships.

Triandis *et al.* (1988) added factor scores on collectivism, and found that this was strongly correlated (inversely) with loneliness, and (positively) with receiving social support.

Origins

Nothing is known about the origins of individual collectivism except that it varies a lot between cultures. Cultural differences are discussed in Chapter 4.

Gender differences in cooperation

Are women more cooperative than men? On the Prisoners' Dilemma Game over 100 studies have examined sex differences, and most of them have found that women are *less* cooperative than men, especially in same-sex pairs. Few investigators believe that this is a genuine finding, however, and a probable interpretation is that the D choice here is simply a cautious choice, or that women are anxious not to look foolish (Colman 1982a).

Measures of masculinity – femininity consist of attributes which are rated as desirable for males or females. In Bem's scales (1974) the following are some of the traits which were found to be more desirable for women or for men.

Males	*Females*
aggressive	affectionate
assertive	sensitive to the needs of others
competitive	sympathetic
independent	understanding
self-sufficient	yielding

Women rate themselves higher on the feminine items, men on the masculine ones. Subjects of either sex with high scores on femininity were more helpful. Those scoring high on masculinity were more independent, and less conforming. However, these dimensions were later found to have little or no relation with self-related masculinity or femininity, they are rather two unrelated dimensions of expressive and instrumental styles of behaviour. Those who score high on both scales, formerly described as 'androgenous', really have two sets of desirable attributes (Brown 1986). In a quite different research tradition, the study of social skills, it has been found that both dimensions are often needed in combination − in leadership, for example (Argyle 1989). Meanwhile, there is a sense in which 'masculine' attributes are more competitive, and 'feminine' ones more cooperative.

Among the personality traits which have been discussed in this chapter, only one had a clear gender difference, and that is empathy. Eisenberg and Miller (1987) carried out a meta-analysis of studies using Mehrabian and Epstein's and other questionnaire measures of empathy, and found a substantial difference: females had higher empathy scores, with an effect size of one standard deviation. Other measures of empathy showed smaller or no sex differences. It is possible that the large self-report difference is partly caused by women replying in accordance with female sex stereotypes.

On extraversion, on the other hand, the questionnaire measure produces no gender differences, but several aspects of extraverted social behaviour show females as more extraverted, for instance in non-verbal behaviour. However, females may have stronger affiliative needs, at least they did in 1976, if not in 1957 (Veroff et al. 1980). And women certainly have stronger needs for intimacy (McAdams 1988).

We turn now to examine several spheres of cooperation, to find out if there are any gender differences.

Gender differences in children's cooperativeness

Knight and Chao (1989) compared the ways in which boys and girls from 3−12 preferred to divide things up: the girls were consistently more cooperative and egalitarian, the boys more competitive. Boys and girls separate and play mainly apart between the ages two and 11, presumably because they want to play in different ways. It has often been found that boys are more aggressive and dominant, more physically active, have more rough-and-tumble play, while girls are concerned with social relationships, are more sensitive and have greater empathy. Boys play in larger groups, which are inevitably hierarchical, while little girls prefer to talk to close friends, getting to know each other, and exchanging self-disclosures. Pepitone (1980) studied mixed volleyball games in several hundred 11-year-old schoolchildren. She found that the boys took a much more active part, making nearly twice as many good throws. As Gilligan (1982) observed:

From the games they play, boys learn both the independence and the organisation skills necessary for coordinating the activities of large and diverse groups of people. By participating in controlled and socially approved competitive situations, they learn to deal with competition in a relatively forthright manner – to play with their enemies and compete with their friends – all in accordance with the rules of the game. In contrast, girls' play tends to occur in smaller, more intimate groups, often the best-friend dyad, and in private places.

However, girls are quite able to play competitive games – but in their own way. A study of 27 11–12-year-old girls and 12 boys playing a ball game over a two-year period, found that the girls talked a lot about 'being nice', 'friendly' and 'not mean'. However, they were also competitive, in a way described as 'nice-mean' and playing 'in-style', which may have resolved the conflict between competition and being nice, and excused the fact that they often lost to the more singleminded boys (Hughes, in press).

In classroom work girls like cooperative tasks more than boys do, and do better at their work than boys under cooperative conditions.

Cooperation in laboratory tasks

It is widely believed that women are more concerned with social relationships, and are more cooperative than men, as shown by studies of gender stereotypes. However, on the Prisoners' Dilemma Game, as we have seen, over 100 studies have found that *men* are more cooperative, though this is often interpreted in terms of men being more risky, women more cautious (see p. 210). Recent studies have investigated gender differences in social dilemmas (n-person PDG), using strangers, but with real money, where if enough people sacrificed five dollars, all would gain 10 dollars. Women were a little more cooperative than men (69 per cent v. 66 per cent, and 47 per cent v. 37 per cent) in two experiments. However, more women said that they were motivated by principles and altruism, and concern for harmonious group relations. The authors conclude that while women are more cooperative than men, the actual difference is smaller than gender stereotypes suggest (Stockard *et al.* 1988).

Helping behaviour, altruism and empathy

Are women more helpful than men? In laboratory experiments on masculinity-femininity it was found that women, and those of either sex high in femininity, were more likely to look after a baby or be kind to a lonely student. Women are more helpful inside the family, especially, of course, in looking after children, and in being sympathetic listeners and providers of social support for husbands (Vanfossen 1981). Within the wider family, it is women who hold the whole structure together, by keeping in contact with each other, giving presents, remembering birthdays, and looking after family members. Women are more often employed in the helping professions, such as nursing and social work, do voluntary work in the community, and occupy 'helpful' jobs in organisations, such as secretaries and research assistants. The skills acquired in these roles may lead to help on other occasions; for example, looking after children.

However, research on helping has concentrated on helping strangers in public situations − for example, where an experimental confederate has collapsed on the underground − and here men do more. Eagley and Crowley (1986) carried out a meta-analysis of studies involving 37,000 subjects in all, and found that men helped more, especially on occasions which fitted the traditional male 'chivalrous' role, that is, helping women, when there was an audience, where danger was involved, other helpers were available and where male skills were needed.

There are substantial gender differences in empathy. One study found that females scored 39.6 and males 16.6 on the Mehrabian and Epstein scale. The same study found that empathy correlated -0.53 with a masculinity-femininity scale, correlating especially with items like 'cries easily', and 0.41 with a femininity scale, especially for items like 'warm in relations with others' (Foushee et al. 1989).

Assertiveness and leadership

Using the Bales or similar categories, women make more socio-emotional moves, while men make task ones, and also initiate more. Men interrupt more (96 per cent in one study), give more orders and rapidly develop stable dominance hierarchies in groups. Women's groups are more egalitarian and cooperative. In groups which initially do not have leaders, men more often emerge as overall leaders, but women more often emerge as social leaders or 'facilitators' (Eagly: meta-analysis, personal communication). A meta-analysis carried out by Eagly of 371 comparisons between male and female styles as appointed leaders found that overall women were somewhat more interpersonally oriented than men, and used a more democratic or participatory style than men. These differences were greater in laboratory experiments and in assessment centres − where relatively untrained leaders were studied, and smaller in organisational settings, where both male and female leaders would have been trained and subjected to the same organisational pressures.

Research on assertiveness, as we have just seen, finds that trainers recommend, and experimental subjects regard as acceptable, a skilled form of assertiveness which takes account of the needs of both sides (see p. 200). It is also found that women are much more concerned with obligations to others. They think that it is important in assertive situations not to threaten others, to be friendly, and not to hurt others' feelings (Wilson 1989).

Verbal communication

Analysis of male and female conversation again finds the greatest difference between same-sex pairs or groups. Women are more active in keeping conversations going, by asking more questions, using more 'tag-questions' (such as 'didn't I?') probably to increase solidarity, and more back-channel signals ('uh-huh') to show interest and attention. While men talk more during the formal part of meetings, women talk as much or more during informal periods. The topics of male and female conversation are also different. Women are said to engage in gossip and trivial topics, and so they do, except that this is important. Women engage in more self-disclosure, and thus achieve greater intimacy than men. Men are more concerned with dominance and status, but they may achieve intimacy and have fun in other ways, by jokes or tall stories, and mildly aggressive banter and teasing (Aries 1987). The whole pattern of female conversation is of cooperation towards the goal of friendship and social support. Men are less obviously cooperative, but they are more concerned with the task anyway; perhaps the formation of a stable hierarchy, with the most competent person in charge, is the most effective way of doing things.

Non-verbal communication

Women emit more positive non-verbal signals: they smile more (50 per cent more of the time in one study), are more expressive in face and hands, look more, and sit or stand closer. This all adds up to a pattern of positive social approach, the same as in extraverts, the opposite of what is found in the lonely and socially withdrawn. The findings about perception of non-verbal communication are also interesting: women look relatively more at faces, the most controlled area, and attend less to tone of voice and bodily movement – the leakier channels. Women have been described as 'polite decoders', since they see what they are intended to see, whereas men attend more to unintended messages. This gender difference is most marked if same-sex pairs are compared, so one explanation has been in terms of male and female subcultures. When women are together they are cooperative, trusting and non-deceptive, where men are competitive, deceptive and try to dominate and outwit one another (Hall 1984).

Summary

All these areas of behaviour show the same pattern. Women seek close, supportive, social relationships, are warm, considerate and trusting, and prefer intimate egalitarian relationships. They could be described as cooperative in the interpersonal sphere, especially with friends and family. Men, on the other hand, are more assertive and independent, prefer larger and hierarchical groups, and are more concerned with tasks than women are. They are less involved in interpersonal activities, and their concern with tasks and group games is often competitive, but also cooperative, though in a non-egalitarian way.

Origins

Why do males and females have these different patterns of behaviour?

1 *Innate differences.* Throughout the animal kingdom females look after children, and males form dominance hierarchies. In all human primitive cultures females look after families, while males cooperate over large tasks, and in governing the community. It is possible that there are some innate, evolved differences here. Some of the gender differences in non-verbal communication may also be innate; for example, women are more accurate receivers at all ages, and the sex difference does not change with age; little girls are very interested in faces (Argyle 1988).

2 *Different parental treatment of boys and girls.* This is perhaps the main source of gender differences. It has been repeatedly found in Britain and the USA that parents allow boys greater independence, have higher expectations for independent task performance, encourage them to compete and not to show their feelings. Parents are warmer towards girls and closer to them, punish them less, encourage physical activity less, and look after them more closely (Huston 1983). This may explain why girls seek closer relationships, but not why boys enjoy larger, more hierarchical groups.

3 *Male and female subcultures.* We have seen that gender differences are greatest when same-sex pairs or groups of males and females are compared. This has led to the theory that there are male and female subcultures. We have seen that women are more 'polite' decoders of non-verbal communication. In verbal communication too women follow different rules, seeking close and equal relationships, showing more concern with friendship and social support than with tasks. Other studies have found that women are most cooperative when with other women, that they are less dominant, condescending and businesslike on TV shows towards other women (Hall 1984). The whole style of female behaviour with other women has a special quality – affiliative, open, rewarding, pleasant, trusting and non-deceptive. Among men, on the other hand, there is greater concern with dominance and competition, and behaviour is more deceptive (Maltz and Borker 1982).

4 *Sociological factors.* But why should there be different male and female subcultures? Men, in the past at least, have usually been dominant and more powerful, and their style of behaviour reflects this. There has traditionally been a major division of labour, where women's work is in the house, men's is outside, men's talk and behaviour are centred on work and decision-taking, women's on looking after members of the family (Aries 1987). Men have to cooperate too, and there is a growing awareness of the importance of interpersonal relationships and social skills at work (Argyle 1989). Nevertheless, the position of women, supported by the kind of

childrearing described above, has resulted in women being the ones concerned with relationships, and in being more cooperative.

Conclusions: What have we learnt about the psychological basis of cooperation

To start with, cooperativeness is commonly recognised as a personality trait, part of a broader trait which can be called 'agreeableness'. It can be measured directly in game situations. The psychological test which comes closest is probably Crandall's Social Interest scale, which has good correlations with cooperation on the PDG, ratings by peers, empathy, volunteering for unpaid help, and negatively with measures of self-centredness and hostility. Empathy, the capacity to share the emotions and see the point of view of others is an important component: it has good correlations with helping behaviour, and clear origins in socialisation.

However, there is a second personality dimension, extraversion, which is independent of social interest and empathy, and which is important for cooperation, in the spheres of friendship and synchrony of social interaction. If Social Interest is a cognitive ability, extraversion is partly a social skill, partly social motivation. The needs for intimacy and affiliation are similar; they have a correlation with rated cooperativeness, and with cooperation in friendship and synchronised interaction, with the avoidance of competition and conflict. Extraversion has a physiological and genetic basis; the needs for affiliation and intimacy are also known to have physiological links. All are connected with the immune system.

Collectivism is possibly a third aspect of cooperation: concern with and generosity towards members of the in-group of family and friends. It is not known how this is related, if at all, to our first two dimensions. And authoritarians, known for their hostility to *out*-groups, would probably score high on this factor, thus creating failure of cooperation beyond the immediate group.

What about those individuals who are very uncooperative? Criminals have low scores on Social Interest (Crandall 1980); psychopaths are known to be very low in empathy. Extraversion is almost a self-report measure of social skill, so those who are socially isolated are likely to have low scores, just as those in occupations like teaching and sales have high scores. Most mental patients are lacking in social skills, and they are very uncooperative. Affiliative motivation predicts affiliative behaviour, but the effect is greater if social skills are also taken into account (McClelland 1987).

On the subject of social skills, it is possible that cooperation is at the heart of many of them, a point hitherto unrecognised. We saw in Chapter 5 how close synchrony and coordination is necessary for social interaction. We saw in Chapter 2 how negotiators have to take account of the goals of both sides. Research on the social skills of leadership has shown how leaders should take account of the needs of subordinates. These are skills which are more closely associated with our second dimension, extraversion and affiliation, rather than with the first, Social Interest and empathy, though they seem to require empathy. How does extraversion, which is partly genetic and which has a clear physiological basis, become associated with social skills? One possible route is suggested by Gray's model (1982). If extraverts amplify rewards, and if other people are the main source of rewards during early childhood, an extraverted individual is drawn to approach people, and is rewarded for successful attempts to deal with them.

Chapter eleven

Promoting cooperation between members of different groups

Common failures of cooperation between groups

Most of the cases of cooperation which have been described so far have been between members of fairly small groups. However, it is notorious that cooperative groups often fail to cooperate with other groups, and that people behave in a less positive and helpful way to members of other groups, and to members of other broad categories of class and nationality.

Effects of conflict between groups

There is extensive evidence to show that people not only favour members of their own group, but are prejudiced against and hostile to those from other groups. Sherif (1961) proposed that this was because of 'realistic conflict' between groups. This theory was supported by his 'robbers' cave' experiment at a summer camp, with 12-year-old boys. New groups were formed by putting boys together in huts so that most of each boy's friends were in the other group. There was evidence of some in-group favouritism as a result of being in the same huts, but this was greatly increased when tug-of-war and other contests were arranged between two groups, and there was real hostility when one group appeared to have frustrated the other. In this and other experiments it has consistently been found that when there is competition, group members think that the products of their own group are superior, and this is especially strong for members of the winning team or group.

On a larger scale war leads to great hostility and prejudice against members of the other side; in the case of British against Germans and Japanese in World War II it took several years before these attitudes subsided. There is a great deal of conflict in industry, between workers and unions on the one side and owners and managers on the other. There is real conflict here; for example, over levels of wages, and laying off workers when work is short. This conflict is manifested in strikes, stoppages, go-slows and even sabotage. There are also conflicts between different groups of workers, who may see themselves as competing for pay and status.

A second source of inter-group conflict is difference in power or status (usually both) between two or more groups. The reason is simple: when there is unequal status the superior group are able to regard the other group or groups as inferior; the low status groups resent their low position and feel hostile towards higher status groups. When there are power differences too, low status groups resent the capacity of other groups to control them.

The most obvious case of status difference is in relations between different racial groups. Usually there are status differences between black and white, or there can be a complex pecking order of ethnic groups, as in the USA and South Africa. Differences between social classes are very similar. In Britain there is a social hierarchy of accents, from 'received pronunciation' downwards, corresponding to differences of social class (Giles and Powesland 1975). One way in which inequality leads to hostility is simply via social norms. Another group, whether higher or lower in status, will have different styles of behaviour (including accent), and is thus seen to deviate from the norm of the in-group. One's own group seems normal, or even universal, and all others are seen as deviates in comparison.

Experiments have thrown further light on antipathy as a result of different power or status. Sachdev and Bourhis (1985) found that in-group bias increased the more power the group had. In several experiments it has been the high status or high power group which showed the most bias. The effect is greater if the status difference is 'illegitimate', that is, undeserved, which is quite irrational in the case of high status groups (Caddick 1982). Low-status groups show little in-group bias in experiments, if the status differences are believed to be legitimate and stable, that is, not likely to change. But if the differences are seen as illegitimate and unstable, low status groups 'may start to assert themselves by displaying in-group favouritism and a rejection of the dominant group's "superiority" ' (Brown 1988).

There is widespread prejudice and holding of negative stereotypes towards members of racial minority groups, and between different ethnic and subcultural groups – blacks and whites in South Africa and the USA, Protestants and Catholics in Northern Ireland, Arabs and Israelis. There is realistic conflict in some of these cases, especially over status and access to good jobs, housing, and other aspects of prosperity. However, there are some important additional features to this kind of conflict. Each group has a long history, which it may feel legitimates its claim to territory or other rights (like Israelis and Afrikaners), or is the basis for complaints of persecution (like black Americans and Roman Catholic Irish). The high status group can thus validate its favoured position, and the low status group can validate its hostility. This cultural history is taught to the young, is included in education, and is celebrated in marches and other ceremonies, even in the religion.

One of the reasons that people dislike other racial and cultural groups is that it is believed that they hold different beliefs and values, think differently, and are therefore incomprehensible, not quite human. Rokeach *et al.* (1960) found that similarity of beliefs was a more important factor than similarity of race, when subjects were asked for their attitudes towards various target persons, presented by verbal descriptions or by photographs. Brown and Abrams (1986) carried out an experiment in which 12-year-old schoolchildren cooperated or competed in groups with children from another school. In both conditions they liked the other children better and cooperated more if told that they had similar attitudes about the relative importance of various school subjects. In the case of culturally different groups the difference may be much more profound than this, and it is likely that people think members of some other groups are different because they communicate and interact differently, a point we shall explore later.

Furthermore, members of different groups are clearly recognisable (even in Northern Ireland), by accent or appearance, and it is easy to categorise people by their obvious group membership, and apply stereotypes to them. There is a tendency to exaggerate the homogeneity of the out-group, and its differences from the in-group, partly since there is little contact with out-group members, who may all 'look the same'. In Britain and the USA hostile racial attitudes and the holding of negative stereotypes is much greater among uneducated people, perhaps because education dispels some hostile myths about other groups, and exposes students to the variations within other racial groups.

Racial attitudes are not just a matter of social norms and socialisation however, since some people in the same community are much more prejudiced than others. These are individuals with an 'authoritarian personality', that is they have rigid ways of thinking, divide other people into good and bad, dislike deviates and members of other groups, especially low-status groups, have often been frustrated themselves, for example, by downward social mobility or other economic failure, and had parents who used punitive methods of discipline without explanation. The frustration may have been from another, more powerful group, but the aggression can be displaced onto a weaker target, such as a racial minority group.

The components of in- and out-group attitudes

Cognition

We have seen that stereotypes are formed, especially about out-groups, and that they usually include negatively-evaluated components. Stereotypes involve the assumption that the out-group is homogenous, more so than the in-group. The main reason for this is that people usually have much less contact with members of other groups, indeed sometimes none at all, and so are not aware of the variability among the members. Different attributions are made to in- and out-group members. For out-group members, good behaviour is given an external attribution, bad behaviour internal, and the opposite for in-group members. Hewstone et al.(1982) asked boys from state and public schools to explain success by one of their own or the other group. Public schoolboys who succeeded were thought to have done it by ability when judged by their own group, but by luck when judged by state schoolboys. Public schoolboys thought that if one of their group failed this was due to not working hard enough, but for a state schoolboy to lack of ability.

Affect

This is at the heart of in- and out-group attitudes: we like one and dislike the other, we evaluate one positively, the other less so. However, things are a little more complex than this. Brewer and Campbell (1976) carried out a survey of 50 members each of 30 tribes in East Africa. Most tribes gave more favourable ratings to their own tribes on scales with some evaluative content, such as 'honest', 'peace-loving', 'virtuous' and 'liking'. On the whole tribes liked adjacent tribes more than non-adjacent ones, and gave them higher ratings – a clear case of social contact leading to liking, perhaps because there would be more trading links. On the other hand, more conflict was also reported with these adjacent tribes – more contact also produces more scope for friction.

Behaviour

Sissons (1981) found English people were much more likely to refuse a request to give change from an Asian requester, though only for same-sex requesters. American studies have shown similar reluctance to help blacks who have collapsed and are in need of help. Sociobiologists explain this in terms of 'inclusive fitness', that is looking after one's own genes and those who share them. There is sometimes aggression towards out-groups, but some studies have found no relationships between in-group favouritism and aggression (Struch and Schwartz, 1989). Football fans appear to behave very aggressively towards the other side's supporters, but most of this turns out to be display and symbolic aggression, intended to humiliate rather than to hurt (Marsh et al. 1978). For aggression to occur, there probably has to be a serious threat, insult or attack.

The effects of categorising people as members of different groups

We have seen how people like and think highly of the members of their own group, and are prejudiced towards and dislike members of other groups. However, so far we have described only groups in some kind of conflict with each other. There is growing evidence that something similar can occur

Table 11.1 Two sample matrices from minimal group experiment

	Reward numbers													
Matrix 1														
Member 72 of Klee group	18	17	16	15	14	13	12	11	10	9	8	7	6	5
Member 47 of Kandinsky group	5	6	7	8	9	10	11	12	13	14	15	16	17	18
Matrix 2														
Member 74 of Klee group	25	23	21	19	17	15	13	11	9	7	5	3	1	
Member 44 of Kandinsky group	19	18	17	16	15	14	13	12	11	10	9	8	7	

Source: Brown 1988

Note: On each page subjects must choose one pair of numbers.

without conflict. Stereotyping is an economical way of summarising social knowledge and providing expectations about members of different groups – except that they often turn out to be mistaken. But why are stereotypes about other groups nearly always negative, compared with those for the in-group? Tajfel (1978) in his 'social identity theory' suggested that it is because our self-image and self-esteem depend partly on the groups to which we belong, so we do our best to see our groups as distinctive and superior in some way to other groups. Tajfel and his colleagues carried out 'minimal group' experiments in which subjects were allocated more or less at random, for instance, by their preferences for the artists Klee and Kandinsky, into 'groups' (which never met) and were asked to allocate rewards to members of the different groups; they always showed favouritism to members of their own group. They were asked to decide how money or points should be allocated, using the kinds of matrix shown in Table 11.1. Typical choices would be 14/9 or 13/10 in favour of a member of the subject's own group.

Moving to real groups, Brown (1978) studied workers in an engineering factory and asked for their preference between different wage settlements. All preferred a situation where they were paid £1 per week more than another department, even though this meant losing £2 a week themselves – £67.30 per week for themselves and £66.30 for the rival department, rather than £69.30 for themselves and £70.30 for the others. The differential was more important than the actual wages (see Table 11.2).

Table 11.2 Matrix used to measure inter-group differentiation in wage comparisons

	Wages				
Toolroom group	£69.30	£68.80	£68.30	£67.80	£67.30
Production and Development groups	£70.30	£69.30	£68.30	£67.30	£66.30

Source: Brown 1978

Gaskell and Smith (1986) interviewed 206 young people, and asked which social groups they felt they belonged to. The answers were 'youth', 'black', 'unemployed' and so on. It was found that the higher the social status of the membership group, the more important was this group to its members – confirming the idea that groups are a source of self-esteem. Young blacks saw their own group as of higher status than that of blacks in general. Mummendey and Simon (1989) found that *out-group* favouritism could take place, on dimensions which were unimportant to the in-group, but important to the out-group, and on which the latter were superior.

However, some of the key predictions from the theory have not always been confirmed. Oakes and Turner (1980) and others found that self-esteem was greater for subjects who were asked to make discriminations between members of different groups in this way. But the results of later studies have not been so clear-cut (Messick and Mackie 1989). Brown *et al.* (1986), in a study of different groups in a factory, tested the hypothesis that identification with the in-group would lead to low evaluation of the out-group, but this gave a very weak prediction: perceived conflict was much more powerful.

It has often been said that attraction towards the in-group goes together with, or results in, prejudice towards out-groups. It is true that when there is competition between two groups, positive bias in favour of the in-group, and negative attitudes towards the out-group develop at the same time, as was found in Sherif's study. And attraction to the in-group produces over-evaluation of this group's products, but it does not lead to under-evaluation of other groups. Dion (1973), using pairs of subjects playing the Prisoners' Dilemma Game, manipulated how similar they believed each other to be, and found that cohesiveness produced increased cooperative choices towards an in-group member, but no reduction of these towards an out-group subject.

Nevertheless, Social Identity Theory does have some possible applications to the reduction of inter-group prejudice. The most obvious application is to weaken the tendency to classify people as members of the two groups, like Jews and Gentiles. Wilder (1986) made a number of suggestions about how this could be done; for example, emphasising cross-cutting categories (like age, class, occupation), and merging two groups into a larger group by removing physical cues like spatial location or appearance. Gaertner *et al.* (1989), in a similar study, found that merging two laboratory groups in this way reduced discrimination against the other group by increasing attraction to it; making members think of themselves as individuals was also effective, but by reducing attraction towards the original group.

I would like to suggest that another explanation for the rejection of out-groups is that they are difficult to communicate and interact with. Critical incident surveys of instances when visitors have got into trouble in another country have produced lists of problems, which have later been built into inter-cultural training courses (see pp. 233ff.). Furnham and Bochner (1986) asked 150 foreign students in England about the difficulties they had experienced in 40 social situations. Greater difficulty was experienced the more remote and culturally different the country of origin. This and other studies show that people often have serious difficultures in the following areas:

1 language
2 non-verbal communication
3 rules of situations
4 rules of relationships
5 social skills, of managing various everyday encounters.

These will be discussed later, in connection with training courses for other cultures.

The effects of sheer contact between groups

The 'contact hypothesis' states that sheer contact between members of two groups is all that is needed to produce positive attitudes between them. Impressive evidence to this effect appeared to be provided from studies of the effects of belonging to mixed black and white companies in the American Army in World War II. Among those who had been in these companies, 64 per cent of white soldiers thought this was a good general policy, compared with 18 per cent of those who had not (Star *et al.* 1965); 51 per cent of black soldiers felt less hostile to whites than before. The recent situation in the US Army, however, is that extensive race relations training is needed to make desegregation work (Landis *et al.* 1984). Desegregated housing is moderately successful. Deutsch and Collins (1951) found that there were usually regular and intimate contacts and relationships between black and white neighbours in the USA, in mixed communities; however, most communities are *not* mixed. Hamilton and colleagues (1984) found that when a black family moved into a white suburb the initial reaction was unfavourable, but that attitudes improved after a year – not as the result of any contact since there was very little, but more because some fears and stereotypes had been disconfirmed. In a big survey in Amsterdam, it was found that the overall effect of housing proximity led to improved attitudes, but also anxiety, irritation and concern, for both Surinams, and for Turks and Moroccans. Frequency of superficial meetings was associated with positive results for both groups, but more intimate contacts – home visits – were associated with positive effects for Surinams, but negative effects for Turks. It seems that close contact with Turks was found too difficult or threatening to the Dutch way of life (Dijker 1987).

Desegregation of schools in the USA was pushed through in the hope that attitudes on both sides would improve. Stephan (1978) reviewed 80 follow-up studies, and concluded (p. 217) that:

(a) desegregation generally does not reduce the prejudices of Whites towards Blacks,
(b) the self-esteem of Blacks rarely increases in desegregated schools,
(c) the achievement level of Blacks sometimes increases and rarely decreases in desegregated schools, and
(d) desegregation leads to increases in Black prejudice towards Whites about as frequently as it leads to decreases.

The main reasons for this failure was that black children did not do very well in class, partly through lack of confidence, partly through lack of verbal skills and other abilities. However, a number of classroom experiments have produced successful results, by using cooperative learning tasks of various kinds, without attempting to equate the ability of white and nonwhite children; low achievers were not rejected under these conditions (Johnson *et al.* 1983, and pp. 101ff.).

Comparison of successful and unsuccessful experiences of contact between groups led social scientists to specify exactly what form this contact should take: it was hypothesised, for example, that it should be equal status, cooperative, intimate, prolonged, and have wider social support; a lot of research has been directed to this issue. The contact hypothesis has been criticised on other grounds, in particular that contact often does not lead to generalisation of positive attitudes to other members of the out-group, apart from those actually encountered. Nevertheless, there has been sufficient faith in the hypothesis for a number of special training methods to have been built on it; for example, cooperative classroom methods, which will be described later.

Equal status has long been regarded as essential: prejudiced and hostile attitudes will be reinforced if members of one group are always in a subordinate position. However, equal status is very difficult to achieve, if there are societal differences, for example between white and black in the USA; attitudes carry over, and whites are more active and influential and dominant. It has even been suggested that change of attitude must come first. Various solutions have been tried – matching mixed classroom groups on ability, giving the subordinate group special coaching, or introducing other sources of status on which the low status group does well. Things are easier in institutional settings, since status depends mainly on job or rank. Harding and Hogrefe (1952) found that attitudes of white department store employees to black workers were more positive, though not much more positive, if there had been equal status contact. Of those who had experienced equal status contact 77 per cent were willing to work in this way, compared with 62.5 per cent of those who had unequal status contact and 48 per cent of those who had no contact with blacks in the store.

Another approach is to arrange for contact with higher-status members of the low-status or minority group; in the US Army, only contact with equal or higher status blacks led to reduced prejudice (Mackenzie 1948). This can add to difficulties of generalisation if such high-status members are not typical, though it can help to break up unfavourable stereotypes.

Experience of cooperation and interdependence will be described in the next section, as one of the main ways of improving relationships between groups. It is effective, but the conditions have to be right. It has been carried out successfully in small-scale studies by Sherif and others, and embodied in several training methods. The main doubt, as we shall see is how far it can succeed with larger groups.

Intimacy. This has often been proposed as an important condition for contact to be successful. It has been suggested that contact should be 'inter-personally' rather than task-oriented. Some of the main failures of contact have been at work. An example from a department store was given above. Another is Minard's finding (1952) that black and white American coal-miners worked together perfectly well down the mine, but did not seek each other's company outside for sociable or leisure purposes. The mixed platoons perhaps created a greater degree of intimacy, or perhaps inter-dependence. Another possibility is that sheer size is a factor. There is more discontent and there are more industrial disputes in larger factories, where contacts between management and workers are more impersonal and bureaucratic (Ingham 1967). It has been found that the larger the factory, the more management attribute leftwing, pro-union attitudes to workers, and vice versa – presumably because they know one another less well (Allen and Stephenson 1983).

Wider social support, for inter-group contact is another likely condition. Inter-group contact may be difficult to produce, and any effects limited if the wider society gives it no support. In industry, for example, managers and workers often have real, conflicting interests, eat in different dining rooms, and earn quite different salaries, so that sheer contact is going to have limited benefits. Similarly, different ethnic, religious, and social class groups may go to different schools, live in different neighbourhoods, even speak different languages, as in Quebec. They may have to live in separate districts by law, as in South Africa. And there may be immense differences of prosperity, housing and opportunities. Nevertheless there can be informal friendships across these divisions. Surveys in Northern Ireland show that in mixed communities there are friendships between Catholics and Protestants. However, inter-group workshops there have been quite unsuccessful (Trew 1986).

Generalisation. We have seen that inter-group contact in the American Army was successful in changing racial attitudes. This was also found on mixed ships. The main failures have been in ordinary work settings. The workers in a mixed department store did not eat together, and miners used different eating places and neighbourhoods above ground. There can also be failure to generalise any changed attitudes to other members of the other group, as Cook (1984) found from his experiments on experiences in cooperative work groups.

It may be suggested that working together is not intimate enough: it requires no self-disclosure, or getting to know others in more than a super-ficial way, often little dependence on one another – though there is in coal-mines. There are a number of leisure activities which might do better than work – team sports, dancing, music, camping, and other highly enjoyable group activities, needing close cooperation.

Wilder (1986) arranged meetings with members of a second, rather dif-ferent, college. More positive evaluation of the other college resulted if the other student behaved in a pleasant way, *and* appeared to be typical, and matched stereotypes of that college (see Figure 11.1).

Figure 11.1 Evaluation of an out-group after contact with a typical or atypical out-group member

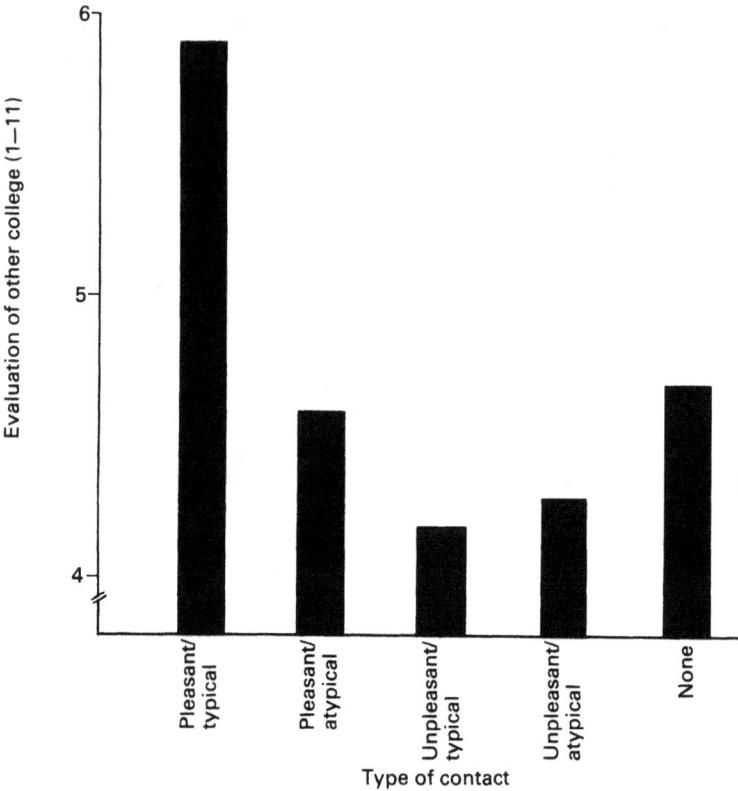

Source: Wilder 1984

Other studies have shown that for generalisation to take place, people have to meet members of the other group who are not only believed to be 'typical', but who are also varied, and who do not display common negative stereotypes (Stephan 1985) – if it is possible to achieve all this at the same time.

It is often the case that one group is, in worldly terms, of higher status or power than another group. The low status group can deal with this in a number of possible ways. Several kinds of 'social creativity' are possible, and have been found in experiments. These are: discovering new dimensions for comparison, on which the in-group does better, deciding that certain attributes which the group possesses are good rather than bad (like 'black is

228

beautiful'), and selecting different out-groups for comparison purposes. This opens the way to a kind of cooperation, where each side selects for emphasis the dimensions where it does well. An example is that South African Hindus see themselves as superior to the whites in spiritual, social and practical spheres, though the whites no doubt see the Hindus as inferior in wealth and social status (Mann 1963). A similar possibility is that cooperation between different groups can make use of a division of labour, reflecting the actual strengths of different groups (Turner 1981).

Why does contact lead to liking?

Most investigators have assumed that it is through changes in knowledge, including greater understanding of the culture of the other group, greater awareness of differences within the group, or information correcting negative stereotypes about the other group. Education and propaganda have been shown to be capable of producing positive effects, but only if done rather skilfully. For example, if the distinctive features of the other group are explained, this has to be done in a way to prevent it from being seen as inadequate and needs to be supplemented by materials showing similarities with the in-group. Sheer contact is likely to increase information about the other group, and this is one possible explanation. Stephan and Stephan (1984) report studies with Anglo and Spanish-speaking schoolchildren in New Mexico. Frequency of contact correlated 0.19 with Anglo knowledge of Chicano culture, which in turn correlated 0.24 with favourable attitudes towards them. This is consistent with a modest causal sequence as suggested, though other explanations are also possible.

However, 'interaction leads to liking' is one of the oldest laws in social psychology, and various explanations of it have been offered in the past. One of these is Zajonc's theory that sheer frequency of exposure to any stimulus increases liking of that stimulus, and there is some experimental evidence that this works for exposure of black faces, though only if shown in a positive context. Certainly sheer exposure has done absolutely nothing for race relations in South Africa or the USA. Other research suggests that sheer frequency of interaction leads to liking only if there is sufficient similarity; people often do not like their neighbours very much, probably because they are often not similar enough.

Another explanation of why interaction leads to liking, is that it gives those involved more time to get to know one another, in establishing patterns of interaction which are rewarding, in finding common interests and possibilities of cooperation, and in greater self-disclosure. It is important to note that interaction does not always lead to liking, though it usually does: some people are 'incompatible', in having different styles of interaction, different interests, different opinions and beliefs (Argyle 1969). It seems very likely that this process, which works for two individuals, could also work for whole groups, in that members of one group become accustomed to the special styles of interaction and concerns of a second group. This could have three effects: first, material help by members of the other group; this is important for foreign students who need locals to show them the ropes; second, self-esteem, being accepted, approved of, by members of a second group – who have no need to do so; third, the establishment of synchronised and coordinated interaction is itself rewarding, and in this case also an achievement.

The effect of cooperative experiences

Cooperation has been used in two ways to improve inter-group relations – cooperation *within* groups of mixed membership, and cooperation *between* groups.

Cooperation within groups

Aronson *et al.* (1978) devised the 'jig-saw classroom', intended to create the optimum conditions for improving attitudes to another group. Groups of six children are formed, including Anglo, Mexican-American and black. Each pupil is taught part of the materials needed for a group project, and then teaches the others; the teachers just help. There is no competition between groups, they meet three times a week for six weeks, and the pupils are marked individually. The results of several follow-up studies were that the jig-saw pupils increased in liking for the other ethnic groups more than those in ordinary classes. They also liked school more and increased in self-esteem.

Another version was devised by DeVries, Edwards and Slavin (1978). Academic tournaments are held between teams of four to five, each containing a mix of races and abilities. The teams hold practice sessions and help each other for the classroom tournaments. In a study of 1,187 pupils, those in the programme achieved a lot more than those taught traditionally, especially in language learning. More important, from our point of view, there were more cross-race friendship choices and interactions during free time.

Johnson and colleagues (1984) carried out meta-analyis of 31 studies of black and white classes in school, and 26 studies of handicapped and non-handicapped classes. The effect of cooperative rewards, compared with competition and individual rewards on inter-group interpersonal attraction is shown:

	black/white	handicapped/normal
cooperative v. competitive	0.54	0.86
cooperative v. individualistic	0.68	0.96

(these figures are ratios of the standard deviation)

Cook (1984) devised cooperative work experience, in mixed black and white groups, incorporating what he thought were the key features which should generate positive attitudes. Groups were formed, consisting of prejudiced whites and blacks of equal educational standing; they were paid to work for sessions of two and a half hours a day for 20 days, on a railway management game; informal lunch-break conversation was encouraged, and the task itself required cooperation; they thought that they were competing against another team. This experience was partially successful, in that 40 per cent of the prejudiced whites showed a real change of attitude, compared with 12 per cent of a control group. Later studies of a similar kind by Cook and others found that members of the low status group were rejected if they were incompetent and the group failed. This is an important problem: if the group fails, there is a danger that minority group members may be blamed. This can be avoided by making sure that they are of equal ability, and that they are not in a minority (Stephan 1985).

Meanwhile, the studies by Cook and others showed that even for very prejudiced whites, nearly half underwent a considerable attitude change after sheer social contact with blacks – provided that the conditions were right.

Cooperation between groups

As we saw earlier, Sherif (1961) created conflict between pairs of groups of boys, by physical segregation, competition and mutual frustration. He then succeeded in restoring good relations between the groups by creating 'superordinate goals'; for example the truck which was to take them back to camp 'broke down' and had to be pulled – pulling together on the same rope which had recently been used in a tug of war, but pulled in opposite directions. Sherif proposed that what was needed was a state of affairs where 'a number of individuals (without previously established interpersonal relations) interact with one another under conditions (a) which situationally embody goals that have common appeal value to the individuals, and (b) which require interdependent activities for their attainment'. Is this the solution to inducing cooperation between groups?

Worchel and his colleagues carried out an important series of laboratory experiments on this matter. Their procedure was to form groups of six to 10 (four in one version) student subjects, who sat round a table in the lab, and worked on a number of tasks. In a second stage two such groups were put together in the same room, and given either cooperative or competitive goals. With the cooperative goal all would receive 50c if the large group did well enough; with the competitive goal only the members of the most successful subgroup would get 50c. All of these experiments found that liking for the other group increased in the cooperative condition. However, this effect was much stronger if the whole group was successful; if it was not, subjects tended to blame the other group. In another experiment, half the subjects tended to blame the other group. In one experiment, half the subjects were put in what was described as a poor environment; here failure did not impair liking of the other, since the environment could be blamed.

In another version, one group wore white coats; this increased in-group attraction, and retarded attraction towards the other group following failure, but did not hinder increased attraction after success (Worchel 1979). Worchel *et al.* (1989) set up pairs of groups of three to do problem-solving tasks, either independently or competitively. In a second phase one group either offered to cooperate with or to help the second: regardless of the prior condition, the second group were more attracted to a group which offered to cooperate rather than to help. While these experiments are very interesting, they did not deal with real group memberships, with long histories of in- and out-group feelings behind them. However, similar results were obtained by Brown and Abrams (1986) in an experiment in which children from two different schools were told either that prize money would depend on the joint performance of the two schools, or that it would go to members of the school which did best. Where the children also thought that the other school was similar in status and attitude, cooperation led to liking.

These positive results from cooperation can be contrasted with the negative effects sometimes produced by helping, either of individuals or nations. The recipient of help will have a negative attitude toward the helper if (a) there is an implication that the person or group helped is less competent, (b) if helping reduces autonomy, freedom of action, or (c) if it is not possible to reciprocate in any way. Furthermore, the motivation to help may be based on this 'dark side' of helping – to seek self-esteem (Fisher *et al.* 1982).

Moving further into real-life inter-group problems, Brown (1978) asked workers in an engineering factory what they would do if the management declared 10 per cent redundancy. He expected that as active trade unionists they would favour a cooperative strategy, but only 20 per cent of workers did, the majority being primarily concerned with defending their own group. Brown later noted a similar failure of large-scale groups to cooperate among the centre parties in British politics in the 1980s. In each of these cases existing groups seem to be mainly concerned with their own welfare and identity, rather than what could be gained by cooperation with other groups. It looks as if the Sherif superordinate goal solution may only be effective in linking rather small social groups. Part of the story may be that groups want to keep their own identity, within the larger one. Brown and Wade (1987) found that there was greater friendliness towards a merged out-group, paid to work on a joint magazine project, if the two groups were given distinctive roles, i.e. cooperated with a division of labour.

Training to deal with other groups

A number of methods of training have been devised, and are in current use, for those going abroad, and in some divided communities. They have been overlooked by research workers in the inter-group tradition, probably because that approach does not have very clear applications for actually ameliorating group conflict situations. These training methods have drawn on two other traditions in social psychology – social skills training and the study of cultural differences in social behaviour (Bochner 1982).

Education and propaganda

Ignorance, misinformation and stereotyping are causes of prejudice towards other groups. It follows that education should be a way of changing such attitudes. Many follow-up studies have been carried out to test the success of films, lectures and other educational methods in improving racial and other inter-group attitudes. A film followed by lecture or discussion is quite successful; lectures are better in small groups and with a prestigious speaker; using several methods is best. Attitude changes have been found in most studies, though the effects are often small and people can easily avoid such propaganda (Stephan 1985). However, it is possible that this avenue has not been fully explored. There is no doubt that cleverly designed propaganda is effective in other spheres, like marketing and politics, so it seems possible that it might be effective here too. Perhaps it should be designed better – to show the basic similarities of the other group, to show its achievements and contributions, to show the range of individuals in it, for example. The inter-group model may be able to make its contribution in the design of such propaganda: this theory suggests de-emphasising the labels distinguishing the two groups, and instead focusing on other categories as described earlier (see p. 224).

Education in this area often emphasises the achievements of the other group – though this must not be overdone – and the similarities of the other group – though there may be obvious differences. The more time is spent on such educational activities, and the greater variety, the more effective they are. The most successful used active involvement, such as role-playing, and this will be discussed later (Stephan and Stephan 1984).

A specialised form of teaching which has been devised for inter-group education is the Culture Assimilator. A 'critical incidents' survey is carried out first of a large sample of difficulties experienced with the other group. This leads to locating 40–100 types of incidents, which are then embodied in a tutor text which takes six to eight hours to work through: each incident is presented as a problem.

One day a Thai administrator of middle academic rank kept two of his assistants about an hour for an appointment. The assistants, although very angry, did not show it while they waited. When the administrator walked in at last, he acted as if he were not late. He made no apology or explanation. After he was settled in his office, he called his assistants in and they all began working on the business for which the administrator had set the meeting.

(Brislin and Pederson 1976: 90–1)

Several explanations are offered, of which the correct one is: 'In Thailand, subordinates are required to be polite to their superiors, no matter what happens, nor what their rank may be'. A number of Culture Assimilators have been constructed, mainly to teach Americans about other cultures, including that of black Americans, also for Australians and Aboriginals. The contents convey a lot of information about the rules, ideas and social relationships of the other culture. Follow-up studies have found positive, though modest improvements in, for example, behaviour in mixed racial groups, though not much change in prejudice (Brislin and Pedersen 1976).

A convenient way of providing information about the other group is in the form of booklets written for tourists. These are sometimes well informed and can be very helpful. Amir and Ben-Ari (1985) studied the effects of reading a booklet about Egyptians for Israeli tourists; visiting Egypt made Israelis on average less pro-Egyptian, but this effect was reduced for those who had read the booklet.

Training based on cultural differences

Cross-cultural research in social psychology has found a number of areas in which styles of social behaviour are different and thus liable to be sources of friction. Training can be based directly on such findings, and may take the form of education or special workshops for those going to work abroad.

Non-verbal communication (NVC)

There are some major differences in this area. In some areas mistakes can lead to the offender being killed.

1 *Proximity, touch, and gaze.* People from non-contact cultures find those from contact cultures disturbingly over-close, and vice versa. Hall (1966) first noticed the difficulty of establishing an agreed distance with Arabs and Latin Americans at international meetings; they appeared to chase a retreating American or European, who would back to a more suitable distance, or rotate to establish a less directly facing position. Greeks (and probably others) are upset when coming to England because people do not stare at them in public and they feel they are being ignored.

2 *Expressiveness.* We find the Japanese difficult because they seem to be so inscrutable, but find blacks disturbing because of their readiness to express negative emotions and attitudes.

3 *Different meanings of gestures.* Violence may result in Greece and southern Italy from using obscene or offensive gestures, like the 'horns'.

4 *Accompaniments of speech.* Black Americans often annoy white interviewers or supervisors by their apparent lack of response while listening.

5 *Symbolic self-presentation.* The meaning of clothes, badges or uniforms may be obscure, with the result that mistakes are made about another's status or occupation.

6 *Rituals.* It is easy to cause offence through ignorance of rules or etiquette – seating guests at the wrong place at table, not bringing gifts, and so on. Pike (1967) reports the case of a missionary girl who got into difficulties with a cannibal chief because she tried to throw him on the floor (shook hands) and laughed at him (smiled). Westerners in Africa and the east often have difficulty in coming to terms with what they regard as dishonest bribery, but which is seen by locals as the customary exchange of gifts.

It is possible to include training in NVC in inter-cultural training. For example, Collett (1971) trained a number of English males to use the NV style of Arabs – closer proximity, touch, high level of gaze and so on. Arabs who met them liked them much more than members of a control group who had merely learnt about the River Nile. At the very least trainees need to know which gestures, or other aspect of NVC, will cause offence, and perhaps to prevent trainees taking unnecessary offence themselves.

Rules

Many difficulties which are experienced abroad are due to not knowing the local rules of behaviour. Here are some of the rules which often cause problems for people working abroad.

1 *Bribery.* In many parts of the world it is normal to pay a commission to civil servants, salesmen or professional people who have performed a service, although they are already receiving a salary. Sometimes there is a regular fee, such as 1–3 per cent of sales. This is regarded locally as a perfectly normal exchange of gifts but in Europe and North America it is often illegal and unethical. Various devices are resorted to in overseas sales, such as paying a 'sales commission' to an intermediary who uses some of the money for a bribe.

2 *Nepotism.* In Africa and other countries people are expected to help their relatives, and this is the local equivalent of social welfare. Sometimes relatives have contributed to an individual's education; when he gets a good job as a result they expect some return. If he is a civil servant or

manager, such favours are regarded by others as nepotism and greatly disapproved of. In fact there are usually local rules which limit the forms which these favours can take.

3 *Gifts.* In all cultures it is necessary to present relatives, friends or work colleagues with gifts on certain occasions, but the rules vary greatly. The Japanese spend a great deal of money on gifts, which must be bought from standard gift shops so that their value can be ascertained and a gift of the same value returned. The gift is not opened in the presence of the giver and a small token present is given immediately in return (Morsbach 1977).

4 *Buying and selling.* There are several alternative sets of rules here: barter, bargaining, fixed-price sales and auction. In cultures where bargaining is used it is normal to establish a relationship first, perhaps while drinking tea, and there are conventions about how the bargaining should proceed.

5 *Eating and drinking.* One of the main problems in ICC (inter-cultural communication) is that there are rules in all cultures about what may not be eaten or drunk, especially certain kinds of meat – like pork, beef or dog – and alcohol. There may be very strong penalties for breaking these rules; for example, those for consuming alcohol in some Arab countries. There are rules about how the eating is performed – with knife and fork, chopsticks, right hand and so on. There are also extensive rules about table manners – when to start eating, how much to leave, how to obtain or refuse a second helping and so on.

6 *Rules about time.* How late is 'late?' This varies greatly. In Britain and North America, one may be five minutes late for a business appointment, but not 15, and certainly not 30 minutes late, which is perfectly normal in Arab countries. On the other hand, in Britain it is correct to be five to 15 minutes late for an invitation to dinner. An Italian might arrive two hours late, an Ethiopian later and a Javanese not at all – he had accepted only to prevent his host losing face (Cleveland *et al.* 1960). A meal in Russia at a restaurant normally takes at least three hours. In Nigeria it may take several days to wait one's turn at a government office, so professional 'waiters' do it for you.

The other side of the coin is that visitors to Britain are likely to have trouble with our not knowing the proper rules of etiquette (Japanese), not liking to form queues, and so on.

Social relationships

In all cultures there are husbands and wives, friends, workmates, supervisors, subordinates and so on, but the ways in which these relationships are conducted may be very different. We carried out a study of relationship rules in Japan, Hong Kong, Italy and England. We found, for example, that in the East there are more rules about obedience, avoiding loss of face, maintaining harmonious relations in groups, and restraining emotional expression (Argyle *et al*. 1986). Other studies show that in cultures outside North America and Western Europe the social distance between levels in hierarchies may be much greater (for instance, in most of Europe), loyalty to primary groups may be greater (China, Japan), it may be almost impossible to speak to women (Arab culture), or sex may be readily available. Friendships may be formal and very demanding (Australian 'mates'), great respect may be paid to elderly relatives (China), and the social networks may be very important (India). In modern societies in the West marriage has changed towards greater equality, and hierarchical work relations to greater use of participation and persuasion.

Language

This is the greatest single barrier between different groups: if two groups cannot communicate, obviously it will be very difficult for them to cooperate or get to know each other. Knowing another group's language is a matter of degree, and it has been found in the USA that the adjustment of overseas students is greatly affected by competence in the language, and in Canada the lack of interaction between English- and French-speaking Canadians is partly due to lack of language skills. There are also variations in language with social class or region which can create communication difficulties, and also mark individuals clearly as belonging to different social classes or other groups. We saw earlier that accommodation may take place, if there are positive attitudes already, but accommodation is only possible for those who can speak in the accent or speech style of the other group.

Languages vary in their polite, colloquial usage. Most cultures have a number of forms of polite usage, which may be misleading. These may take the form of exaggeration or modesty. Americans ask questions which are really orders or requests ('Would you like to . . . ?'). And in every culture, in many situations, there are special forms of words, or types of conversation, which are thought to be appropriate – for example, to ask a girl for a date, to disagree with someone at a committee, to introduce people to each other and so on. Americans prefer directness, but Mexicans regard openness as a form of weakness or treachery, and think one should not allow the outside world to know one's thoughts. Frankness by Peace Corps volunteers in the Philippines leads to disruption of smooth social relationships (Brein and David 1971).

There are cultural differences in the sequential structure of conversations. The nearly universal question-answer sequence is not found in some African cultures where information is precious and not readily given away (Goody 1978). In Japan it is rude to say 'no', therefore wrong to ask a question for which this might be the answer. Saying 'no' may be avoided simply by changing the topic, while 'yes' can mean 'no' or 'perhaps'. Saying 'no' would lead to loss of face by the other. Therefore, indirect forms of negation may be used, such as serving a banana (an unsuitable object) with tea to indicate that a marriage was unacceptable (Cleveland *et al.* 1960). The episode structure of conversations varies a lot: Arabs and others have a 'run-in' period of informal chat for about half an hour before getting down to business.

Intercultural workshops

These are fairly intensive courses for training for adults, sometimes from one culture to learn about another, sometimes drawn from two cultures. Kelman and Cohen (1979) describe a series of such workshops carried out at Harvard, designed for influential individuals, though in a private capacity, and drawn from two or three cultures, such as India, Pakistan and Bangladesh. The trainers were neutral, in this case Jewish. The three groups met both separately and together, and spent their time analysing the problems and looking for solutions. Although no quantitative follow-up was carried out, there was a clear impression that a common terminology was developed, and that each side understood better and accepted the claims and points of view of the others. This method has been used for a number of other conflicts around the world (Stephan 1985).

Role-playing, including role reversal, has been used, mainly with children and students. For example, white schoolchildren play the role of being black, and have the experience of being discriminated against. In other versions trainees role-play various cross-cultural encounters, or quite complex roles such as that of a black policeman at the Watts riot. These methods have been used to give greater insight into cultural differences, and the problems of people in other groups. It is also possible to teach trainees the social skills needed in the other culture (Furnham and Bochner 1986). A good example of this is a scheme by La Fromboise and Rowe (1983) to teach American Indians the skills they need to cope with encounters with white Americans. Standard social skills training methods were used – modelling and videotape playback – and training in non-verbal communication was included.

The BAFA-BAFA game is intended to teach sensitivity to any other culture. It is now marketed as a game. Two teams of about 10 are needed, and they spend the first hour learning two arbitrary 'cultures'. One is authoritarian and warm, permission is needed from a leader before a conversation can begin, and it must start by talking about a male relative. The other culture is cold and competitive, devoted to making money by a card game; no speech is allowed, only a new gesture language. A series of visitors are then exchanged; at first these get on badly and are rejected, but gradually each culture learns about the other, and later visitors are more successful.

Integrated schemes

Most serious programmes of inter-cultural training have used a combination of methods. For example, the Peace Corps established a centre in Hawaii for those going to South East Asia, with a replica Vietnamese village complete with water buffaloes. The training included (Guthrie 1966):

1 basic linguistics, so that trainees could pick up local dialects quickly; later this was replaced by teaching specific dialects
2 lectures by experts on different aspects of the new culture
3 physical and survival training at the Puerto-Rican jungle camp; later this was replaced by training in the culture itself.

The American Navy built up a number of three-day courses; for example, for those going ashore in Japan. These included lectures, role-playing and a field trip, but no language learning, and were quite successful.

In Britain training for diplomats and other high-level visitors abroad is given at Farnham Castle. In addition to educational materials such as books and films, there are meetings with returned expatriots and, where possible, natives of the area to be visited. Similar schemes for managers include case studies of typical management problems likely to be encountered; training is often provided for wives – who may otherwise be the first to crack in a foreign posting.

The role of mediating persons

If members of group A are being trained to deal with group B, it is useful to have a trainer who is familiar with the cultures of both groups, who feels comfortable and is accepted by both. Such people have been called 'mediating persons' by Bochner (1981) – 'people who have the ability to act as links between different cultural systems, bridging the gap by intoducing, translating, representing and reconciling the cultures to each other'. Trainers are often this kind of person; there are others – for example, tour guides.

Interpreters are a special kind of mediating person, in that they are familiar with two or more languages, and can translate one into another. To do this well requires some depth of understanding of each culture as well, since the ideas and thought categories of each culture are embodied in the language. Mediating persons often have to be interpreters too.

It is the ultimate goal of inter-cultural training that as many people as possible shall become mediating persons. Hutnik (1986) studied Asian students in Birmingham, and asked about their preference for English and Indian friends, food, clothes and music. While many had a clear preference for one or the other, about 25 per cent liked both, and can thus be regarded to some extent as mediating persons, who are evidently quite common in this community.

Chapter twelve

Conclusions

An extended definition of cooperation

We offered a new definition which includes social activity at work, leisure and in relationships, and coordination over joint activities, communication and social interaction. This extends cooperation to include encounters and relationships where the goal and end-product is simply the relationship itself, or is the joint activity, as in making music. It also includes communication and interaction, where the cooperation consists of coordination, in the service of other goals. There is a sense in which *all* social behaviour is cooperative, since in the most minimal case it takes two to send and receive a message; however, some situations, relationships and cultures are more cooperative than others.

Criticism of the rational economic model

We have discussed several spheres where the economic model does not seem to work. One of these is helping behaviour and altruism. Even in the animal kingdom there are many cases of cooperation and help where there is no gain to the individuals concerned, and where there can be considerable loss or risk. Examples are the giving of warning calls, helping another animal in a fight, grooming another, and sharing food. We have seen how such instances can be explained by evolutionary mechanisms like inclusive fitness and reciprocal altruism.

The rational economic model also fails for close relationships. We have seen that in romantic love, family, and other close or 'communal' relationships, people are not primarily seeking rewards for themselves, but are concerned for the welfare of the other, and for the relationship itself.

People also become bonded, or attached, to organisations and this results in further non-rational or non-economic activity. In studies of 'organisational commitment' among industrial workers, it is found that this depends partly on the expectation of future rewards, but also on affective and non-instrumental attachment to the organisation (Argyle 1989). Involvement and action on behalf of leisure, voluntary and professional organisations depends partly on rational assessment of costs and benefits, but also on affective bonding and internalisation of values.

There are individual differences in such non-economic concern for individuals or groups. Karylowski (1982) devised a projective test in which a subject chooses the reasons why individuals in pictures might help another. One category of reasons he called 'exocentric' – concern with the needs of the other.

Adler (1979) thought that patients benefit from becoming involved in concerns directed towards others and to tasks, which he called 'social interest' or 'feeling of community'. Erickson (cited by Wallach and Wallach 1983) managed to cure the disengagement of an expert card-player by playing crazy games of cards in front of him. 'One would be playing poker, another bridge, another pinochle. One would say, "What's wild?" the other would reply, "I'll bet you two trump." They put one card on another with no reference to each other.' Eventually he could stand it no more and organised a proper game of cards. Social interest has subsequently been developed into an individual difference measure, which predicts cooperativeness.

The main types of cooperation

We have surveyed a wide range of types of cooperation, and suggested a classification of them, as follows:

1 For work, for external rewards, usually because the job is too large for one person alone. However, this leads to social relationships between workers.
2 In some close relationships there is no such external goal:
  (a) *Family*. Here there is a kind of 'biological cooperation' to look after each other, and to produce and educate the next generation; however, this behaviour is motivated by sexual and other motivations rather than by remote group goals.
  (b) *Friends*. There is some mutual help and a lot of conversation, but the main activities are leisure, where the product is the performance itself.
3 Interaction and communication require a special kind of cooperation, often called 'coordination', in the service of other joint goals and activities.

These kinds of cooperation are found in all human societies, including those labelled 'individualistic' or 'competitive' by anthropologists. The early rational economic model of shared group goals only applies to the first kind.

Criticism of early experiments

The Prisoners' Dilemma Game and similar experimental procedures have very limited application, since they simply do not fit most cases of real-life cooperation. It takes some ingenuity to think of any such situations, apart from the original one with the two prisoners, in which two people have to make simultaneous choices, in ignorance of what the other will do, and without any communication with each other. The 'tragedy of the commons' *does* have more obvious parallels to situations where people can choose to pay taxes or bus fares, or to drop litter and so on, but this is more a matter of conformity and public morals than cooperating with other individuals.

Are humans innately cooperative?

There is no doubt that we are generally cooperative in the ways listed above. Animals are cooperative too, and for them this is almost entirely unlearnt, the product of evolutionary processes. But it does not follow that human cooperation has the same origins – it could be due to socialisation, and to social evolution. It can be argued that some aspects of human evolution fit the predictions of evolutionary models. For example, we help our kin a great deal, we are much less likely to harm biological children compared with adopted or stepchildren, and in promiscuous societies men do more for the children of their sisters than those of their wives. However, some of these findings could be explained in other ways; concern for children could be due to early attachment processes rather than to shared genes.

The coordination found in social interaction provides stronger evidence for unlearnt processes. Interaction depends on the possession of equipment for social signalling – faces and voices, and the muscles to operate them; this is certainly unlearnt. And infants in the first days and weeks of life show an impressive readiness to communicate, interact and relate to other people. There is a great deal of learning, mainly in the course of close interaction with the mother or other caretaker, but this rests on a foundation of innate equipment and primitive social responsiveness.

The social evolution and learning of cooperation

All kinds of cooperation have a universal, possibly innate, part which is much the same in all cultures. In addition there are variations between cultures, showing the effects of historical development, or social evolution, passed on not by genes but by socialisation and education.

In all cultures people cooperate over work, for jobs which need more than one person. In modern societies work is carried out in large and complex organisations, with a management hierarchy, rules, incentives and the rest. 'Workers' cooperatives', based on simple ideas of cooperation and equality, often fail, especially if there is no clear leadership structure. Families everywhere have marriage, parents and children, siblings, who eat together and share living quarters and property. But there are cultural variations in who may marry, where they live when they do, how many wives or husbands are allowed, and how many relatives are recognised. Such rules have important consequences; for example, exogamy leads to bonds being formed between different groups. Friendship between non-kin is found everywhere, but again with variations. In Australia, for example, the institution of 'mateship' developed, partly because of a shortage of women in the early days in the bush, and because of the need for a reliable companion under harsh conditions.

Variations in social interaction and communication are perhaps smaller. There are different languages in different cultures, but they all have a similar structure. There is some variation in non-verbal communication – for example, different gestures – but the main signals of face and voice do not vary much. And social interaction is very similar in all cultures, apart from some variations in the amount of back-channel signals and rules of politeness.

Whole societies have been compared for their overall level of cooperativeness. Even for very simple primitive societies this is not easy, since those societies judged to be individualistic or competitive are also cooperative in many ways, as we have seen. It is possible to measure 'collectivism' in modern societies by survey methods, and this corresponds to greater attachment to immediate groups of family and friends, but not to wider groupings. Many attempts have been made to create ideal cooperative and egalitarian communities; the kibbutz is perhaps the most successful example, but there are many tensions there now. Such communities have only proved possible on a fairly small scale, below 500 adults. They need firm socialisation of children, a strong ideological commitment, and a clear social structure. The sharing of property, in units larger than the family, is often a point of tension.

What are the benefits of cooperation?

The most obvious benefit is that many things are possible which otherwise could not be done at all: at work – large tasks; in the family – the procreation of children; among friends – most leisure activities. Some things which could be done alone are done better: at work – division of labour leads to more expert performance, and group decisions are found to be better decisions; in the family – two can cope better than one, if only because someone is needed to mind the nest while someone else looks for food; among friends – sport and games, music and most other leisure activities, where they could be done alone, attain a higher level of complexity and satisfaction when done with other people.

Cooperation produces immediate emotional rewards; evolution has favoured such rewards for biologically important activities. In cooperative working groups job satisfaction is greater; in couples, sex causes intense joy and married people are happier than unmarried; meetings with friends are a major source of joy. Cooperation leads to joy because the others provide help, affection and social support, and because positive verbal and non-verbal messages are received, and because affiliative needs are satisfied.

There are benefits for health and mental health. Social support at work reduces the effect of stress on mental health; married people are in better health and mental health, and live longer; and the rate of heart attacks is lower in collective cultures and communities. The explanation is partly that cooperative social support helps to cope with stress or makes it less stressful; it removes negative emotions and loss of self-esteem. Individuals with strong intimacy needs are found to have stronger immune systems, suggesting a more fundamental biological reward for cooperation.

Cooperation also creates social bonds with the others concerned. In working groups where there are cooperative incentives, or an interdependent work-flow, people like each other more; in families the close cooperation over mutual care leads to life-long bonding; many friends are drawn from leisure settings where there has been cooperation over sport, music or dancing. Part of the explanation is that cooperation involves help, so that the others behave in a rewarding way and are therefore liked; the experience of collaborating over shared goals may be an additional factor. Close synchrony of behaviour, it has been suggested, is a basic biological source both of joy and attachment.

Individual differences in cooperativeness

Some individuals are definitely more cooperative than others, as assessed by their performance at laboratory games, ratings of their real-life behaviour, and by self-report questionnaires. Such people are judged to be more socially skilled, and cooperation is an essential part of all skills, including assertiveness and leadership. Among familiar personality dimensions, extraversion has the highest correlation with cooperation; the needs for affiliation and intimacy also correlate. This kind of sociability is partly innate, as shown by twin studies, partly the result of early attachment to mothers. Empathy is another predictor, and one that is unrelated to extraversions. Empathy could be regarded as a kind of ability, extraversion more a kind of social motivation.

Women are in some ways more cooperative than men. They have higher scores on empathy (but not on extraversion), and their whole social style is more directed to the formation of close relationships, rather than to hierarchical ones or to task activity.

Coming back to cooperation as part of social competence, what exactly are the social skills required?

1 Extraversion suggests that general positive motivation is important – the desire to interact and relate to other people, the capacity to be rewarding to them.
2 Empathy suggests sensitivity to the emotions, thoughts and situations of others, resulting in a concern for their welfare.
3 The cooperative skills involved in leadership, assertiveness and negotiation include the skills of integrating the goals of the two sides, so that an integrative solution is found in which both benefit.
4 The study of interaction and communication skills shows the importance of skilled synchronising. Socially unskilled people are often deficient at this level of cooperation.

Applications of research on cooperation

Social skills training

SST is widely practised for mental patients and in professional skills training for teachers, doctors and others. In the case of patients, the level of success has been modest, less than some of us had previously hoped. Many neurotic patients are lonely and isolated, difficult to get on with. They are often egocentric, lack interest in other people, can't see others' points of view. They are lacking in rewardingness and fail to deliver positive non-verbal signals. They are poor at assertiveness, and often lacking in synchronising skills. This adds up to a general failure of cooperativeness, and suggests some new kinds of therapy. One is training in cooperative groups, by using group incentives, combined with the usual coaching and video playback. Another is micro-SST, using slowed-down videotape, to give detailed feedback at the micro level.

Inter-group conflict

We have seen that most approaches to this problem have had rather limited success or none at all. The study of cooperation defines the problem as extending cooperation beyond the confines of the in-group to embrace members of other groups as well. Sheer social contact is successful, but only under the right conditions; one of these conditions is that it should be cooperative. Success is reported with the jig-saw classroom and similar experience of cooperation with other ethnic groups at school. Part of the problem may lie in the difficulties of interacting with people from another culture, with a different language, different no-verbal signals and so on. Success has been obtained in training people to work abroad, by inter-cultural training, and the same methods could be used for relations with ethnic or other groups at home.

Human nature and morals

We have seen that in many ways human nature is cooperative. We are more like ants and wolves than like cats. We readily join groups and form attachments, and receive powerful biological and emotional rewards for doing so. Our cooperative tendencies are culturally universal, partly innate, the result of evolution.

We have seen that human beings are not entirely egoistic, and we have argued that earlier economic models of men were mistaken. Animals often behave in an altruistic way, and we too form social relations where there is great concern for others.

Our behaviour is partly directed by rational considerations and calculations, but partly not. When riding a bicycle we may plan what is the best route to take, but have little conscious insight into how to stay upright. If we count the rewards and costs we are usually more aware of the immediate ones than of the long-term consequences of cooperative behaviour. While the long-term consequences of sex are fairly well known, the consequences of marriage rules are not.

Cooperation is only partly the result of genetic evolution; it is partly due to social evolution, passed on by socialisation, and encouraged by social rules. Rules develop, like the rule of the road, because they solve problems and enhance the general good. We have seen that the informal rules of relationships include rules about being cooperative, in general and in detail. Politeness rules give some specific guidance about how to be cooperative in social life. Some of these rules have an emotive, moral quality, such as rules about helping, and looking after people in close relationships.

In addition to rules, skills have to be learned, in order to be able to cooperate effectively. This is particularly true at the level of interaction and communication. Grice's 'cooperative principle' looks like a set of rules, but can better be seen as a guide to conversational skills. Some interaction skills are at a micro level, governing the detailed synchrony and coordination of verbal and non-verbal signals. Special training may be needed for those who get these wrong.

Earlier psychological theories assumed an egoistic and non-cooperative model of man, and encouraged the seeking of individual rewards. Psychoanalytic theory not only assumed it, but popularised the view that people should not be repressed, and should satisfy their needs. Later clinical theories, such as those of Maslow and Carl Rogers, encouraged people to fulfil themselves by 'self-actualisation' – but without any reference to other people (Wallach and Wallach 1983). Exchange theory offered a view of relationships, even close relationships, which supposes that partners seek the best balance of rewards over costs that they can get. We have seen that these views are wrong as empirical accounts, and it follows that the moral guidance offered is also mistaken.

Recent research with laboratory games has offered another basis of morals – tit-for-tat, a new version of 'an eye for an eye and a tooth for a tooth'. This is said to be better than unconditional reciprocity, since non-cooperators will be punished (Axelrod 1984). I have objected to the empirical foundations on which tit-for-tat is based, and have tried to show that cooperation is a different and more complex matter. How then should non-cooperators be dealt with? As shown above, the social evolution side of cooperation has produced rules, and rules often have sanctions. On the other hand, training in the necessary skills may be more useful than punishment.

Research on helping behaviour by social psychologists is more in line with Christian ethics than with the Jewish approach of tit-for-tat. However, we have seen that people often help partly to demonstrate their superior competence, and that help is not always gratefully received if the recipient feels humiliated or constrained, and it can lead to a hostile relationship between helper and helped. A cooperative relationship, including mutual help, in the course of joint action, has more positive consequences.

Christian ethics commands us to 'love our neighbours as ourselves'. In practice we do a lot for members of our in-group, that is family, close friends, and sometimes neighbours, but are much less willing to do anything for members of other groups, and sometimes dislike them very much. Ways of reducing such prejudice towards out-groups were discussed above, and this can be regarded as a moral problem too, a topic for rules. Again, rules and punishments are not enough, it is necessary to acquire the right skills too.

References

Abrams, P. and McCulloch, A. (1976) *Communes, Sociology and Society*, Cambridge: Cambridge University Press.

Adams, B.N. (1968) *Kinship in an Urban Setting*, Chicago: Markham.

Adler, A. (1979) *Superiority and Social Interest: a Collection of Later Writings*, H.L. Ansbacher and R.R. Ansbacher (eds), 3rd edn, New York: Norton.

Ainsworth, M.D.S. (1989) 'Attachments beyond infancy', *American Psychologist* 44: 709–16.

Ainsworth, M.D.S., Blehar, M.C., Water, E. and Wall, S. (1978) *Patterns of Attachment*, Hillsdale, N.J: Erlbaum.

Alexander, R.D. (1979) *Darwinism and Human Affairs*, Seattle: University of Washington Press.

Allan, G.A. (1979) *A Sociology of Friendship and Kinship*, London: Allen & Unwin.

Allen, P.T. and Stephenson, G.M. (1983) 'Inter-group understanding and size of organisations', *British Journal of Industrial Relations* 21: 312–29.

Amir, Y. and Ben-Ari, R. (1985) 'International tourism, ethnic contact, and attitude change', *Journal of Social Issues* 41: 105–15.

Arbric, J.C. (1982) 'Cognitive processes underlying cooperation', in V.J. Derlega and J. Grzelak (eds) *Cooperation and Helping Behavior*, New York: Academic Press.

Argyle, M. (1969) *Social Interaction*, London: Methuen.

—— (1975, 1988) *Bodily Communication*, London: Methuen.

—— (1983) *The Psychology of Interpersonal Behaviour*, 4th edn, Harmondsworth: Penguin.

—— (1987) *The Psychology of Happiness*, London: methuen.

—— (1989) *The Social Psychology of Work*, 2nd edn, Harmondsworth: Penguin.

Argyle, M. and Cook, M. (1976) *Gaze and Mutual Gaze*, Cambridge: Cambridge University Press.

Argyle, M. and Furnham, A. (1982) 'The ecology of relationships: choice of situation as a function of relationship', *British Journal of Social Psychology* 21: 259–62.

—— (1983) 'Sources of satisfaction and conflict in long-term relationships', *Journal of Marriage and the Family* 45: 481–93.

Argyle, M. and Henderson, M. (1985) *The Anatomy of Relationships*, London: Heinemann and Harmondsworth: Penguin.

Argyle, M. and Lu, L. (in press) 'The happiness of extraverts', *Personality and Individual Differences*.

Argyle, M., Graham, J.A., Campbell, A. and White, P. (1979) 'The rules of different situations', *New Zealand Psychologist* 8: 13–22.

Argyle, M., Furnham, A. and Graham, J.A. (1981) *Social Situations*, Cambridge: Cambridge University Press.

Argyle, M., Henderson, M. and Furnham, A. (1985) 'The rules of social relationships', *British Journal of Social Psychology* 24: 125–9.

Argyle, M., Henderson, M., Bond, M., Contarello, A. and Iizuka, Y. (1986) 'Cross-cultural variations in relationship rules', *International Journal of Psychology* 21: 287–315.

Aries, R. (1987) 'Gender and communication', in P. Shaver and C. Hendrick (eds) *Sex and Gender: Review of Personality and Social Psychology*, 7: 149–76, London: Sage.

Aronson, E., Blaney, N., Stephan, C., Sikes, J. and Snapp, M. (1978) *The Jigsaw Classroom*, Beverly Hills: Sage.

Aronsson, K., Jönsson, L. and Linell, P. (1987) 'The courtroom hearing as middle ground: speech accommodation by lawyers and defendants', *Journal of Language and Social Psychology* 6: 99–115.

Austin, J.L. (1962) *How to do Things with Words*, Cambridge, Mass.: Harvard University Press.

Avedon, E.M. and Sutton-Smith, B. (eds) (1971) *The Study of Games*, New York: Wiley.

Axelrod, R. (1984) *The Evolution of Cooperation*, New York: Basic Books.

Axelrod, R. and Hamilton, W.D. (1984) 'The evolution of cooperation in biological systems', in R. Axelrod *The Evolution of Cooperation*, New York: Basic Books.

Badhwar, N.K. (1987) 'Friends as ends in themselves', *Philosophy and Phenomenological Research* 48: 1–23.

Bakan, D. (1966) *The Duality of Human Existence*, Boston: Beacon.

Barker, R.G. and Wright, H.F. (1955) *Midwest and its Children*, New York: Harper & Row.

Barnett, M.A. (1987) 'Empathy and related responses in children', in N. Eisenberg and J. Strayer (eds) *Empathy and its Development*, Cambridge: Cambridge University Press.

Baron, R.A. (1986) *Behavior in Organizations*, 2nd edn, Boston: Allyn & Bacon.

Batson, C.D. (1987) 'Prosocial motivation: is it ever truly altruistic?' *Advances in Experimental Social Psychology*, 20: 65–122.

Batson, C.D., Fultz, J. and Schoenrade, P.A. (1987) 'Adults' emotional reactions to the distress of others', in N. Eisenberg and J. Strayer (eds) *Empathy and its Development*, Cambridge: Cambridge University Press.

Baumann, G. (1987) *National Integration and Local Integrity*, Oxford: Clarendon Press.

Baumrind, D. (1980) 'New directions in socialization research', *American Psychologist* 35: 639–52.

Beattie, G.W. (1983) *Talk: An Analysis of Speech and Non-verbal Behaviour in Conversation*, Milton Keynes: Open University Press.

Bem, S.L. (1974) 'The measurement of psychological androgeny', *Journal of Consulting and Clinical Psychology* 42: 155–62.

Ben-Rafael, E. (1988) *Status, Power and Conflict in the Kibbutz*, Aldershot: Avebury.

Bentler, R.M. and Speckart, G. (1979) 'Models of attitude–behavior relations', *Psychological Review* 86: 452–64.

Berkman, L.F. and Syme, S.L. (1979) 'Social networks, host resistance, and mortality: a nine year follow-up study of Alameda county residents', *American Journal of Epidemiology* 109: 186–204.

Bernstein, B. (1959) 'A public language: some sociological implications of a linguistic form', *British Journal of Sociology*, 10: 311–26.

Berscheid, E. and Dion, K. (1971) 'Physical attractiveness and dating choice: a test of the matching hypothesis', *Journal of Experimental Social Psychology* 7: 173–89.

Berscheid, E. and Walster, E. (1974) 'Physical attractiveness', *Advances in Experimental Social Psychology* 7: 158–216.

Bethlehem, D.W. (1982) 'Anthropological and cross-cultural perspectives', in A.M. Colman (ed.) *Cooperation and Competition in Humans and Animals*, Wokingham: Van Nostrand.

Bilous, F.R. and Krauss, R.M. (1988) 'Dominance and accommodation in the conversational behaviours of same- and mixed-gender dyads', *Language and Communication* 8: 183–94.

Birch, F. (1979) 'Leisure patterns 1973 and 1977', *Population Trends* 17: 2–8.

Blakar, R.M. (1985) 'Towards a theory of communication in terms of preconditions: a conceptual framework and some empirical explorations', in H. Giles and R.N. St Clair (eds) *Recent Advances in Language, Communication and Social Psychology*, London: Erlbaum.

Bochner, S. (1981) *The Mediating Person: Bridges between Cultures*, Cambridge, Mass.: Schenkman.

—— (ed.) (1982) *Cultures in Contact*, Oxford: Pergamon.

Bond, M.H. and Hwang, K-K. (1986) 'The social psychology of the Chinese people', in M.H. Bond (ed.) *The Psychology of the Chinese People*, Hong Kong: Oxford University Press.

Bowlby, J. (1971) *Attachment and Loss: Vol. 1. Attachment*, London: Pelican Books.

Boyd, R. and Richerson, P.J. (1985) *Culture and the Evolutionary Process*, Chicago: University of Chicago Press.

Bracey, H.E. (1964) *Neighbours*, London: Routledge & Kegan Paul.

Braiker, H.B. and Kelley, H.H. (1979) 'Conflict in the development of close relationships', in R.L. Burgess and T.L. Huston (eds) *Social Exchange in Developing Relationships*, New York: Academic Press.

Brein, M. and David, K.H. (1971) 'Intercultural communication and the adjustment of the sojourner', *Psychological Bulletin* 76: 215–30.

Brenner, M. (1981) 'Skills in the research interview', in M. Argyle (ed.) *Social Skills and Work*, London: Methuen.

Bretherton, I., McNew, S. and Beeghly-Smith, M. (1981) 'Early person knowledge as expressed in gestural and verbal communication: when do infants acquire a "theory of mind"?' in M.E. Lamb and L.R. Sherrod (eds) *Infant Social Cognition*, Hillsdale, N.J: Erlbaum.

Brewer, M.B. and Campbell, D.T. (1976) *Ethnocentrism and Intergroup Attitudes*, New York: Wiley.

Brislin, R.W. and Pederson, P. (1976) *Cross-cultural Orientation Programs*, New York: Gardner Press.

Bronfenbrenner, U. (1970) *Two Worlds of Childhood*, New York: Sage.

Brown, G.W. and Harris, T. (1978) *Social Origins of Depression*, London: Tavistock.

Brown, P. and Levinson, S. (1978) 'Universals in language usage: politeness phenomena', in E.N. Goody (ed.) *Questions and Politeness: Strategies in Social Interaction*, Cambridge: Cambridge University Press.

Brown, Roger (1986) *Social Psychology*, London: Collier Macmillan.

Brown, Rupert J. (1978) 'Divided we fall: an analysis of relations between sections of a factory work-force', in H. Tajfel (ed.) *Differentiation Between Social Groups*, London: Academic Press.

—— (1988) *Group Processes*, Oxford: Blackwell.

Brown, Rupert J. and Abrams, D. (1986) 'The effects of intergroup similarity and goal interdependence on intergroup attitudes and task performance', *Journal of Experimental Social Psychology* 22: 78–92.

Brown, Rupert J. and Wade, G. (1987) 'Superordinate goals and intergroup behaviour: the effect of role ambiguity and status on intergroup attitudes and task performance', *European Journal of Social Psychology* 17: 131–42.

Brown, Rupert J., Condon, S., Mathews, A., Wade, G. and Williams, J. (1986) 'Explaining intergroup differentiation in an industrial organization', *Journal of Occupational Psychology* 59: 273–86.

Bruner, J.S. (1977) 'Early social interaction and language acquisition', in H.R. Schaffer (ed.) *Studies in Mother–Infant Interaction*, London: Academic Press.

Bulmer, M. (1986) *Neighbours: the Work of Philip Abrams*, Cambridge: Cambridge University Press.

Burnett, R. (1986) 'Conceptualisation of personal relationships', D.Phil. thesis, Oxford University.

Buss, D.M. (1988) 'The evolution of human intrasexual competition: tactics of mate attraction', *Journal of Personality and Social Psychology* 54: 616–28.

—— (1989) 'Sex differences in human mate preferences: evolutionary hypotheses tested in 37 cultures', *Behavioral and Brain Sciences* 12: 1–49.

Buunk, B.P., Janssen, P.P.M. and Vanyperen, N.W. (1989) 'Stress and affiliation reconsidered: the effects of social support in stressful and non-stressful work units', *Social Behaviour* 4: 155–71.

Caddick, B. (1982) 'Perceived illegitimacy and intergroup relations', in H. Tajfel (ed.) *Social Identity and Intergroup Relations*, Cambridge: Cambridge University Press.

Capella, J.N. (1981) 'Mutual influence in expressive behaviour: adult-adult and infant-adult dyadic interaction', *Psychological Bulletin* 89: 101–32.

Carroll, D.W. (1986) *Psychology of Language*, Monterey, Calif.: Brooks/Cole.

Chadwick-Jones, J.K. (1976) *Social Exchange Theory*, New York and London: Academic Press.

Chapman, A.J. and Foot, H.C. (eds) (1977) *It's a Funny Thing, Humour*, Oxford: Pergamon.

Cialdini, R.B. and Kenrick, D.T. (1976) 'Altruism and hedonism: a social developmental perspective on the relationship of negative mood state and helping', *Journal of Personality and Social Psychology* 34: 907–14.

Clark, H.H. (1985) 'Language use and language users', in G. Lindzey and E. Aronson (eds) *Handbook of Social Psychology*, New York: Random House.

Clark, H.H. and Clark, E.V. (1977) *Psychology and Language*, New York: Harcourt Brace.

Clark, M.S. (1986) 'Evidence for the effectiveness of manipulation of communal and exchange relationships', *Personality and Social Psychology Bulletin* 12: 414–25.

Clark, M.S. and Mills, J. (1979) 'Interpersonal attraction and communal relationships', *Journal of Personality and Social Psychology* 37: 12–24.

Clark, M.S. and Reis, H.T. (1988) 'Interpersonal processes in close relationships', *Annual Review of Psychology* 39: 609–72.

Clark, R.A. and Delia, J.G. (1976) 'The development of functional persuasive skills in childhood and early adolescence', *Child Development* 47: 1008–14.

Clarke, D.D. (1983) *Langue and Action*, Oxford, Pergamon.

Clarke-Stewart, K.A. (1983) 'Early childhood programs', in P.H. Mussen (ed.) *Handbook of Child Psychology, vol. 2*, New York: Wiley.

—— (1988) 'Parents' effects on children's development: a decade of progress?' *Journal of Applied Developmental Psychology* 9: 41–84.

Cleveland, H., Magone, G.J. and Adams, J.G. (1960) *The Overseas Americans*, New York: McGraw-Hill.

Clutton-Brock, T.H. and Harvey, P.H. (1976) 'Evolutionary rules and primate societies', in P.P.G. Bateson and R.A. Hinde (eds) *Growing Points in Ethology*, Cambridge: Cambridge University Press.

Cochrane, R. (1988) 'Marriage, separation and divorce', in S. Fisher and J. Reason eds) *Handbook of Life Stress, Cognition and Health*, Chichester: Wiley.

Cohn, J.F. and Tronick, E.Z. (1988) 'Mother-infant face-to-face interaction: influence is bidirectional and correlated to periodic cycles in either partner's behavior', *Developmental Psychology* 24: 386–92.

Collett, P. (1971) 'On training Englishmen in the non-verbal behaviour of Arabs: an experiment in intercultural communication', *International Journal of Psychology* 6: 209–15.

Colman, A. (1982a) *Game Theory and Experimental Games*, Oxford: Pergamon.

—— (ed.) (1982b) *Cooperation and Competition in Humans and Animals*, Wokingham: Van Nostrand.

Cook, S.W. (1984) 'Cooperative interaction in multiethnic contexts', in N. Miller and M.B. Brewer (eds) *Groups in Contact*, Orlando: Academic Press.

Costa, P.T. and McCrae, R.R. (1988) 'Personality in adulthood: a six-year longitudinal study of self-reports and spouse ratings on the NEO Personality Inventory', *Journal of Personality and Social Psychology* 54: 853–63.

Coupland, N. (1984) 'Accommodation at work: some phonological data and their implications', *International Journal of the Sociology of Language* 46: 5–32.

Crandall, J.E. (1980) 'Adler's concept of social interest: theory, measurement and implications for adjustment', *Journal of Personality and Social Psychology* 39: 481–95.

Crossley-Holland, P. (1966) 'History of Music', in *Chambers Encyclopedia* 9: 608–21.

Csikszentmihalyi, M. (1975) *Beyond Boredom and Anxiety*, San Francisco: Jossey Bass.

Cunningham, M.R. (1988) 'Does happiness mean friendliness? Induced mood and heterosexual self-disclosure', *Personality and Social Psychology Bulletin* 14: 283–97.

Dabbs, J.M. (1969) 'Similarity of gestures and interpersonal influence', *Proceedings of the Annual Convention of the A.P.A.* 4: 337–8.

Daly, M. and Wilson, M. (1988) 'Evolutionary social psychology and family homocide', *Science* 242: 519–24.

Davis, D. and Perkowitz, W.T. (1979) 'Consequences of responsiveness in dyadic interaction: effects of probability of response and proportion of content-related responses on interpersonal attraction', *Journal of Personality and Social Psychology* 37: 534–51.

Davis, M.H. and Oathout, H.A. (1987) 'Maintenance of satisfaction in romantic relationships: empathy and relational competence', *Journal of Personality and Social Psychology* 53: 397–410.

Dawkins, R. (1976) *The Selfish Gene*, Oxford: Oxford University Press.

Deloache, J.S. and Plaetzer, B. (1985) 'Tea for two: joint mother-child symbolic play', Paper at Society for Research in Child Developmnt, Toronto, April.

Deutsch, M. (1949) 'A theory of cooperation and competition', *Human Relations* 2: 129–39. 'An experimental study of the effects of cooperation and competition upon group processes', *Human Relations* 2: 199–231.

—— (1958) 'Trust and suspicion', *Journal of Conflict Resolution* 2: 265–79.

Deutsch, M. and Collins, M. (1951) *Interracial Housing: a Psychological Evaluation of a Social Experiment*, Minneapolis: University of Minnesota Press.

Deutsch, M. and Gerard, H.B. (1967) *Foundations of Social Psychology*, New York: Wiley.

Deutsch, M. and Krauss, R.M. (1960) 'The effect of threat upon interpersonal bargaining', *Journal of Abnormal and Social Psychology* 6: 181–9.

DeVore, I. (ed.) (1965) *Primate Behavior*, New York: Holt, Rinehart & Winston.

DeVries, D., Edwards, K. and Slavin, R. (1978) 'Biracial learning teams and race relations in the classroom: four field experiments on teams-games-tournaments', *Journal of Educational Psychology* 70: 356–62.

De Waal, F.B.M. (1982) *Chimpanzee Politics: Power and Sex among Apes*, New York: Harper & Row.

Dijker, A.J.M. (1987) 'Emotional reactions to ethnic minorities', *European Journal of Social Psychology* 17: 305–25.

Dion, K.K. and Dion, K.L. (1985) 'Personality, gender and the phenomenology of romantic love', *Review of Personality and Social Psychology* 6: 209–39.

Dion, K.L. (1973) 'Cohesiveness as a determinant of ingroup-outgroup bias', *Journal of Personality and Social Psychology* 28: 163–71.

Dittmar, H. (1989) *Material Possessions and Identity*, D.Phil. thesis, University of Sussex.

Dodge, K.A. (1985) 'Facets of social interaction and the assessment of social competence in children', in B.H. Schneider *et al.* (eds) *Children's Peer Relations: Issues in Assessment and Intervention*, New York: Springer-Verlag.

Dreman, S.B. and Greenbaum, C.W. (1973) 'Altruism or reciprocity: sharing behavior in Israeli kindergarten children', *Child Development* 44: 61–8.

Dunn, J. (1988) *The Beginnings of Social Understanding*, Oxford: Blackwell.

Durkheim, E. (1893, 1960) *The Division of Labor in Society*, Glencoe, Ill.: Free Press.

Eagly, A.H. and Crowley, M. (1986) 'Gender and helping behavior: a meta analytic review of the social psychological literature', *Psychological Bulletin*, 100: 283–308.

Eder, D. (1988) 'Building cohesion through collaborative narrative', *Social Psychology Quarterly* 51: 225–35.

Eisenberg, N. and Miller, P.A. (1987) 'The relation of empathy to prosocial and related behaviors', *Journal of Personality and Social Psychology* 52: 91–119.

Eisenberg, N. and Strayer, J. (eds) (1987) *Empathy and its Development*, Cambridge: Cambridge University Press.

Eiser, J.R. and Bhavnani, K-K. (1974) 'The effect of situational meaning on the behaviour of subjects in the Prisoners' Dilemma Game', *European Journal of Social Psychology* 4: 93–7.

Elder, G.H. (1968) *Adolescent Socialization and Personality Development*, Chicago: Rand McNally.

—— (1974) *Children of the Great Depression*, University of Chicago Press.

Ellis, A. and Beattie, G. (1986) *The Psychology of Language and Communication*, London: Weidenfeld & Nicholson.

Emlen, S.T. (1984) Cooperative breeding in birds and mammals, in J.R. Krebs and N.B. Davies (eds) *Behavioural Ecology*, 2nd edn, Oxford: Blackwell.

Eysenck, H.J. and Cookson, D. (1970) 'Personality in primary school children: 3. Family background', *British Journal of Educational Psychology* 40: 117–31.

Eysenck, H.J. and Eysenck, M.W. (1985) *Personality and Individual Differences*, New York: Plenum.

Farabough, S.M. (1982) 'The ecological and social significance of duetting', in D.E. Kroodsma *et al.* (eds) *Acoustic Communication in Birds*, New York: Academic Press.

Farnsworth, P.R. (1969) *The Social Psychology of Music*, 2nd edn, New York: Dryden.

Feshbach, N.D. and Feshbach, S. (1982) 'Empathy training and the regulation of aggression', *Academic Psychology Bulletin* 4: 399–413.

Festinger, L., Pepitone, A. and Newcomb, T. (1952) 'Some consequences of de-individuation in a group', *Journal of Abnormal and Social Psychology* 47: 382–9.

Firth, R., Hubert, J. and Forge, A. (1969) *Families and Their Relatives*, London: Routledge & Kegan Paul.

Fisher, J.D., Nadler, A. and Whitcher-Alagna, S. (1982) 'Recipient reactions to aid', *Psychological Bulletin* 91: 27–54.

Flanders, N.A. (1970) *Analyzing Teaching Behavior*, Reading, Mass.: Addison-Wesley.

Flinn, M. (1981) 'Uterine vs. agnatic kinship variability and associated marriage preferences: an evolutionary biological analysis', in R.D. Alexander and D.W. Tinkle (eds) *Natural Selection and Social Behavior*, Oxford: Blackwell.

Floderus-Myrhed, B., Pederson, N. and Rasmuson, I. (1980) 'Assessment of heritability for personality, based on a short-form of the Eysenck Personality Inventory: a study of 12,898 twin pairs', *Behavior Genetics* 10: 153–62.

Forgas, J.P. and Bond, M. (1985) 'Cultural influences on the perception of interaction episodes', *Personality and Social Psychology Bulletin* 11: 75–88.

Forys, S.K. and McCune-Nicolich, L. (1984) 'Shared pretend: sociodramatic play at 3 years of age', in I. Bretherton (ed.) *Symbolic Play*, Orlando: Academic Press.

Foushee, H.C., Davis, M.H. and Archer, R.L. (1989) 'Empathy, masculinity and femininity', University of Texas at Austin (unpub.).

Fox, R. (1972) 'Alliance and contrast: sexual selection in the evolution of human kinship systems', in R.G. Campbell (ed.) *Sexual Selection and the Descent of Man*, Chicago: Aldine.

Fox, S. (1984) 'The sociability aspect of extraversion as a situation-specific dimension', *Social Behaviour and Personality* 12: 7–10.

French, D.C. (1977) 'Effects of cooperative, competitive and individualistic sets on performance in children's groups', *Journal of Experimental Child Psychology* 24: 1–10.

Furman, W. and Buhrmester, D. (1985) 'Children's perceptions of the personal relationships in their social networks', *Developmental Psychology* 21: 1016–24.

Furnham, A. (1981) 'Personality and activity preference', *British Journal of Social Psychology* 20: 57–68.

Furnham, A. and Bochner, S. (1986) *Culture Shock*, London: Methuen.

Gaertner, S.L. *et al.* (1989) 'Reducing intergroup bias: the benefits of recategorisation', *Journal of Personality and Social Psychology* 57: 239–49.

Gallo, P.S. (1966) 'Effects of incrased incentives upon the use of threat in bargaining', *Journal of Personality and Social Psychology* 4: 14–20.

Gallois, C. and Callan, V.J. (1988) 'Communication accommodation and the prototypical speaker: predicting evaluations of status and solidarity', *Language and Communication* 8: 271–83.

Gamson, W.A. (1964) 'Experimental studies of coalition formation', *Advances in Experimental Social Psychology* 1: 82–110.

Ganchrow, J.R., Steiner, J.E. and Daher, M. (1983) 'Neonatal facial expressions in response to different qualities and intensities of gustatory stimuli', *Infant Behavior and Development* 6: 473–84.

Garvey, C. (1974) 'Some properties of social play', *Merrill-Palmer Quarterly* 20: 163–80.

—— (1977) *Play*, London: Open Books.

Gaskell, G. and Smith, P. (1986) 'Group membership and social attitudes of youth:

an investigation of some implications of social identity theory', *Social Behaviour* 1: 67–77.

Geertz, C. (1973) *The Interpretation of Cultures*, New York: Basic Books

General Household Survey (1986) London: HMSO.

Giddens, A. (1982) *Profiles and Critiques in Social Theory*, London: Macmillan.

Giles, H. and Powesland, P.F. (1975) *Speech Style and Social Evaluation*, London: Academic Press.

Gilligan, C. (1982) *In a Different Voice*, Cambridge, Mass.: Harvard University Press.

Ginsburg, G.P. and Kilbourne, B.K. (1988) 'Emergence of vocal alternation in mother-infant interchanges', *Journal of Child Language* 15: 221–35.

Goffman, E. (1967) *Interaction Ritual: Essays in Face-to-Face Behavior*, Garden City, NY: Doubleday.

Goldman, I. (1937) 'The Kwakiutl of Vancouver Island', in M. Mead (ed.) *Co-operation and Competition among Primitive Peoples*, New York: McGraw-Hill.

Goody, E.N. (1978) 'Towards a theory of questions?' in E.N. Goody (ed.) *Questions and Politeness*, Cambridge: Cambridge University Press.

Gove, W.R. *et al.* (1980) 'Playing dumb: a form of impression management with undesirable side effects', *Social Psychology Quarterly* 43: 89–102.

Gray, J.A. (1982) *The Neuropsychology of Anxiety*, Oxford: Clarendon Press.

Graziano, W.G., Feldesman, A.B. and Rahe, D.F. (1985) 'Extraversion, social cognition, and the salience of aversiveness in social encounters', *Journal of Personality and Social Psychology* 49: 971–80.

Greenbaum, C.W. and Kugelmass, S. (1980) 'Human development and socialization in cross-cultural perspective: issues arising from research in Israel', in N. Warren (ed.) *Studies in Cross-Cultural Psychology* 2, London: Academic Press.

Greenberg, L. (1979) 'Genetic component of bee odor in kin recognition', *Science* 206: 1095–7.

Grice, H.P. (1968) 'Utterer's meaning, sentence-meaning, and word-meaning', *Foundations of Language* 4: 225–42.

—— (1975) 'Logic and conversion', in P. Cole and J.L. Morgan (eds) *Syntax and Semantics vol. 3 Speech Acts*, New York: Academic Press.

Grusec, J.E. and Lytton, H. (1988) *Social Development*, New York: Springer-Verlag.

Guthrie, G.M. (1966) 'Cultural preparation for the Philippines', in R.B. Textor (ed.) *Cultural Frontiers of the Peace Corps*, Cambridge, Mass.: MIT Press.

Hall, E.T. (1966) *The Hidden Dimension*, New York: Doubleday.

Hall, J.A. (1984) *Nonverbal Sex Differences*, Baltimore: Johns Hopkins University Press.

Hall, J.R. (1988) 'Social organization and pathways of commitment: types of communal groups, rational choice theory, and the Kanter thesis', *American Sociological Review* 53: 679–92.

Hamilton, D.L., Carpenter, S. and Bishop, G.D. (1984) 'Desegregation of suburban neighbourhoods', in N. Miller and M.B. Brewer (eds) *Groups in Contact*, Orlando: Academic Press.

Hamilton, W.D. (1964) 'The evolution of social behavior', *Journal of Theoretical Biology* 7: 1–52.

—— (1972) 'Altruism and related phenomena, mainly in social insects', *Annual Review of Ecological Systems* 3: 193–232.

—— (1975) 'Innate social aptitudes of man: an approach from evolutionary genetics', in R. Fox (ed.) *Biosocial Anthropology*, New York: Wiley.

Hampson, S.E. (1988) *The Construction of Personality*, 2nd edn, London: Routledge.

Hampton, P.J. (1945) 'The emotional element in music', *Journal of General Psychology* 33: 237–50.

Harding, J. and Hogrefe, R. (1952) 'Attitudes of white department store employees towards negro co-workers', *Journal of Social Issues* 8, no. 1: 18–28.

Harlow, H.F. and Harlow, M.K. (1965) 'The affectional systems', in A.M. Schrier, H.F. Harlow and F. Stollnitz (eds) *Behavior of Nonhuman Primates, vol. 2*, New York: Academic Press.

Harré, R. and Secord, P. (1972) *The Explanation of Social Behaviour*, Oxford: Blackwell.

Hatfield, E., Utne, M.K. and Traupmann, J. (1979) 'Equity theory and intimate relationships', in R.L. Burgess and T.L. Huston (eds) *Social Exchange in Developing Relationships*, New York: Academic Press.

Harris, P.L. (1989) *Children and Emotion*, Oxford: Blackwell.

Hays, R.B. (1985) 'A longitudinal study of friendship development', *Journal of Personality and Social Psychology* 48: 909–24.

Hazan, C. and Shaver, P. (1987) 'Romantic love conceptualised as an attachment process', *Journal of Personality and Social Psychology* 52: 511–24.

Henderson, M. and Argyle, M. (1985) 'Social support by four categories of work colleagues: relationships between activities, stress and satisfaction', *Journal of Occupational Behavior* 6: 229–39.

Hetherington, E.M. and Morris, W.M. (1978) 'The family and primary groups', in W.H. Holtzman (ed.) *Introductory Psychology in Depth: Developmental Topics*, New York: Harper's College Press.

Hewstone, M.R.C., Jaspars, J. and Lalljee, M. (1982) 'Social representations, the intergroup images of "public" and "comprehensive" schoolboys', *European Journal of Social Psychology* 12: 241–69.

Hill, R. *et al.* (1970) *Family Development in Three Generations*, Cambridge, Mass.: Schenkman.

Hinde, R.A. (1979) *Towards Understanding Relationships*, London: Academic Press.

—— (1984) 'Why do the sexes behave differently in close relationships?' *Journal of Social and Personal Relationships* 1: 471–501.

—— (1987) *Individuals, Relationships and Culture*, Cambridge: Cambridge University Press.

Hirschleifer, J. and Coll, J.C.M. (1988) 'What strategies can support the evolutionary emergence of cooperation?' *Journal of Conflict Resolution* 32: 367–98.

Hobfoll, S.E. (1988) *The Ecology of Stress*, New York: Hemisphere.

Hoffman, L.W. and Manis, J.D. (1982) 'The value of children in the United States', in F.I. Nye (ed.) *Family Relationships*, Beverly Hills: Sage.

Hofstede, D. (1984) *Culture's Consequences*, Beverly Hills: Sage.

Hogg, M.A. and Turner, J.C. (1985) 'When liking begets solidarity: an experiment on the role of interpersonal attraction in psychological group formation', *British Journal of Social Psychology* 24: 267–82.

Holloway, M. (1966) *Heavens on Earth*, New York: Dover.

Homans, G.C. (1950) *The Human Group*, London: Routledge & Kegan Paul.

Hornstein, H.A. (1982) 'Promotive tension: theory and research', in V.J. Derlega and J. Grzelak (eds) *Cooperation and Helping Behavior*, New York: Academic Press.

House, J.S. (1981) *Work Stress and Social Support*, Reading, Mass.: Addison-Wesley.

Howes, C. (1988) 'Peer Interaction of Young Children', *Monographs of Society for Research in Child Development* 53: no. 1.

Hrdy, S.B. (1977) *The Langurs of Abu: Female vs Male Strategies of Reproduction*, Cambridge, Mass.: Harvard University Press.

Hughes, L.A. (in press) '"But that's not *really* mean"': competing in a cooperative mode', *Sex Roles*.

Hui, C.H. and Triandis, H.C. (1986) 'Individualism-collectivism: a study of cross-cultural researchers', *Journal of Cross-Cultural Psychology* 17: 225–48.

Humphreys, A.P. and Smith, P.K. (1984) 'Rough-and-tumble in preschool and playground', in P.K. Smith (ed.) *Play, in Animals and Humans*, Oxford: Blackwell.

Huntingford, F. (1982) 'The evolution of cooperation and altruism', in A.M. Colman (ed.) *Cooperation and Competition in Humans and Animals*, Wokingham: Van Nostrand.

Huston, A.C. (1983) 'Sex-typing', in E.M. Hetherington (ed.) *Handbook of Child Psychology, Vol. 4*, New York: Wiley.

Hutnik, N. (1986) *Ethnic minority identity: the case of second generation South Asians in Britain*, Oxford D.Phil. thesis.

ICOM (1987) *No Single Model*, Leeds: ICOM.

Ingham, A.G. *et al.* (1974) 'The Ringelmann effect: studies of group size and group performance', *Journal of Experimental Social Psychology* 10: 371–84.

Ingham, G.K. (1967) 'Organisation size, orientations to work and industrial behaviour', *Sociology* 1: 239–58.

Jacobs, M.K. and Goodman, G. (1989) 'Psychology and self-help groups', *American Psychologist* 44: 536–45.

Johnson, D.W. (1975) 'Affective perspective taking and cooperative predisposition', *Developmental Psychology* 11: 869–70.

Johnson, D.W. *et al.* (1981) 'Effects of cooperative, competitive, and individualistic goal structures on achievement: a meta-analysis', *Psychological Bulletin* 89: 47–62.

Johnson, D.W. *et al.* (1983) 'Are low achievers disliked in a cooperative situation? A test of rival theories in a mixed ethnic situation', *Contemporary Educational Psychology* 8: 189–200.

Johnson, D.W., Johnson, R.T. and Maruyama, G. (1984) 'Goal interdependence and interpersonal attraction in heterogeneous classrooms: a meta-analysis', in N. Miller and M.B. Brewer (eds.) *Groups in Contact*, Orlando: Academic Press.

Johnson, R.C. *et al.* (1989) 'Cross-cultural assessment of altruism and its correlates', *Personality and Individual Differences* 10: 855–68.

Kabanoff, B. (1985) 'Potential influence structures as sources of interpersonal conflicts in groups and organizations', *Organizational Behavior and Human Decision Processes* 36: 113–41.

Kagan, J. (1989) 'Temperamental contributions to social behavior', *American Psychologist* 44: 668–74.

Kane, T.R., Suls, J.M. and Tedeschi, J. (1977) 'Humour as a tool of social interaction', in A.J. Chapman and H.C. Foot (eds) *It's a Funny Thing, Humour*, Oxford: Pergamon.

Kanter, R.M. (1968) 'Commitment and social organization: a study of commitment mechanisms in utopian communities', *American Sociological Review* 33: 499–517.

—— (ed.) (1973) *Communes*, New York: Harper & Row.

Karylowski, J. (1982) 'Two types of altruistic behavior: doing good to feel good or to make the other feel good', in V.J. Derlega and J. Grzelak (eds) *Cooperation and Helping Behavior*, New York: Academic Press.

Kaye, K. (1977) 'Toward the origin of dialogue', in H.R. Schaffer (ed.) *Studies in Mother-Infant Interaction*, London: Academic Press.

Kayser, E., Schwinger, T. and Cohen, R.L. (1984) 'Laypersons' conceptions of social relationships: a test of contract theory', *Journal of Social and Personal Relationships* 1: 433–58.

Kelley, H.H. and Stahelski, A.J. (1970) 'Social interactive basis of cooperators' and competitors' beliefs about others', *Journal of Personality and Social Psychology* 16: 66–91.

Kelman, H.C. and Cohen, S.P. (1979) 'Reduction of international conflict: an international approach', in W.G. Austin and S. Worchel (eds) *The Social Psychology of Intergroup Relations*, Monterey, Calif.: Brooks/Cole.

Kendon, A. (1967) 'Some functions of gaze direction in social interaction', *Acta Psychologica* 26: 22–63.

—— (1970) 'Movement coordination in social interaction: some examples considered', *Acta Psychologica* 32: 1–25.

Kendon, A. and Ferber, A. (1973) 'A description of some human greetings', in R.P. Michael and J.H. Crook (eds) *Comparative Ethology and Behavior of Primates*, London: Academic Press.

Kenrick, D.T. and Trost, M.R. (1989) 'A reproductive model of heterosexual relationships: putting proximate economics in ultimate perspective', *Review of Personality and Social Psychology* 10: 92–118.

Kephart, W.H. (1967) 'Some correlates of romantic love', *Journal of Marriage and the Family* 29: 470–4.

Kitchener, R.F. (1981) 'Piaget's social psychology', *Journal for the Theory of Social Behaviour* 11: 253–77.

Knight, G.P. and Chao, C-C. (1989) 'Gender differences in the cooperative, competitive, and individualistic values of children', *Motivation and Emotion* 13: 125–41.

Kobrin, F. and Hendershot, G. (1977) 'Do family ties reduce morality: evidence from the United States 1966–68', *Journal of Marriage and the Family* 39: 737–45.

Krauss, R.M. (1987) 'The role of the listener: addressee influences on message formulation', *Journal of Language and Social Psychology* 6: 81–98.

Krauss, R.M. and Weinheimer, S. (1964) 'Changes in reference phrases as a function of frequency of usage in social interaction: a preliminary study', *Psychonomic Science* 1: 113–14.

Kraut, R.E. and Johnston, R.E. (1979) 'Social and emotional messages of smiling: an ethological approach', *Journal of Personality and Social Psychology* 37: 1539–53.

Kuhlman, D.M. and Marshello, A.F.J. (1975) 'Individual differences in game motivation as moderators of pre-programming strategy effects in prisoners' dilemma game', *Journal of Personality and Social Psychology* 32: 922–31.

Laffal, J. (1965) *Pathological and Normal Language*, New York: Atherton.

La Fromboise, T.D. and Rowe, W. (1983) 'Skills training for bicultural competence: rationale and application', *Journal of Counseling Psychology* 30: 589–95.

La Gaipa, J.J. and Wood, H.D. (1981) 'Friendship in disturbed adolescents', in S. Duck and R. Gilmour (eds) *Personal Relationships, vol. 3: Personal Relationships in Disorder*, London: Academic Press.

Lakoff, R. (1973) 'The logic of politeness; or minding your p's and q's', in *Papers from the Ninth Regional Meeting of the Chicago Linguistic Society*: 292–305, Chigago: Chicago Linguistic Society.

Landis, D., Hope, R.O. and Day, H.R. (1984) 'Training for disintegration in the military', in N. Miller and M.B. Brewer (eds) *Groups in Contact*, New York: Academic Press.

Langer, S.K. (1942) *Philosophy in a New Key*, Cambridge, Mass.: Harvard University Press.

—— (1953) *Feelings and Form*, London: Routledge & Kegan Paul.

Lanzetta, J.T. and Englis, B.G. (1989) 'Expectations of cooperation and competition and their effects on observers' vicarious emotional responses', *Journal of Personality and Social Psychology* 56: 543–54.

Lawler, E.E. and Hackman, J.R. (1969) 'The impact of employee participation in the development of pay incentive systems: a field experiment', *Journal of Applied Psychology* 53: 467–71.

Leech, G.N. (1983) *Principles of Pragmatics*, London: Longman.

Levinson, S.C. (1983) *Pragmatics*, Cambridge: Cambridge University Press.

Lewicki, R.J. and Litterer, J.A. (1985) *Negotiation*, Homewood, Ill.: Irwin.

Liebrand, W.B.G. and McClintock, C.G. (1988) 'The ring measure of social values: a computerized procedure for assessing individual differences in information processing and social value orientation', *European Journal of Personality* 2: 217–30.

Lindskold, S. (1986) 'GRIT: reducing distrust through carefully introduced conciliation', in S. Worchel and W.G. Austin (eds) *Psychology of Intergroup Relations*, 2nd edn, Chicago: Nelson.

Lindskold, S. and Han. G. (1988) 'GRIT as a foundation for integrative bargaining', *Personality and Social Psychology Bulletin* 14: 335–45.

Loomis, C.P. and Beagle, J.A. (1950) *Rural Social Systems: a Textbook in Rural Sociology and Anthropology*, Englewood Cliffs, N.J: Prentice-Hall.

Luce, R.D. and Raiffa, H. (1957) *Games and Decisions*, New York: Wiley.

McAdams, D.P. (1980) 'A thematic coding system for the intimacy motive', *Journal of Research in Personality* 14: 413–32.

—— (1988) 'Personal needs and personal relationships', in S. Duck (ed.) *Handbook of personal Relationships*, Chichester: Wiley.

McAdams, D.P. and Bryant, F.B. (1987) 'Intimacy motivation and subjective mental health in a nationwide sample', *Journal of Personality* 55: 395–413.

McClelland, D.C. (1986) 'Some reflections on the two psychologies of love', *Journal of Personality* 54: 334–53.

—— (1987) *Human Motivation*, Cambridge: Cambridge University Press.

McClintock, C.G. and Van Avermaet, E. (1982) 'Social values and rules of fairness: a theoretical perspective', in V.J. Derlega and J. Grzelak (eds) *Cooperation and Helping Behavior*, New York: Academic Press.

Maccoby, E.E. and Martin, J.A. (1983) 'Socialization in the context of the family: parent-child interaction', in P.H. Mussen (ed.) *Handbook of Child Psychology*, vol. 4: 1–101, New York: Wiley.

Macdonald, D.W. (1986) 'A meerkat volunteers for guard duty so its comrades can live in peace', *Smithsonian* April: 55–65.

McDowall, J.J. (1978) 'Interactional synchrony', *Journal of Personality and Social Psychology* 36: 963–75.

Mackenzie, B.K. (1948) 'The importance of contact in determining attitudes towards negroes', *Journal of Abnormal and Social Psychology* 43: 417–41.

McLaughlin, M.L. (1984) *Conversation: How Talk is Organized*, Beverly Hills: Sage.

McPhail, P. (1967) 'The development of social skills in adolescents', Oxford Department of Education, cited by Argyle (1983).

Madsen, M.C. (1971) 'Developmental and cross-cultural differences in the cooperative behavior of young children', *Journal of Cross-Cultural Psychology* 2: 365–71.

Maltz, D.N. and Borker, R.A. (1982) 'A cultural approach to male-female miscommunication', in J.J. Gumperz (ed.) *Language and Social Identity*, Cambridge: Cambridge University Press.

Mann, J.W. (1963) 'Rivals of different rank', *Journal of Social Psychology* 61: 11–28.

Mann, L. (1980) 'Cross-cultural studies of small groups', in H. Triandis (ed.) *Handbook of Cross-Cultural Psychology, vol. 5*, Reading, Mass.: Addison-Wesley.

Marcus, R.F. (1986) 'Naturalistic observation of cooperation, helping, and sharing and their association with empathy and affect', in C. Zahn-Waxler, E.M. Cummings and R. Iannotti (eds) *Altruism and Aggression*, Cambridge: Cambridge University Press.

Marcus, R.F., Roke, E.J. and Bruner, C. (1985) 'Verbal and nonverbal empathy and prediction of social behavior of young children', *Perceptual and Motor Skills* 60: 299–309.

Marler, P. (1965) 'Communication in apes and monkeys', in J. DeVore (ed.) *Primate Behavior*, New York: Holt, Rinehart & Wilson.

——— (1976) 'Social organization, communication and graded signals: the chimpanzee and the gorilla', in P.P.G. Bateson and R.A. Hinde (eds) *Growing Points in Ethology*, Cambridge: Cambridge University Press.

Marriott, R. (1968) *Incentive Payment Systems*, London: Staples.

Marsh, P., Rosser, E. and Harré, R. (1978) *The Rules of Disorder*, London: Routledge & Kegan Paul.

Marwell, G. (1982) 'Altruism and the problem of collective action', in V.J. Derlega and J. Grzelak (eds) *Cooperation and Helping Behavior*, New York: Academic Press.

Marwell, G. and Schmitt, D.R. (1975) *Cooperation, an Experimental Analysis*, New York: Academic Press.

Mauss, M. (trans. 1985) 'A category of the human mind: the notion of person; the notion of self', in M. Carrithers *et al.* (eds) *The Category of the Person*, Cambridge: Cambridge University Press.

Maxwell, G.M. and Cook, M.W. (1985) 'Postural congruence and judgments of liking and perceived similarity', *New Zealand Journal of Psychology* 14: 20–26.

May, M.A. and Doob, L.W. (1937) *Competition and Cooperation: a Report*, New York: Social Science Research Council.

Maynard-Smith, J. (1974) 'The theory of games and the evolution of animal conflict', *Journal of Theoretical Biology* 47: 209–21.

Mead, M. (ed.) (1937) *Cooperation and Competition among Primitive Peoples*, New York: McGraw-Hill.

Mehrabian, A. and Epstein, N. (1972) 'A measure of emotional empathy', *Journal of Personality* 40: 525–43.

Mellor, M., Hannah, J. and Stirling, J. (1988) *Worker Cooperatives in Theory and Practice*, Milton Keynes: Open University Press.

Messick, D.M. and Brewer, M.B. (1983) 'Solving social dilemmas: a review', *Review of Personality and Social Psychology* 4: 11–44.

Messick, D.M. and Mackie, D.M. (1989) 'Intergroup relations', *Annual Review of Psychology* 40: 45–81.

Messick, D.M. and McClintock, G.G. (1968) 'Motivational bases of choice in experimental games', *Journal of Experimental Social Psychology* 4: 1–25.

Miller, K.I. and Monge, P.R. (1986) 'Participation, satisfaction and productivity: a meta-analytic review', *Academy of Management Journal* 29: 727–53.

Miller, N., Brewer, M.B. and Edwards, K. (1985) 'Cooperative interaction in desegregated settings: a laboratory analogue', *Journal of Social Issues* 41: 63–79.

Minard, R.D. (1952) 'Race relationships in the Pocahontas coal field', *Journal of Social Issues* 8: 29–44.

Mintz, A. (1951) 'Non-adaptive group behavior', *Journal of Abnormal and Social Psychology* 46: 150–9.

MORI (1982) *Loneliness*, London: Market and Opinion Research International

Morley, I.E. and Hosking, D.M. (1984) 'Decision-making and negotiation', in M.

Gruneberg and T. Wall (eds) *Social Psychology and Organizational Behaviour*, Chichester: Wiley.

Morley, I.E. and Stephenson, G.M. (1977) *The Social Psychology of Bargaining*, London: Allen & Unwin.

Morsbach, H. (1977) 'The psychological importance of ritualized gift exchange in modern Japan', *Annals of the New York Academy of Science* 293: 98–113.

Muir, H.C. and Marrison, C. (1989) 'Human factors in cabin safety', *Aerospace* April: 18–21.

Mummendey, A. and Simon, B. (1989) 'Better or different? III. The impact of importance of comparison dimension and relative in-group size upon intergroup discrimination', *British Journal of Social Psychology* 28: 1–16.

Murray, L. and Trevarthen, C. (1985) 'Emotional regulation of interactions between two-month-olds and their mothers', in T.M. Field and N.A. Fox (eds) *Social Perception in Infants*, Norwood, NJ: Ablex.

Nash, A. (1988) 'Ontogeny, phylogeny, and relationships', in S. Duck (ed.) *Handbook of Personal Relationships*, Chichester: Wiley.

Neale, M.A. and Bazerman, M.H. (1985) 'The effects of framing and negotiator confidence on bargaining behaviours and outcomes', *Academy of Management Journal* 28: 34–49.

Newson, J. and Newson, E. (1973) *Infant Care in an Urban Community*, London: Allen & Unwin.

—— (1968) *Four Years Old in an Urban Community*, London: Allen & Unwin.

—— (1976) *Seven Years Old in the Home Environment*, London: Allen & Unwin.

Nisbett, R.E. and Wilson, T.D. (1977) 'Telling more than we know: verbal reports on mental processes', *Psychological Review* 84: 231–59.

Noller, P. (1984) *Nonverbal Communication and Marital Interaction*, Oxford: Pergamon.

Norman, W.T. (1963) 'Toward an adequate taxonomy of personality attributes: replicated factor structure in peer nomination personality ratings', *Journal of Abnormal and Social Psychology* 66: 574–88.

Oakes, P.J. and Turner, J.C. (1980) 'Social categorization and intergroup behaviour: does minimal intergroup discrimination make social identity more positive?' *European Journal of Social Psychology* 10: 295–301.

O'Keefe, B.J. and Delia, J.G. (1985) 'Psychological and interactional dimensions of communicative development', in H. Giles and R.N. St Clair (eds) *Recent Advances in Language, Communication, and Social Psychology*, London: Erlbaum.

Opie, I. and Opie, P. (1969) *Children's Games in Street and Playground*, Oxford: Clarendon Press.

Osgood, C.E. (1962) *An Alternative to War or Surrender*, Urbana, Ill.: University of Illinois Press.

Packer, C. (1977) 'Reciprocal altruism in olive baboons', *Nature* 265: 441–3.

Parke, R.D. *et al.* (1989) 'Family and peer systems: in search of the linkages', in K. Kreppner and R.M. Lerner (eds) *Family Systems and Life-span Development*, Hillsdale, NJ: Erlbaum.

Parten, M.B. (1932) 'Social participation among preschool children', *Journal of Abnormal and Social Psychology* 27: 243–69.

Passingham, R.E. (1982) *The Human Primate*, Oxford: W.H. Freeman.

Peck, J. (1989) 'Friendship and the evolution of cooperation', Oxford Dept of Zoology, unpublished.

Pepitone, E.A. (1980) *Children in Cooperation and Competition*, London: Gower.

Piaget, J. (1932) *The Moral Judgment of the Child*, London: Routledge & Kegan Paul.

Pike, K. (1967) *Language in Relation to a Unified Theory of Human Behavior*, The Hague: Mouton.

Plomin, R. (1986) *Development, Genetics, and Psychology*, Hillsdale, NJ: Erlbaum.

Pope, K.S. *et al.* (eds) (1980) *On Love and Loving*, San Francisco: Jossey-Bass.

Potter, S. (1947) *The Theory and practice of Gamesmanship*, London: Hart-Davis.

Pruitt, D.G. (1981) *Negotiation Behavior*, New York: Academic Press.

Radke-Yarrow, M., Zahn-Waxler, C. and Chapman, M. (1983) 'Children's prosocial dispositions and behavior', in P.H. Mussen (ed.) *Handbook of Child Psychology, vol. 4*: 469–45, New York: Wiley.

Rapoport, A. and Chammah, A. (1965) *Prisoner's Dilemma*, Ann Arbor: University of Michigan Press.

Rheingold, H.L. (1982) 'Little children's participation in the work of adults, a nascent social behaviour', *Child Development* 53: 114–25.

Riesman, D., Glazer, N. and Denney, R. (1950) *The Lonely Crowd*, New Haven: Yale University Press.

Rigby, A. (1974) *Alternative Realities: a Study of Communes and Their Members*, London: Routledge & Kegan Paul.

Rinn, W.E. (1984) 'The neuropsychology of facial expression: a review of the neurological and psychological mechanisms for producing facial expressions', *Psychological Bulletin* 95: 52–77.

Roberts, K. (1983) *Leisure*, 2nd edn, London: Longman.

Rokeach, M., Smith, P.W. and Evans, R.I. (1960) 'Two kinds of prejudice or one?' in M. Rokeach (ed.) *The Open and Closed Mind*, New York: Basic Books.

Rommetveit, R. (1974) *On Message Structure*, New York: Wiley.

Rosenfeld, H.M. (1978) 'Conversational control functions of non-verbal behavior', in A.W. Siegman and B. Pope (eds) *Nonverbal Behavior and Communication*, Hillsdale, NJ: Erlbaum.

Roy, D. (1959) 'Banana time: job satisfaction and informal interaction', *Human Organisation* 18: 158–68.

Rubin, J.Z. and Brown, B.R. (1975) *The Social Psychological of Bargaining and Negotiation*, New York: Academic Press.

Rubin, K.H., Fein, G.G. and Vandenberg, B. (1987) 'Play', in P.H. Mussen (ed.) *Handbook of Child Psychology, vol. 4*: 693–744, New York: Wiley.

Rubin, Z. (1970) 'Measurement of romantic love', *Journal of Personality and Social Psychology* 16: 263–73.

Rushton, J.P. (1989) 'Genetic similarity, human altruism, and group selection', *Behavioral and Brain Sciences* 12: 503–18.

Rushton, J.P., Littlefield, C.H. and Lumsden, C.J. (1986) 'Gene-culture coevolution of complex social behavior: human altruism and mate choice', *Proceedings of the National Academy of Science* 83: 7340–3.

Rutter, D.R. (1987) *Communicating by Telephone*, Oxford: Pergamon.

Rutter, M. *et al.* (1979) *Fifteen Thousand Hours: Secondary Schools and their Effects on Children*, London: Open Books.

Saarni, C. (1979) 'Children's understanding of display rules for expressive behavior', *Developmental Psychology* 15: 424–9.

Sachdev, I. and Bourhis, R.Y. (1985) 'Social categorisation and power differentials in group relations', *European Journal of Social Psychology* 15: 415–34.

Sacks, H., Schegloff, E. and Jefferson, G. (1974) 'A simplest systematics for the organization of turn-taking in conversation', *Language* 50: 696–735.

Sampson, R.J. (1988) 'Local friendship ties and community attachment in mass society: a multilevel systemic model', *American Sociological Review* 53: 766–79.

Scaife, M. and Bruner, J.S. (1975) 'The capacity for joint visual attention in the infant', *Nature* 253: 265–6.

Schaffer, H.R. (1984) *The Child's Entry into a Social World*, London: Academic Press.

Schaffer, H.R. and Emerson, P.E. (1964) 'The development of social attachments in infancy', *Monographs of the Society for Research on Child Development* 29: no. 3.

Schanck, R. and Abelson, R.P. (1977) *Scripts, Plans, Goals, and Understanding*, Hillsdale, NJ: Erlbaum.

Scherer, K.R., Wallbott, H.G. and Summerfield, A.B. (1986) *Experiencing Emotions*, Cambridge: Cambridge University Press.

Schwartz, J.C. and O'Connor, C.J. (1984) 'The social ecology of memorable emotional experiences', Paper at Second International Conference on Personal Relationships, Madison.

Schwartz, S.A. (1988) 'Individualism and collectivism: critique and proposed refinements', Paper at International Congress of Psychology, Sydney.

Semeonoff, B. (1940) 'A new approach to testing musical ability', *British Journal of Psychology* 30: 326–40.

Shaver, P.R. and Hazan, C. (1988) 'A biased overview of the study of love', *Journal of Social and Personal Relationships* 5: 473–501.

Sherif, M. *et al.* (1961) *Intergroup Conflict and Cooperation: The Robber's Cave Experiment*, Norman: University of Oklahoma.

Shomer, R.W., Davis, A.H. and Kelley, H.H. (1966) 'Threats and the development of coordination: further studies of the Deutsch and Krauss trucking game', *Journal of Personality and Social Psychology* 4: 119–26.

Shouval, R. *et al.* (1975) 'Anomalous reactions to social pressure of Israeli and Soviet children raised in family versus collective settings', *Journal of Personality and Social Psychology* 32: 477–89.

Siegal, S. and Fouraker, L.E. (1960) *Bargaining and Group Decision Making*, New York: McGraw-Hill.

Sissons, M. (1981) 'Race, sex and helping behaviour', *British Journal of Social Psychology* 20: 285–92.

Slavin, R.E. (1983) 'When does cooperative learning increase student achievement?' *Psychological Bulletin* 94: 429–45.

Slugoski, B.R. (1985) *Grice's Theory of Conversation as a Social Psychological Model*, Oxford: D.Phil. thesis.

Slugoski, B.R. and Turnbull, W. (1988) 'Cruel to be kind: sarcasm, banter and social relations', *Journal of Language and Social Psychology* 7: 102–21.

Snow, C.E. (1977) 'The development of conversations between mother and babies', *Journal of Child Language* 4: 1–22.

Social Trends (1989) London: HMSO.

Sroufe, L.A., Fox, N.E. and Pancake, V.R. (1983) 'Attachment and dependency in developmental perspective', *Child Development* 54: 1615–27.

Star, S.A., Williams, R.M. and Stouffer, S.A. (1965) 'Negro infantry platoons in white companies', in H. Proshanky and B. Seidenberg (eds) *Basic Studies in Social Psychology*, New York: Holt, Rinehart & Winston.

Staub, E. (1978) *Positive Social Behavior and Morality*, New York: Academic Press.

Stebbins, R.A. (1979) *Amateurs*, Beverly Hills: Sage.

Stephan, K.H. and Stephan, G.E. (1973) 'Religion and the survival of utopian communities', *Journal for the Scientific Study of Religion* 12: 89–100.

Stephan, W.G. (1978) 'School desegregation: an evaluation of predictions made', in *Brown v. the Board of Education*, *Psychological Bulletin* 85: 217–38.

———— (1985) 'Intergroup relations', in G. Lindzey and E. Aronson (eds) *Handbook of Social Psychology, vol. 2*, 3rd ed, New York: Random House.

Stephan, W.G. and Stephan C.W. (1984) 'The role of ignorance in intergroup relations', in N. Miller and M.B. Brewer (eds) *Groups in Contact*, Orlando: Academic Press.

Stern, D. (1977) *The First Relationship*, Cambridge, Mass.: Harvard University Press.

Stockard, J., Van de Kragt, A.J.C. and Dodge, P.J. (1988) 'Gender roles and behavior in social dilemmas: are there sex differences in cooperation and its justification?', *Social Psychology Quarterly* 51: 154–63.

Stone, A.A. *et al.* (1987) 'Evidence that secretory ISA antibody is associated with daily mood', *Journal of Personality and Social Psychology* 52: 988–93.

Straus, M.A., Gelles, R.J. and Steinmetz, S.K. (1980) *Behind Closed Doors: Violence in the American Family*, New York: Doubleday.

Stroebe, W. and Stroebe, M.S. (1987) *Bereavement and Health*, New York: Cambridge University Press.

Struch, N. and Schwartz, H. (1989) 'Intergroup aggression: its predictors and distinctness from in-group bias', *Journal of Personality and Social Psychology* 56: 364–73.

Sundstrom, E. (1986) *Work Places*, Cambridge: Cambridge University Press.

Sutton-Smith, B. and Kelly-Byrne, D. (1984) 'The idealization of play', in P.K. Smith (ed.) *Play in Animals and Humans*, Oxford: Blackwell.

Swenson, C.H. (1972) 'The behavior of love', in H.A. Otto (ed.) *Love Today, a New Exploration*, New York: Association Press.

Tajfel, H. (1978) *Differentiation between Social Groups*, London: Academic Press.

Tedeschi, J.T., Schlenker, R. and Bonoma, T.V. (1973) *Conflict, Power, and Games*, Chicago: Aldine.

Termine, N.T. and Izard, C.E. (1988) 'Infants' responses to their mother's expressions of joy and sadness', *Developmental Psychology* 24: 223–9.

Thomas, E.J. (1957) 'Effects of facilitative role interdependence on group functioning', *Human Relations* 10: 347–66.

Thompson, R.A. (1987) 'Empathy and emotional understanding: the early development of empathy', in N. Eisenberg and J. Strayer (eds) *Empathy and its Development*, Cambridge: Cambridge University Press.

Thorne, A. (1987) 'The press of personality: a study of conversation between introverts and extraverts', *Journal of Personality and Social Psychology* 53: 718–26.

Tickle-Degnen, L. and Rosenthal, R. (1987) 'Group rapport and nonverbal behavior', *Review of Personality and Social Psychology* 9: 113–36.

Tiger, L. (1969) *Men in Groups*, London: Nelson.

Tönnies, F. (1887, 1959) *Community and Society*, New York: Harper.

Totman, R. *et al.* (1980) 'Predicting experimental colds in volunteers from different measures of recent life stress', *Journal of Psychosomatic Research* 24: 155–63.

Trevarthen, C. (1980) 'The foundations of intersubjectivity: development of interpersonal and cooperative understanding in infants', in D.R. Olson (ed.) *The Social Foundations of Language and Thought*, New York: Norton.

Trew, K. (1986) Catholic-Protestant contact in Northern Ireland, in M. Hewstone and R. Brown (eds) *Contact and Conflict in Intergroup Encounters*, Oxford: Blackwell.

Triandis, H.C. *et al.* (1988) 'Individualism and collectivism: cross-cultural perspectives on self-ingroup relationships', *Journal of Personality and Social Psychology* 54: 323–8.

Trist, F.L., Higgins, G.W., Murray, H. and Pollock, A.B. (1963) *Organizational Choice*, London: Tavistock.

Trivers, R.L. (1971) 'The evolution of reciprocal altruism', *Quarterly Review of Biology* 46: 35–57.

—— (1985) *Social Evolution*, Menlos Park, Calif.: Benjamin/Cummings.

Troll, L.E., Miller, S.J. and Atchley, R.C. (1979) *Families in Later Life*, Belmont, Calif.: Wadsworth.

Tubbs, M.E. (1986) 'Goal-setting: a meta-analytic examination of the empirical evidence', *Journal of Applied Psychology* 71: 474–83.

Turnbull, C.M. (1973) *The Mountain People*, London: Cape.

Turnbull, W. and Slugoski, B.R. (1988) 'Conversational and linguistic processes in causal attribution', in D. Hilton (ed.) *Contemporary Science and Natural Explanation*, Brighton: Harvester.

Turner, J.C. (1981) 'The experimental social psychology of intergroup behaviour', in J.C. Turner and H. Giles (eds) *Intergroup Behaviour*, Oxford: Blackwell.

—— (1987) *Rediscovering the Social Group*, Oxford: Blackwell.

Underwood, B. and Moore, B. (1982) 'Perspective-taking and altruism', *Psychological Bulletin* 91: 143–73.

Vanfossen, B.E. (1981) 'Sex differences in the mental health effects of spouse support', *Journal of Health and Social Behavior* 22: 130–43.

Van Zelst, R.H. (1952) 'Validation of a sociometric regrouping procedure', *Journal of Abnormal and Social Psychology* 47: 229–301.

Vernon, P.E. (1930) 'The phenomena of attention and visualisation in the psychology of musical appreciation', *British Journal of Psychology* 21: 50–63.

Veroff, J. *et al.* (1980) 'Comparison of American motives: 1957 v. 1976', *Journal of Personality and Social Psychology* 39: 1249–62.

Veroff, J., Douvan, E. and Kulka, R.A. (1981) *The Inner American*, New York: Basic Books.

Walker, C. (1977) 'Some variations in marital satisfaction', in R. Chester and J. Peel (eds) *Equalities and Inequalities in Family Life*, London: Academic Press.

Walker-Andrews, A. (1988) 'Infants' perception of the affordance of expressive behavior', *Advances in Infancy Research* 15: 174–221.

Wall, T.D. and Lischeron, J.A. (1977) *Worker Participation*, London: McGraw-Hill.

Wallach, M.A. and Wallach, L. (1983) *Psychology's Sanction for Selfishness*, San Francisco: W.H. Freeman.

Walster, E. and Walster, G.W. (1978) *A New Look at Love*, Reading, Mass.: Addison-Wesley.

Warner, W.L. and Lunt, P.S. (1941) *The Social Life of a Modern Community*, New Haven: Yale University Press.

Washburn, S.L. and Hamburg, D.A. (1965) 'The implications of primate research', in I. DeVore (ed.) *Primate Behavior: Field Studies of Monkeys and Apes*, New York: Holt, Rinehart & Winston.

Webber, R.A. (1974) 'The relationship of group performance to the age of members in homogeneous groups', *Academy of Management Journal* 17: 570–4.

Weiss, R.F. *et al.* (1971) 'Altruism is rewarding', *Science* 171: 1262–3.

Wheeler, L., Reis, H.T. and Bond, M.H. (1989) 'Collectivism-individualism in everyday social life: the middle kingdom and the melting pot', *Journal of Personality and Social Psychology* 57: 79–86.

Wheeler, L., Reis, H. and Nezlek, J. (1983) 'Loneliness, social interaction and social roles', *Journal of Personality and Social Psychology* 45: 943–53.

White, S. (1989) 'Backchannels across cultures: a study of Americans and Japanese', *Language in Society* 18: 59–76.

Wichman, H. (1972) 'Effects of isolation and communication in a two-person game', in L.S. Wrightsman, J. O'Connor and N.J. Baker (eds) *Cooperation and Competition*, Belmont: Brooks/Cole.

Wicker, A.W. (1973) 'Undermanning theory and research: implications for the study of psychological and behavioral effects of excess human populations', *Representative Theory and Research* 4: 185–206.

Wiggins, J.S. (in press) 'Agency and communion as conceptual coordinates for the understanding and measurement of interpersonal behavior', in D. Cichetti and W. Grove (eds) *Thinking Critically in Psychology*, New York: Cambridge University Press.

Wilder, D.A. (1986) 'Social categorization: implications for creation and reduction of intergroup bias', *Advances in Experimental Social Psychology* 19: 291–355.

Wilke, H.A.M. and Braspenning, J. (1989) 'Reciprocity shift in a social trap', *European Journal of Social Psychology* 19: 317–26.

Williamson, G.M. and Clark, M.S. (1989) 'Providing help and desired relationship type as determinants of changes in moods and self-evaluations', *Journal of Personality and Social Psychology* 56: 722–34.

Wilson, E.O. (1971) *The Insect Societies*, Cambridge, Mass.: Belknap.

—— (1975) *Sociobiology, the New Synthesis*, Cambridge, Mass.: Belknap.

Wilson, G. (1981) *The Coolidge Effect: an Evolutionary Account of Human Sexuality*, New York: Morrow.

Wilson, L.K. (1989) *Assertion and its Social Context*, Ph.D. thesis, University of Queensland.

Wintermantel, M. and Siegenstetter, J. (1988) 'Hearer questioning and instruction', *Journal of Language and Social Psychology* 7: 213–27.

Wolfe, R.N. and Krasmer, J.A. (1988) 'Type versus trait: extraversion, impulsivity, sociability, and preferences for cooperative and competitive activities', *Journal of Personality and Social Psychology* 54: 864–71.

Wolfendon, G.E. (1973) 'Nesting and survival in a population of Florida scrub jay', *Living Bird* 12: 25–49.

Worchel, S. (1979) 'Cooperation and the reduction of intergroup conflict: some determining factors', in W.G. Austin and S. Worchel (eds) *The Social Psychology of Intergroup Relations*, Monterey, Calif.: Brooks/Cole.

Worchel, S.W., Wing, F.Y. and Scheltema, K.E. (1989) 'Improving group relations: comparative effects of anticipated cooperative and helping on attraction for an aid-giver', *Social Psychology Quarterly* 52: 213–9.

Yamagishi, T. (1988) 'Seriousness of social dilemmas and the provision of a sanctioning system', *Social Psychology Quarterly* 51: 32–42.

Yizher, U. (1989) 'Kibbutz in crisis – a new direction rather than a new model', *Kibbutz Studies* 29: 14–19.

Young, M. and Wilmott, P. (1973) *The Symmetrical Family*, London: Routledge & Kegan Paul.

Zahn-Waxler, C. and Radke-Yarrow, M. (1982) 'The development of altruism: alternative strategies', in N. Eisenberg (ed.) *The Development of Prosocial Behavior*, New York: Academic Press.

Zajonc, R.B. (1968) 'Attitudinal effects of sheer exposure', *Journal of Personality and Social Psychology Monographs Supplement* 9: 2–27.

Name index

Abelson, R.P. 183
Abrams, D. 220, 232
Abrams, P. 82, 85
Adams, B.N. 145
Adler, A. 166, 167, 197, 242
Ainsworth, M.D.S. 92, 136
Alexander, R.D. 54, 65
Allan, G.A. 152
Allen, P.T. 227
Amir, Y. 234
Arbric, J.C. 30
Argyle, M. 9, 11, 18, 61, 62, 63, 73, 77, 80, 110, 112, 113, 116, 118, 119, 122, 123, 126, 127, 130, 132, 134, 135, 138, 140, 141, 142, 143, 148, 150, 152, 153, 167, 168, 176, 183, 188, 190, 192, 197, 198, 199, 200, 203, 211, 215, 229, 237, 241
Aries, R. 214, 215
Aronson, E. 230
Aronsson, K. 181
Austin, J.L. 181
Avedon, E.M. 158
Axelrod, R. 13, 30, 51, 52, 248

Badhwar, N.K. 152, 153
Bakan, D. 6, 166
Barker, R.G. 100
Barnett, M.A. 104, 209
Baron, R.A. 43
Batson, C.D. 6, 103, 208
Baumann, G. 68
Baumrind, D. 93
Bazerman, M.H. 41
Beagle, J.A. 71
Beattie, G. 178, 180, 189
Bem, S.L. 210

Ben-Ari, R. 234
Ben-Rafael, E. 87
Bentler, R.M. 9
Berkman, L.F. 153
Bernstein, B. 190
Berscheid, E. 134
Bethlehem, D.W. 21, 67, 68, 69, 70
Bhavani, K.-K. 31
Bilous, F.R. 183
Birch, F. 158
Blakar, R.M. 181
Bochner, S. 224, 233, 238, 239
Bond, M.H. 73
Borker, R.A. 215
Bourhis, R.Y. 219
Bowlby, J. 92
Boyd, R. 54
Braiker, H.B. 137
Braspenning, J. 34
Brein, M. 237
Brenner, M. 194
Bretherton, I. 104
Brewer, M.B. 32, 34, 221
Brislin, R.W. 234
Bronfenbrenner, U. 75
Brown, B.R. 43
Brown, G.W. 140
Brown, P. 186
Brown, Roger 211
Brown, Rupert J. 219, 220, 222, 223, 224, 232
Bruner, J.S. 90, 91
Bryant, F.B. 206
Buhrmester, D. 148
Bulmer, M. 77
Burnett, R. 10
Buss, D.M. 63, 135, 136
Buunk, B.P. 129

Subject index

For Product Safety Concerns and Information please contact our EU
representative GPSR@taylorandfrancis.com
Taylor & Francis Verlag GmbH, Kaufingerstraße 24, 80331 München, Germany

www.ingramcontent.com/pod-product-compliance
Lightning Source LLC
Chambersburg PA
CBHW070608270326
41926CB00013B/2462

* 9 7 8 0 4 1 5 8 3 8 1 9 1 *